G000272736

THE GREAT WESTERN AT WEYMOUTH

BY THE SAME AUTHOR

Railways of Dorset

UNIFORM WITH THIS VOLUME

The Golden Years of the Clyde Steamers (1889–1914)

SS *Reindeer* on arrival at Weymouth landing stage from the Channel Islands; steam launch *Armine* and coal barge going alongside (September 1921)

THE GREAT WESTERN AT WEYMOUTH

A Railway and Shipping History

by

J. H. LUCKING

DAVID & CHARLES : NEWTON ABBOT

ISBN 0 7153 5135 4

Printed in Great Britain by
Clarke Doble & Brendon Limited Plymouth
for David & Charles (Publishers) Limited
South Devon House Railway Station
Newton Abbot Devon

CONTENTS

ILLUSTRATIONS

PLATES

IN TEXT

INTRODUCTORY NOTE

THE Great Western Railway—unique in this as in many other ways—operated cross-channel services on two distinct fronts: to Ireland and across the English Channel. This book is an account of the latter, centred on Weymouth. France comes into it but first and foremost *The Great Western at Weymouth* means the Channel Islands—early potatoes, holidaymakers, tomatoes and flowers. In the realm of cross-channel shipping the passage to the islands ranks high in interest, complicated by a double port of call and enlivened by inter-railway rivalry and hazardous navigation. Island waters, a malevolent combination of rock and tide, have been the scene of numerous wrecks. Also unique, in its way, is the port of Weymouth. The harbour is municipally owned but for a hundred years and more it has been effectively a railway port, by virtue of a 'marriage of convenience' in which one party has been largely relieved of day-to-day responsibility for an asset which it has never shown much desire to exploit independently while the other has enjoyed basic facilities on beneficial terms. This relationship was inherited by British Rail and still exists today.

In the interests of completeness the account extends back to the days of the government packets and forward to today, but before 1845 and after 1947 it is necessarily much condensed.

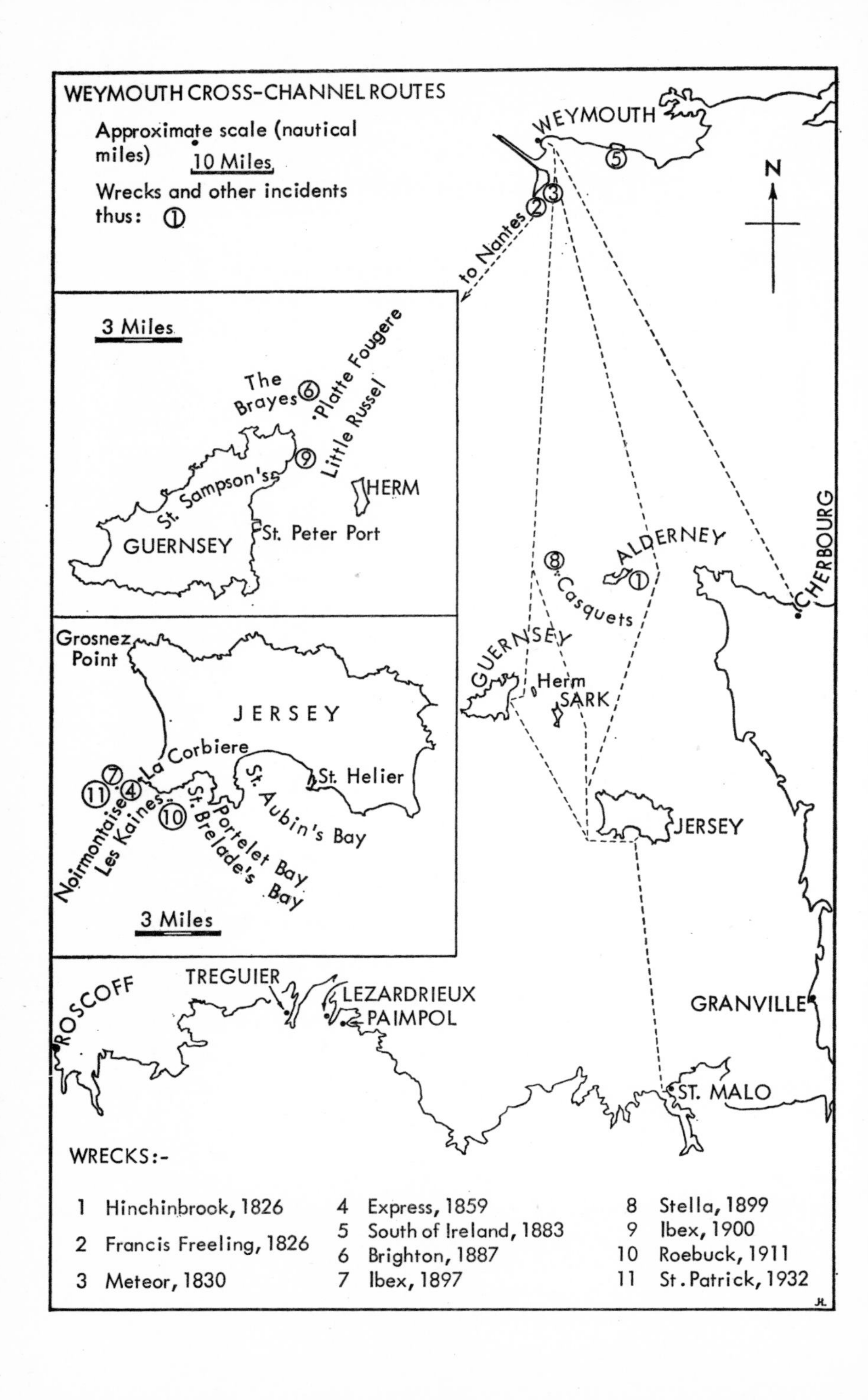
WEYMOUTH CROSS-CHANNEL ROUTES
Approximate scale (nautical miles)
10 Miles
Wrecks and other incidents thus: ①
WEYMOUTH
N
to Nantes
3 Miles
The Brayes
Platte Fougere
Little Russel
St. Sampson's
HERM
St. Peter Port
GUERNSEY
ALDERNEY
Casquets
CHERBOURG
GUERNSEY
Herm
SARK
Grosnez Point
JERSEY
La Corbiere
St. Helier
St. Aubin's Bay
Noirmontaise
Les Kaines
St. Brelade's Bay
Portelet Bay
3 Miles
JERSEY
ROSCOFF
TREGUIER
LEZARDRIEUX
PAIMPOL
GRANVILLE
ST. MALO
WRECKS:-
1 Hinchinbrook, 1826
2 Francis Freeling, 1826
3 Meteor, 1830
4 Express, 1859
5 South of Ireland, 1883
6 Brighton, 1887
7 Ibex, 1897
8 Stella, 1899
9 Ibex, 1900
10 Roebuck, 1911
11 St. Patrick, 1932

CHAPTER ONE

THE CHANNEL ISLANDS PACKETS (1794-1845)

IN 1794, 63 years before Weymouth became part of the Great Western Railway, there appeared in *The London Gazette*[1] the following notice:

General Post Office
February 3, 1794

Notice is hereby given, that a Packet will sail every Thursday from Weymouth for the Islands of Guernsey and Jersey, and a Mail with the Letters for these Islands will be made and sent from this Office every Wednesday Night. The First Mail is to sail if possible on Thursday the 6th Instant.

The Course the Packet will take, and the Times of her Stay and Return, will be in general, and, unless in Cases of particular and occasional Orders to the contrary, the same as in the last War, namely, to sail to Guernsey and drop her Letters there, to proceed immediately to Jersey, there to deliver her Letters, and to stay Three Days for the Answers, then to return to Guernsey, deliver her Letters, stay there Two Days, and return to Weymouth.

By Command of the Postmaster General. Anth. Todd, Sec.

This service was the outcome of persistent pressure by the Channel Islands governors for reliable communications at a time when wars with France made the islands important militarily, but once established it lasted well into the railway age. It and others like it were the direct forerunners of the railway cross-channel shipping of more modern times and some account of the vessels concerned, and of the conditions under which they operated, provides an appropriate introduction to the chapters that follow.

SAILING PACKETS

While a Channel Islands mail service was being considered, several south coast ports had been in the running to become the

English station, notably Southampton, which handled most of the islands' ordinary trade. Weymouth was chosen because it offered the shortest and most direct crossing.[2] The actual date of the first sailing was Thursday 13 February 1794 and the vessel concerned was the Dover packet *Royal Charlotte*, Captain James Wood, one of two which were available for transfer to Weymouth because the Dover–Calais service was temporarily interrupted by war. The other was the *Rover*, Captain Joseph Bennett. Subsequently the proceedings were regularised by act of Parliament.[3]

The early Channel Islands packets, typical of their kind, were workmanlike vessels some 50 or 60ft long, with bluff bow, broad beam and square stern. Cutter rig—single mast rigged fore and aft with a square topsail added—ensured speed for the mails. The usual crew consisted of the captain, a mate and about sixteen seamen. Packets were not allowed to compete with commercial vessels by carrying cargo but were permitted to take passengers, and the fare between Weymouth and either Jersey or Guernsey was fixed at £1 6s 0d (£1·30).[4] Of that, half-a-guinea (52½p) was remitted to the Revenue. The partial remission is accounted for by the fact that the packets, although usually designated 'HM', were not owned by the Post Office but merely hired from private owners, the owner invariably being the captain. He was indemnified against his vessel's capture in wartime but all other risks and expenses were expected to come out of the hire charge. In practice this was inadequate and passenger receipts were relied on to make good the difference.

In June 1795 Wood transferred to a new packet, the *Earl of Chesterfield*. The *Rover* and the *Earl of Chesterfield* then maintained a weekly service with fair regularity until 1806, when the latter was in turn superseded by the *Chesterfield*. 'Fair regularity', it should be added, was relative. The round trip was expected to take about a week and with a fair wind, and luck, Guernsey might be made in about twelve hours from Weymouth. But twenty or thirty hours was more usual, particularly in winter when a gale could make the crossing a perilous business—'like to be very fatal', as Bennett once put it in a letter to the Post

Office.[5] Other causes of disruption at one time or another included arbitrary interference with sailing times by the island governors and seizure of the packets for smuggling. Smuggling was endemic. The seamen alleged that without it they could not maintain their families and the captains turned a blind eye; often, indeed, they were deeply involved on their own account.

The Bye-boat

In addition to the two regular packets there was another, the *Alert*, which was known as the bye-boat. That term was sometimes used to denote a stand-by Post Office vessel but the *Alert* was a 'pirate' operated between Weymouth and Guernsey by a local merchant and shipping agent, one Nicholas Robilliard. As she entered the harbour at St Peter Port instead of merely heaving to outside as the packets did, on their way to Jersey, her popularity in Guernsey was assured. Unofficially Robilliard also handled letters, and Guernsey merchants were wont to instruct their correspondents 'direct to us care Mr. Nichs Robilliard, Weymouth, without putting Guernsey, otherwise it will not come by the bye-boat'.[6]

The Post Office naturally disapproved of the *Alert* and in 1806 estimated that annual passenger receipts had fallen from £700 to only £400 as a result of Robilliard's intervention. Though reluctant to admit any inadequacy in the official service they now felt obliged to run an additional packet, and in October 1806 hired the Guernsey cutter *General Doyle*, Captain Charles Pipon, for a year's trial. The augmented service, leaving Weymouth on Wednesdays and Saturdays, was so successful that it was decided to make the arrangement permanent and a new regular packet was built. This, the *Francis Freeling*, entered service under Pipon's command at the end of 1809 and within months the *Alert* went out of business.

A Privateer

More frequent sailings began to encourage tourism, and intending visitors were assured by an island guide book of 1809 that 'the danger of capture by the French Privateers is next to nothing, so numerous are the British Cruisers in the Channel'.[7] The Admiralty had been directed at the outset to ensure that 'His Majesty's Cruizers . . . keep an eye on the Jersey & Guernsey Packets . . .'[8] and that assurance was a tribute to their success. Nevertheless, complacency was unwise. On 29 October 1811 the *Chesterfield* was on passage to the islands when she fell prize to a Cherbourg privateer, *L'Epervier*, an incident still remembered for the notoriety attached to its sequel.

On receiving compensation, as provided for in his agreement, the *Chesterfield*'s captain, Starr Wood (James's son and successor), laid down a replacement of the same name, meanwhile taking as a temporary command the cutter *Rapid*. All went well until one day in October 1812, by which time the new vessel was nearing completion and due for inspection by the inspector of packets. Certain last-minute details wanting attention, and 'do-it-yourself' being as good a way of cutting costs then as now, Wood repaired to the shipyard with four of his men. In his absence the *Rapid* put to sea without him, with the mate in charge and with a depleted crew. Even that might have passed unnoticed had the mate not been incapably drunk, as a result of which the crossing appears to have been a hair-raising experience. Through the Lieutenant-Governor of Guernsey the passengers complained to the postmaster general. The mate was summarily dismissed and, after the inevitable inquiry, which found them both 'highly culpable', Wood and the agent were also dismissed.

Wood appealed, unsuccessfully, and then made a nuisance of himself by flying a flag very much like that of the Post Office and sometimes succeeding in booking passengers who had intended taking the official packet. In 1814 he was granted a licence to run between the islands and Southampton but his opposition remained 'very injurious' to the Post Office as he undercut the Weymouth fares.[9]

His successor at Weymouth was Robert Naylor, who had previously commanded one of the ocean-going packets at Falmouth and now had the *Countess of Liverpool*, specially built for the station. This vessel, however, was rather too large to be economical on the Channel Islands run and Naylor got into debt. By degrees her ownership passed to his creditors until, in 1816, they seized her outright. Withheld from service, since the Post Office recognised no other owner, the *Countess of Liverpool* was replaced by the *Sir William Curtis*, of Ramsgate, Captain John Batten—until Batten got mixed up in Naylor's affairs and was himself imprisoned for debt. In June 1817 he was succeeded by Robert White, a local man, and under White's command the *Countess of Liverpool* resumed service.

Proposals for Steam Packets

It was at about this time that cross-channel routes were beginning to be served by steam vessels. The first to visit the Channel Islands was the *Medina*, which crossed from Southampton to Guernsey on the night of 9–10 June 1823; from there, the following day, she ran an excursion to Jersey.[10] This was an isolated occurrence and not directly concerned with Weymouth, but it aroused such interest that a month later Sir Colin Halkett, Lieutenant-Governor of Jersey, wrote to the postmaster general to urge the use of steam for the island mails. He favoured a contract service based on Southampton or Portsmouth, and the same idea was advocated by at least one commercial operator. The Post Office, however, insisted that if the mails went by steam it would be in official packets and that these would sail from Weymouth. The shorter crossing could be run by smaller vessels, which were cheaper.

Treasury approval for the establishment of steam packets at Weymouth was given in December 1824. The Post Office proposed to transfer two from Milford, the *Ivanhoe* and *Meteor*, and lay down a third, whose completion would enable sailings to be increased to three times a week. The new steamer was ordered in March 1825 and it was hoped to make the change to steam during that year, but the *Ivanhoe* and *Meteor* both needed refitting and there was no further development.

The new steamer was launched on 9 May 1826, with the name

Watersprite, and on 26 June made a trial crossing to Guernsey carrying G. H. Freeling, the assistant secretary responsible for packet administration, and various other postal officials. During the next few months both she and the *Ivanhoe* put in further appearances at Weymouth but despite agitation in the islands there was still no sign of their taking up the mail run. The excuse this time was that both were more urgently needed for the Irish mails. Meanwhile commercial steamers sailing to the islands from Southampton and Portsmouth were taking most of Weymouth's passengers, intensifying the old competition.

Two Wrecks

Earlier in 1826, on 2 February, the partnership of the three sailing packets had been broken prematurely when one of them, the *Hinchinbrook*, struck a reef in the Race of Alderney and sank. The night was fine but very dark and blowing hard, and it appears that while hove-to the captain, Thomas Quirk, underestimated the strength of the current and let the vessel drift. All aboard were landed safely in the ship's boat, the mails and passengers being taken forward to Guernsey in a local vessel while Quirk and his crew returned to Weymouth in the *Francis Freeling*. As a replacement Quirk provided a temporary packet, the *Queen Charlotte*, which ran until the following July. He was then pensioned off, aged sixty-seven.

The loss of the *Hinchinbrook* was shortly followed by a far more serious accident. On 6 September 1826 the *Francis Freeling* left Weymouth for the islands and disappeared with all hands. Exactly what happened was never definitely established but she was thought to have been run down off Portland Bill by a Swedish brig which afterwards reported such an incident. The loss of life so shocked the town that a disaster fund was set up for the crew's dependants and later the postmaster general granted them an annual allowance.

It was a strange twist of fate that Weymouth, having lost only one packet in thirty years, and that by enemy action, should now lose two in quick succession at a time when the end of sail had

Page 17: *(above)* PS *Cygnus* in her original form, under steam and sail, 1857; *(below)* GWR paddle steamers at Weymouth c 1880; nearer the camera is the *Aquila* (Channel Islands service) and astern of her the *South of Ireland* (Cherbourg service)

Page 18: *(above)* PS *Gael* swinging in Weymouth harbour in the summer of 1884; *(below)* PS *Great Western* (1867) at Weymouth, c 1878

been decreed anyway. With steam imminent the gap was filled by further temporary packets—the *Iris*, a former Milford packet latterly kept in reserve at Holyhead; the *Samuel and Julia*, a local lugger which traded to the islands; and the *Dove*.

INTRODUCTION OF STEAM

Steam was introduced the following summer, the *Ivanhoe* and *Watersprite* being formally appointed to the station as from 5 July 1827. When the first official Channel Islands mail to be carried by steam put to sea, on the night of Saturday 7 July, it was the *Watersprite*, under Captain Frederick White, which had the honour. The *Iris* returned to Holyhead and the sole survivor of the regular packets, the *Countess of Liverpool*, was later sent round to the Thames and sold.

That this service, in difficult waters, had been maintained by sailing vessels with so little serious misfortune for thirty-three years, during much of which time England and France were at war, was most creditable. Nevertheless, where a schedule has to be maintained the limitations of sail are not to be denied and with the introduction of steam both speed and reliability improved significantly. The *Dorset County Chronicle* was quick to give the new régime its blessing:[11]

> His Majesty's Steam Packets are now regularly fixed for this station to convey the Mails and Passengers to Guernsey and Jersey; and such is the rapid expedition of these vessels, that on Wednesday last, two gentlemen having taken their breakfast in London, departed by the Magnet coach, and arrived at the Golden Lion, Weymouth, the same evening, in good time for the packet, so that on the following morning, they were seated at their breakfast at Payn's hotel, Guernsey, all accomplished within 24 hours. They are dispatched on Wednesday's and Saturday's at nine o'clock in the evening, and return to Weymouth every Sunday and Wednesday morning.
>
> We understand his Majesty's steam packets at Weymouth are not permitted to interfere with the mercantile or shipping interest of the town, as no goods are permitted on board except the

> passenger's luggage. We highly approve of this regulation, for to permit opposite interests to impinge upon, or interfere with, each other, is to excite a spirit of intrigue and animosity, which it should be the object of legislation to prevent.

In Jersey, the captains of the commercial steamers failed to echo this ponderous approval. Rather was their reaction one of 'intrigue and animosity'. The Jersey harbour committee ordered the extremity of the south quay—the best deep water berth—to be reserved for the packets, but the commercial captains resented this ruling and consistently disregarded it. If they supposed that their attitude might encourage the Post Office to reconsider a contract service they were soon disillusioned, however. In January 1828 G. H. Freeling reported that the station was functioning satisfactorily and the postmaster general thereupon fixed the agent's salary at £300 a year—just double the old figure—and those of the captains at £280. Two months later it was decided to start the third weekly sailing.

The Meteor

The packet brought in for the additional sailing was the *Meteor*, which would have been at Weymouth earlier had the introduction of steam not been delayed until after the completion of the *Watersprite*. As one of the two packets which had inaugurated steam at Holyhead, in June 1821, the *Meteor* was a noteworthy vessel. She and her partner, the *Lightning*, were built on 'Seppings's Improved Principle'[12] and by crossing the Irish Sea regularly throughout the winter convinced the Post Office of steam's reliability. Freeling attributed their success to the strength of their construction, describing them as 'nothing but masses of wood and copper'. The other 'Irish' packet now at Weymouth, the *Ivanhoe*, was also of more than usual interest. Launched on 17 February 1820, she was one of the earliest seagoing steamers and was bought by the Post Office in November 1821, after running privately. She was built of fir (Scots pine) instead of the more usual oak and was described by the Post Office at the time of purchase as 'not as strong as the Post Office packets but as strong as most ordinary vessels'. She served at Holyhead from June 1822 until July 1824, when both she and the *Meteor* were transferred to Milford.

The latter's transfer to Weymouth was effective from 5 April 1828 and she made her first passage on the 13th. The revised programme, 'out' on Tuesday, Thursday and Saturday evenings and 'home' on Mondays, Thursdays and Saturdays, was authorised as an experiment for the summer but in 1829 the additional sailing was discontinued as the increase in receipts did not cover the increase in costs. Three steamers were retained, 'one to lay up and act as reserve'; the *Meteor*, however, was not long one of them. On the morning of 23 February 1830 she left Guernsey roads under the command of Lt Ross Connor, passed the Casquets at 12.30 pm, in thick haze, and continued on her course at about 7 knots. About 8 pm, when near Church Ope, Portland, she went aground. There was no loss of life but as the tide fell a large crowd descended on the wreck and set about looting the passengers' baggage. (Portlanders, closely acquainted with the notorious Chesil Beach, were practised wreckers). The mail reached Weymouth overland, at 2 am the next day. Afterwards the machinery and gear were salvaged and the wreck sold, a move that earned reproof for the agent for his omitting to obtain the postmaster general's consent. An inquiry was held but no report of it has survived, so this apparently casual loss—of a local vessel in moderate conditions—remains something of a mystery.

The Flamer

A replacement for the *Meteor* was ordered the following August. Named *Flamer* she was launched on 29 April 1831 and arrived at Weymouth at the end of July. Through a builder's error her beam was 2in greater than the designed figure, equivalent to an extra 12 tons. This was expected to make her a better ship and on entering service she was acclaimed as a marked improvement on the older packets—though only the contract tonnage was paid for, it may be added! Her total cost, including engines, was £7,190 (compared with £9,658 for the *Watersprite*).

In spite of her extra inches the *Flamer* soon proved to be an indifferent sea-boat, rolling badly and often getting into trouble. One crossing in December 1833, a particularly nasty one, was nearly her last. Leaving Weymouth on Thursday evening she was no sooner at sea than she had to put into Portland roads for shelter; from there, in the morning, she returned to Weymouth. At 7 pm she tried again, and by the following morning had got as far as Alderney. Unable to make any further headway against the gale she was still there some hours later and her captain, William Roberts, then gave up and turned about for Weymouth. At 1 pm on Saturday, more than thirty-six hours after she had first left, the *Flamer* was twenty miles off the Casquets when an outsize wave carried away all the deck gear and the ship's boat and flooded the cabin, obliging the twelve passengers to huddle together on the companion ladder—the only safe spot between the waters within and the waters without. On the Sunday afternoon she crawled back into the safety of Weymouth harbour with Roberts and five other men seriously injured, one fatally. It was said that neither of the other packets would have survived such a battering.

When conditions were as bad as this a week might pass with no mail but, through all but the worst, the captains adhered to their schedules with great regularity, in the best traditions of the public service. Their reputation in another respect was less creditable, however; they were tough but they were also rough, and incivility was as often occasion for complaint as courage was for praise. The 'broadside of insults' which the captain of the *Watersprite* was alleged to have let loose on a gentleman passenger 'who had had the misfortune to soil the bridge a little' seems to have been fairly typical. The captain in question, Frederick White, was afterwards taken to task in the island newspapers for his 'brusque manners'.[13] In Jersey the captains' surly attitude served to aggravate what the Post Office came to regard as a 'Southampton bias' (suspected to stem initially from local financial interest in the

HIS MAJESTY'S POST OFFICE

STEAM  PACKETS.

One of these Packets with the Mails and Passengers, leaves Weymouth for the Islands of GUERNSEY and JERSEY, every Wednesday and Saturday, at 9 o'clock, P. M. weather permitting, and leaves the Islands for Weymouth, every Tuesday and Saturday, the time being dependant on the tides.

RATES OF PASSAGE MONEY.

Cabin Passengers, each..................	£1	1	0
Female Servants, each	0	15	0
Male Servants, each	0	12	6

Children under Ten years of age, to be charged half the rates paid by their Parents.

Carriages with Four Wheels, each	3	0	0
Ditto, Two Wheels, each	1	10	0
Horses, each	1	10	0
Dogs, with their Owners, each...........	0	2	6
Ditto, on Freight, each.................	0	5	0
Parcels of or under 30lbs. weight........	0	2	6
Cash or Bullion, per Thousand Pounds ..	1	1	0

The above Rates to be paid in British Money, and the Freight of all Parcels must be paid for at the time they are received on board.

These Packets possess every accommodation for Passengers, are remarkably fine Vessels, and the Captains Gentlemen of great skill in their profession.

RESIDENT AGENT,

CAPT. J. AGNEW STEVENS, R. N.

COMMANDERS,

Capt. ROBERT WHITE, *Watersprite*,

Capt. LIVEING, *Flamer*,

Capt. COMBEN, *Ivanhoe*.

Weymouth–Channel Islands steam packet notice, 1835 (*Commins's New Weymouth Guide*) private steamers) and in 1832 the postmaster general issued a general warning, remarking 'the fact cannot be denied that they are exceedingly gross and violent persons'.

PARLIAMENTARY CENSURE

The management of a sizeable fleet of steam vessels was a specialised job for which the Post Office was quite unfitted and which it had never relished. When the first steam packets appeared the cutter captains had declined ownership, having had no experience of navigating or maintaining steamers. Commercial contract was considered unreliable, so Crown ownership became the only choice. Time had revealed the system's defects. Most of the packets were out-of-date, undersized and ill-equipped, and whereever the existence of a competing service offered direct comparison with commercial vessels, as in the case of the Channel Islands, the comparison was always to the packets' detriment. Rightly the Post Office's first concern was with the mails, but failure to study passenger interests drove traffic away and inflated costs. In 1830 a government commission reported 'improvident outlay on steamers and defective management and control'.[14] Two years later another inquiry condemned Post Office responsibility altogether and recommended that the packets should be transferred to the Admiralty.[15] But nothing was done.

The effect of this situation at Weymouth was increasingly to divert passengers to Southampton. The steamers there, under the stimulus of competition between rival companies, went from strength to strength. Better built, better found and better engined than the packets, they carried not only more passengers but, unofficially, many letters, as they provided a better transit to and from London.[16]

In 1836 came yet another report, covering Weymouth and five other Post Office stations.[17] All ran at a loss, but it is interesting to read that Weymouth's was comparatively modest and that the incompetence and fraud that were rife elsewhere were entirely absent. The inquiry found 'the accounts kept with great regularity and a very efficient and proper control exercised . . . as far as depended upon the agent'. The agent was Captain James Agnew Stevens, Lieut RN, a former Holyhead steam packet captain well qualified by training and experience to manage a seagoing service.[18]

Giving evidence before the inquiry, Stevens made the usual recommendations for improving the packets—greater length and greater power—and suggested that thus altered they could easily extend their summer range to St Malo or Granville; Captain Liveing, of the *Flamer*, said that the lack of power was such that in a head sea the wheels 'could be turned at all only with difficulty'; and Captain White, of the *Watersprite*, complained of lack of publicity, pointing out that he had often brought back to Weymouth passengers who, from such westerly places as Bristol, had gone to the islands via Southampton ignorant that any other service existed. One disadvantage that was peculiar to Weymouth was its distance from Holyhead, where the Post Office dockyard was situated. Once in about four years each packet had to make a voyage of nearly 400 miles, right round Land's End, even though there was a naval dockyard as near as Portsmouth.[19]

ADMIRALTY TAKEOVER

As a result of this report a general transfer of responsibility to the Admiralty was ordered, and this took effect on 16 January 1837. Post Office jurisdiction was thereafter limited to deciding departure times and routes. In October 1836, preparatory to the transfer, Stevens reported on the three Weymouth packets as follows:[20]

> 'Watersprite' 186 tons has been lengthened by the Bow 20ft which has added to her former tonnage (162) 24 Tons, she is now receiving Additional Steam Power at Blackwall which will give her Engines of about 75 horses power, until she is tried it will be impossible to Report fully on her, but I think that she will prove a fast and efficient Vessel, and as sound as the day she was first launched.
>
> 'Flamer' 165 Tons 60 horse power, is only 5 years old, in perfectly good order strong and well built in the bottom but

slight and requires strengthening above the waterline, she is too narrow and wants stability in bad weather, is capable when strengthened of receiving the same additional Steam Power as the 'Watersprite', and would then be a fast and, but for her want of stability and body, a fine efficient Vessel.

'Ivanhoe' 185 Tons [*sic*] 60 horse power, was built in 1818 [*sic*] and purchased by Government (I believe) in 1822 is very much out of order both in Hull and Machinery from long Service, is very slow, and in my opinion not worth a general repair.

The lengthening of the *Watersprite* had been taken in hand by White's of Gosport the previous June. On returning to Weymouth, in December 1836, she was reported by the *Jersey Times* as 'wonderfully improved in speed since her lengthening', a view borne out by the respective passage times and coal consumptions of the three packets at the time of handing over to the Admiralty:

Packet	*Average passage each way**	*Tons of coal carried*	*Consumption per hour*
Flamer	14h 29m	17	7cwt
Ivanhoe	14h 57m	20	8cwt
Watersprite	11h 50m	19	$6\frac{3}{4}$cwt

The Admiralty's first move at Weymouth was to withdraw the *Ivanhoe*. 'Leaky and exhibiting the marks of age' she was sent to Woolwich for repairs at the end of January 1837 but closer inspection confirmed Stevens's opinion and she did not return. Renamed *Boxer* she lasted on minor naval duties until about the end of 1841. In May the other two steamers were renamed, *Flamer* becoming *Fearless* and *Watersprite* becoming *Wildfire,* while an outward sign of improved discipline was the appearance of the packet captains in cocked hats and wearing swords.

During the next few months there were frequent changes of vessel on the station: in September 1837 *Fearless* was sent to Chatham for the improvements recommended by Stevens and was temporarily replaced by the Admiralty steam vessel *Pluto*; on 27

* Including calling off Guernsey

H.M. MAIL PACKET ***DASHER,*** 1838 - COMPOSITE DECK PLAN

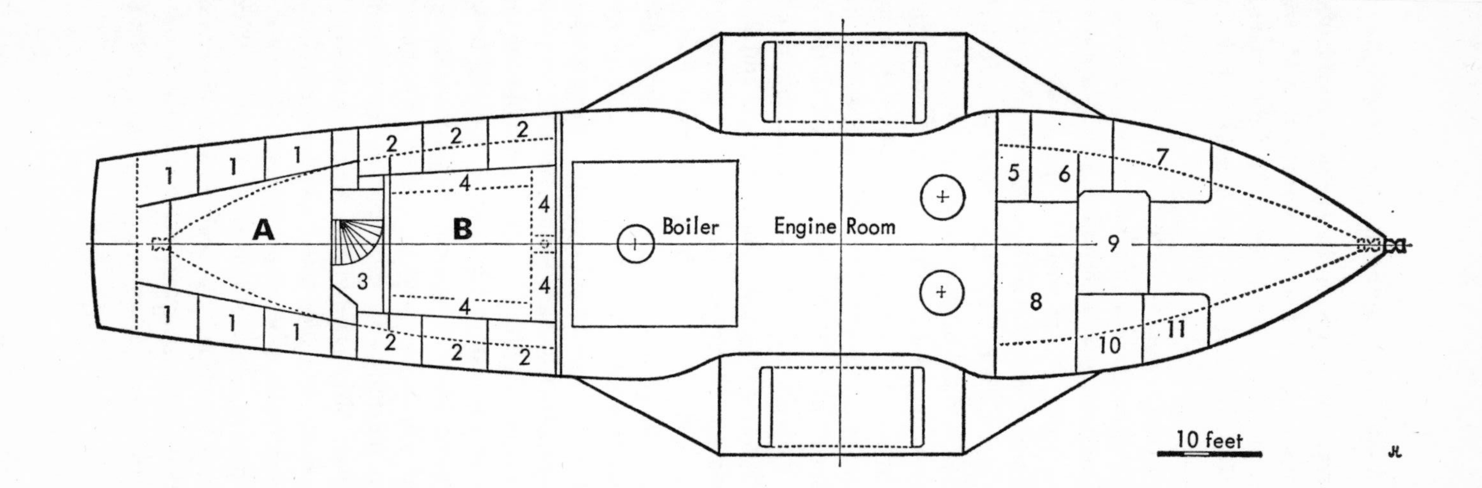

A	Ladies' Cabin	3	Steward's Room	8	Horse & Luggage Room
B	Gentlemen's Cabin	4	Couch	9	Commander
		5	Mail Room	10	Sleeping Berth
1	Bed Place	6	2nd Master	11	Pilot
2	Two Bed Places	7	Engineer		

(based on original drawings in the National Maritime Museum, Greenwich, by courtesy of the trustees)

December *Dasher*, replacement for the *Ivanhoe*, was launched at Chatham; in January 1838 *Fearless* returned; and, lastly, in April 1838 *Dasher* arrived at Weymouth, *Pluto* returned to Portsmouth and *Wildfire* was sent to Woolwich for repairs and re-boilering. *Pluto* was considerably larger than the regular packets but her performance appears to have been unremarkable. She was, in fact, not liked, as extra hands had to be hired to man her.

Dasher's first appearance in Guernsey drew the approval of at any rate one newspaper, which wrote: 'The Dasher appears to be an excellent sea-boat and in good calm weather should reach Weymouth in six hours'. But a few days later, perhaps reflecting that in other than 'good calm weather' the packets had a rather tarnished reputation, the same paper made the comforting observation 'a newly invented and very elegant lifebuoy hangs over the stern in constant readiness'.[21] She was undoubtedly the best packet on the service though still not fully equal to the job. An improvement in November 1838 was the fitting of cycloidal paddle wheels, which gave 7½ knots in a cross sea and 9 in calm water. This was considered very satisfactory.

In the summer of 1839 it was finally decided that *Fearless* would have to be replaced. With her new engines she could manage 4 knots in a strong head sea but the increase in power was a mixed blessing as it increased her coal consumption. Extra supplies had to be carried in bags on the deck and that in turn aggravated her instability. She was sent to Woolwich and performed minor naval duties until 1875, when she was broken up.

Her replacement at Weymouth was the *Cuckoo*, lately in reserve at Holyhead. *Cuckoo* arrived in August 1839 but did not enter service until the following October, on completion of repairs and repainting. Although by then an oldish vessel, having been in service since April 1824, when she inaugurated steam at Milford, she appears to have been well thought of at Weymouth and 'not to be surpassed in her qualities as a sea-boat'. Her cabin accommodation was described as 'replete with every comfort' and she once beat the Southampton steamer *Lady de Saumarez* by fourteen minutes between Guernsey and Jersey, to the *County*

Chronicle's unconcealed satisfaction. Until taken over by the Admiralty she was named *Cinderella*.

COMMERCIAL OPPOSITION

A quite different development in 1839 was the appearance, for a few weeks, of a commercial rival to the packets. A company called the Commercial Steam Packet Company had for some time been running a coastal service between London, Southampton and Weymouth. In April 1839 they advertised the steamers *Calpe* and *City of Glasgow* to extend that service on alternate Tuesdays to Cherbourg:

> Day voyage to France in seven hours (weather permitting) at 9 a.m. precisely. Saloon 15/-, Fore cabin 10/-. Carriages £3.3.0, Horses £2.2.0. Returning from Cherbourg the following evening, Wednesday, at 7 p.m. No landing from Boats at Weymouth or Cherbourg.[22]

And in September these sailings (by the *Kent*, not, as advertised, the *Calpe*) were extended to Alderney and Guernsey.

The *City of Glasgow*, and also the *Grand Turk*, were still advertised to Cherbourg until at least March 1840—a link which is itself of interest, both as Weymouth's first commercial cross-channel steamer service and in the light of the Great Western's association forty years later—but the Channel Islands calls lasted only until 1 November 1839.

Further opposition now threatening the packets was far more serious, however. The completion in May 1840 of the London & South Western Railway brought Southampton to within about three hours of London and before long letters were being carried that way with the Post Office's approval, provided that they were suitably endorsed, eg 'by private steamer'.

The possibility of Southampton becoming the Channel Islands packet station had been the object of rumour while the 'rail-road' was still being built and in 1841 the Admiralty appointed a committee to look into the question.[23] While conceding that Southampton now provided a quicker transit to and from London the committee considered that on balance the advantage still lay with Weymouth, commercially because it was nearer Falmouth, and thus a better link with the ocean mails, and navigationally for reasons already well known. Little importance was attached to the shallowness of the harbour as Weymouth Corporation had promised dredging. Crossing to the islands in the *Dasher* the committee found her 'deficient in size and power' and recommended the building of three new vessels of about 400 tons and 180hp, to run three times a week.

Reading the report today, one is struck by the absence of direct reference to Southampton's railway, evidence that its significance had been largely missed. Stevens had revealed an awareness of railway potential in cross-channel transport as far back as 1836, when he referred in his evidence before the Commissioners of Inquiry to 'the apparent certainty of a railroad being very shortly constructed from Weymouth to Bath, joining the Great Western one', and of this probably resulting in 'the considerable enlargement of Weymouth harbour'. But six years later a Weymouth railway had still to get beyond the talking stage, and it was with Southampton that the real advantage now lay.

SOUTHAMPTON TAKEOVER

In 1843 a London & South Western subsidiary, the South Western Steam Packet Company, took over the now bankrupt Commercial Steam Packet Company and the resulting integration of rail and sea produced a service that Weymouth could not match. Proposals for bigger packets were clearly too late. The transfer in September 1843 of many ocean mails from Falmouth to Southampton weakened the case for Weymouth packets anyhow and by the beginning of 1844 the truth was out. The Post Office, 'backed by the giant shareholders of the London & South Western' was negotiating a Channel Islands mail contract via Southampton.

Protest meetings and constant press disparagement of the Southampton steamers were unavailing, and in March 1845 the

Instructions, No. **11**, **1845**.

By Command of the Postmaster General.

NOTICE TO THE PUBLIC,

AND

Instructions to all Postmasters, Sub-Postmasters, and Letter Receivers.

GENERAL POST OFFICE,
April, 1845.

ON and after the **26th** instant, the Mails for the **CHANNEL ISLANDS** will be conveyed from *Southampton* instead of from Weymouth as at present.

The Mails will be made up and dispatched from Southampton on the *Evenings* of *Tuesday, Thursday*, and *Saturday*.

Channel Islands mails announcement, 1845 (*Post Office*)

County Chronicle announced its deep regret that the packet crews had received twenty-eight days notice. Ironically there was at last some real hope of a Weymouth railway; two bills, indeed, were even then before Parliament. But at least another year must elapse before any construction could be expected, and by then the packets would be gone.

The end came in April. On the 5th, *Dasher* left for Woolwich to pay off. Her commander, Robert White, was afterwards presented with a testimonial by the mayor and other leading citizens. The next to go was *Wildfire*, which alone had served at Weymouth from beginning to end. Having, as the *Watersprite*, taken out the first mail she might appropriately have brought home the last, but her final crossing was on Saturday 19 April; on the 24th she too departed for Woolwich. The last mail, on the 26th, was thus brought in by the *Cuckoo*. That night the outward Channel Islands mails went from Southampton, as they would continue to do for many years. On 5 May *Cuckoo* left for Woolwich. As it turned out, Weymouth's railway was not a year or two away but nearly twelve.

Dasher afterwards spent many more years in Channel Islands waters, on fishery protection, a service performed for a time by *Cuckoo* also; *Wildfire* became a tender at Sheerness. *Cuckoo* was sold for breaking up in October 1864, *Dasher* towards the end of 1885 and *Wildfire* in December 1888.[24]

Notes to this chapter are on page 220

CHAPTER TWO

ARRIVAL OF THE RAILWAY, AND RIVAL STEAMERS (1845-59)

TWO LINES

FOR Weymouth, withdrawal of the packets was a blow to civic pride and a commercial loss. The town was aggrieved, and looked for redress to the coming of the railway. What, then, were the prospects?

The two lines in the offing in April 1845 were the Wilts Somerset & Weymouth, nominally independent but with Great Western backing, and the Southampton & Dorchester; the latter was planned to reach Weymouth by way of a junction at Dorchester and running powers over the former. At one time the Great Western had had an interest in the Southampton line as well but had relinquished it to the London & South Western. The drive for Weymouth thus became part of the long west-country rivalry between those two companies, a rivalry that was nowhere keener than between their steamer services to the Channel Islands.

Both railways were authorised in 1845 and an amending bill deposited for the following session by the WS&W provided for an extension to the harbour, about a mile beyond the station. Alternative proposals with the same object emanated from the S&D and from a westward extension of that line, the Exeter Dorchester Weymouth Junction Coast Railway. All three could not succeed, of course, but the last-mentioned being dropped, and the S&D's bill being held over to 1847, the field was left to the WS&W, whose extension was authorised on 3 August 1846.

As far as the lines to Weymouth itself were concerned all seemed set fair. The Southampton line reached Dorchester in 1847 and the WS&W was going well. Weymouth's hopes ran high.

But in the wake of the 'railway mania' came the slump and, when the Weymouth line had got as far as Westbury, all work stopped. The town was thus left railway-less and re-establishment of the packets apparently as far away as ever.[1]

The South Western shows interest

Meanwhile the abandonment of the short-sea route was the cause of some official misgiving. In 1848 the LSWR applied to Parliament for its own steamer powers and it was stated in support of the bill that 'the Post Office are desirous that we should run a boat from Weymouth to the Channel Islands'.[2] Two years previously the South Western Steam Packet Co had been reconstituted as the New South Western Steam Navigation Co and, on being granted powers,[3] the LSW took a formal lease of the Navigation Co's fleet. This regularised the existing close relationship and made the vessels concerned railway steamers in all but name.

The principal effect of this development was, of course, to strengthen the competitive position of Southampton, but the act also named five other ports from which services might be run if the company wished. One of these was Weymouth and just two years later, on 14 August 1850, the steamer *South Western* started a weekly service between Weymouth and St Malo via Guernsey, Jersey and Granville. As passengers had to travel to and from Dorchester by bus this attempt to reopen the route was, however, premature. Patronage was slender and at the end of the year the *South Western* went back to Southampton.[4]

More significantly, in March 1850 the WS&W was taken over by the Great Western and work re-started. Progress was still extremely slow and powers had to be twice renewed, but towards the end of 1856 completion was at last in sight. Despite competition afforded by regular Channel Islands sailings from London, Shoreham and Plymouth, as well as the thrice-weekly Southampton mail service, prospects for Weymouth looked brighter than for years.

Although the new line was owned by the Great Western, only the South Western possessed the necessary powers and organisa-

Page 35: *(above)* PS *Cygnus* in her final form, alongside the Albert Pier, Jersey, c 1883; *(below)* PS *Brighton* in her final form, 1886

Page 36: The Lynx class: *(above)* in passenger service; the *Antelope*, c 1910; *(below)* as converted for cargo; the *Lynx*, c 1920. Note the removal of superstructure

tion to run a steamer service and it was the latter which now took the initiative. In November 1856 two Southampton captains, Goodridge and Cook, visited Weymouth to weigh up the prospects. The quayside and harbour generally were in a poor state of repair after years of minimal attention but the captains appeared to be satisfied with what they found and, after talking things over with the mayor, returned home to complete their plans. James Goodridge, already well known in Southampton, later became South Western agent in Weymouth.

In another two months the railway was ready, Great Western and South Western trains entering the town on the same day, 20 January 1857. There was, after all, no harbour extension, the powers obtained in 1846 having lapsed, but the way to a new steamer service was now open.

The Great Western lends a hand

The Great Western does not appear initially to have thought much about the question of running a steamer service, but that was not surprising. Merely getting to Weymouth had required an excessive outlay, which promised only a limited return, and rapid expansion in other directions had further stretched the company's resources. There was, however, no lack of interest in Jersey, where dissatisfaction with the Southampton monopoly had for some time nourished ideas of reopening the Weymouth route once the town was on the railway. A group of local merchants and other influential residents contemplated building 'two first-class iron steamers with all modern improvements' to run in connection with the Weymouth trains.

In November 1856 Captain Stevens, by then retired to Jersey but still loyally interested in his old station, had put similar proposals to William Eliot, a Weymouth alderman. He had heard, he wrote, that when the South Western started running from Weymouth they would use their two slowest and worst boats, the *South Western* (of the short-lived 1850 service) and the *Atalanta*, to discredit the route, and urged that if Weymouth were ever again to be a serious contender for the Channel Islands trade it was 'now or never'. 'The Great Western,' he continued, 'should study their own interest and lend a hand.'

In spite of their earlier indifference the Great Western proved, on being approached, to be quite ready to lend a hand, and as soon as the line was opened two directors, F. N. Micklethwait and D. Ogilvy, went round Weymouth and the islands addressing public meetings to drum up support for a proposed new company. A prospectus was issued in the name of the Weymouth & Channel Islands Steam Packet Company Limited, extolling Weymouth's familiar advantages and contemplating a journey time between London and Jersey of twelve hours. As the best trains by either line then took about five hours to Weymouth, the sea crossing would have been allowed only seven, including a Guernsey call, and transfer between the station and the steamer nothing at all! This rather careless promise was afterwards explained away as a 'miscalculation of distances'.

In the islands, particularly in Jersey, the response was enthusiastic, but Weymouth was apathetic, Micklethwait complaining to Charles Saunders, the Great Western secretary, that the 'Weymouth gentlemen' were 'devoid of spirit and money'. Nothing daunted, the promoters pushed ahead and early in 1857 decided to obtain second-hand tonnage instead of waiting to build new.

The choice fell on two paddle steamers then lying idle at Victoria Dock, London. Named *Aquila* and *Cygnus* these had been built in 1854 for an unsuccessful Harwich–Antwerp service started by the North of Europe Steam Navigation Co and were now offered at £9,000 each or on charter on agreed terms. Both were reported to need some attention but to be generally in sound condition, with satisfactory engines and boilers. After some deliberation it was decided to charter them for eighteen months for £50 a week each, with an option to purchase within six months at the offering price less whatever might have been paid in charter fees. So far, so good. But the company still had no legal existence, and, having hoped to commence sailings on 11 April, the promoters now reluctantly accepted the need for a month's postponement.

Meanwhile, with an established organisation to call upon, the South Western held the advantage and on 26 March 1857 Archibald Scott, the traffic manager, informed Saunders that their service would start on Monday 13 April. Pious pronouncements had been made about friendly relations between the two companies but friction arose right at the outset over the question of fares. The South Western announced publicly that they would charge 35s first class (£1·75) and 25s second class (£1·25) between London and Guernsey or Jersey, and proposed interavailability of tickets. This announcement was made without prior consultation with the Great Western and was interpreted by Saunders as intended to prejudice the Weymouth route, current fares via Southampton, inclusive of port charges of 1s (5p), being only 31s and 21s respectively (£1·55 and £1·05). The South Western refused to raise the Southampton fares but, when Saunders stood firm and announced the Packet Co's intention to charge 31s and 21s, they were obliged to follow suit. Interavailability was abandoned.

Scott's announcement precipitated a flurry of activity in the Packet Company camp. At Lowestoft, where the *Aquila* and *Cygnus* were being refitted by the owners under the supervision of Captain William Prowse RN, one of the company's nominated directors, feverish efforts were being made to prepare them for sea. Work often continued late into the night. By 11 April they were ready and when they underwent trials Prowse happily described them as 'real beauties'. *Aquila* logged 12½ knots, but *Cygnus* could manage only 11¼, owing to 'stiffness in her machinery'.

The Express

Back in Weymouth the South Western's arrangements went smoothly ahead. The paddle steamer *Express*, having arrived from Southampton on 8 April, lay open for public inspection before entering service. On the 13th, as promised, she sailed for the islands. The *Dorset County Chronicle* describes the occasion with side-whiskered solemnity:[5]

> On Monday the South Western Railway Co's Steamer the Express, Captain Harvey, opened the campaign of steam communication from Weymouth to Guernsey and Jersey . . . The extreme coldness and severity of the weather would have rendered a sea voyage anything but delightful, therefore none but those impelled by necessity accompanied the Express on her first trip from our harbour . . . The manner in which the noble vessel steamed through the bay, showed her to be admirably calculated for her work, and even in much more boisterous weather her very great steadiness of motion will tend to obviate many of the 'disagreeables' attendant on salt water travelling . . . the Express . . . will doubtless secure a good share of public support.

The crossing took ten hours, and the actual number of passengers 'impelled by necessity' was just seven. On the return crossing the following day there were eight.

As the *Express* was leaving Weymouth the *Cygnus* and *Aquila* were preparing to leave Lowestoft, the former for Weymouth, the latter for Jersey direct, so that the Packet Co's service could start from both sides on the same date. Both experienced the bad weather that marred the passage of the *Express* and off Beachy Head the crew of the *Cygnus* had to bale with buckets when the pumps failed—evidence, perhaps, of over-hurried preparation. But Captain Prowse brought his ship safely into Weymouth on the afternoon of 14 April and, after showing her off in the bay, berthed alongside the Custom House where, like the *Express* the previous week, the ship was exhibited to the public's admiring gaze. In Jersey spirits ran high and when, that same evening, after a rough passage lasting over thirty hours, the *Aquila* entered St Helier 'in gallant style' she too, we are told, was much admired by the local populace.

The Steam Packet Company Incorporated

The 14th also saw the culmination of much activity behind the scenes, with the Weymouth & Channel Islands Steam Packet Company being formally incorporated. The authorised capital was £40,000, in £10 shares, with provision to increase that figure to £100,000 by special resolution; 2,000 shares were allotted to

Jersey, 1,000 to Guernsey, and 500 each to Weymouth and the Great Western. The shares were quickly taken up except, as predicted by Micklethwait, in Weymouth, where half the allotment remained untaken. It is of interest in passing that the original Great Western shareholding included both Brunel and Gooch.

Twelve provisional directors were nominated, two of whom, Micklethwait and Ogilvy, represented the Great Western. Weymouth was represented by four, including Prowse; Jersey also by four, one of whom, Elias Neel, a banker and States deputy, was nominated chairman; and Guernsey by two. Immediately the company was incorporated plans were changed again, and on 16 April an advertisement in the *County Chronicle* announced that sailings would start the following day.

The departure of the *Cygnus* seems to have attracted comparatively little attention. With the *Express* already crossing regularly it must have been something of an anti-climax. Also, as the opening date had not long previously been advertised as 15 May the public were unprepared. Nevertheless, to be fully operational so soon after the South Western was quite an achievement, considering that all was new and untried and that the company had been in existence for only three days.

Unfortunately the hasty start had left many things unsettled. There had, for example, been difficulty in manning the ships; it was nearly three months before the company appointed a captain of their own to the *Aquila*. Far worse, there had been no time to make proper arrangements with the owners, with the result that the charter rested upon the personal guarantee of a single shareholder, a certain Mr Mills. Nor was the relationship with the Great Western based on anything more substantial than a gentleman's agreement.

This situation was the cause of much heartburning among the shareholders, especially in Guernsey. The two gentlemen who had been nominated as that island's directors, Henry Tupper and Thomas Priaulx, withdrew their support, and although Priaulx did afterwards consent to stand, mischief had been done to the

WEYMOUTH & CHANNEL ISLANDS

STEAM PACKET COMPANY LIMITED.

STEAM COMMUNICATION BETWEEN

WEYMOUTH

AND THE

CHANNEL ISLANDS

THE **IRON** **OF THIS**  **FAST** **Steamboats** **COMPANY.**

'AQUILA' & 'CYGNUS'

Fitted up in the most splendid style, with every requisite accommodation, and making DAYLIGHT PASSAGES both ways, now ply between Weymouth and the Channel Islands as follows:—

FROM WEYMOUTH TO JERSEY, CALLING OFF GUERNSEY,

Every Tuesday, Thursday, Friday, and Saturday at 7 A. M.

FROM JERSEY TO WEYMOUTH, CALLING OFF GUERNSEY,

Every Monday, Wednesday, Friday and Saturday, at ½ past 6 A. M.

☞ **Passengers are requested to be on Board a quarter of an hour before the times fixed for departure.**

FARES.

	1st Class.	2nd Class.
London to Guernsey or Jersey, or vice versa,	**31s.**	**21s.**
Weymouth to Guernsey or Jersey, or vice versa,	**18s.**	**12s.**

CHILDREN under Two Years of Age, Free. **DITTO** above Two and under Twelve, Half-price

Tickets from LONDON to GUERNSEY and JERSEY, or vice versa, are available for three days; they include Railway and Steam packet Fares only, and are not transferrable.

BAGGAGE.

All Goods other than personal baggage, belonging to passengers, although not entered on the Manifest as Merchandise, to pay accustomed freight. Passengers are requested to have all Packages composing their Luggage distinctly marked with their names and addresses, and to take the whole on board with them. The Company is not liable for any loss or damage to Baggage.

STEWARDS' FEES.

First Class, 2s.; Second Class, 1s.; Children under 2 Years of age, free—above 2 and under 12, half Fees.

PROVISIONS MAY BE OBTAINED ON BOARD AT MODERATE RATES.

☞ To prevent delay in the Shipment of Goods, particulars of the contents and value of each Package should be forwarded by Post to the Company's Agents, as under. In the case of BONDED or EXCISEABLE GOODS, the Goods WITHOUT SUCH ADVICE CANNOT BE SHIPPED.

The Company are not liable for unavoidable delays, accidents, or sea-risks of any kind whatsoever. The Company do not undertake to carry Passengers or Goods by any particular Vessel, or by any Train in particular.

FOR FURTHER PARTICULARS APPLY TO THE FOLLOWING AGENTS, VIZ:—IN

WEYMOUTH - - - - - **Captain Wm. ROBERTS.**
GUERNSEY - - - - - - **Mr. John JONES.**
JERSEY - - - - - - **Mr. RENOUF,**

Also at the PADDINGTON STATION, LONDON; and all other Stations of the Great Western Railway Company.

BY ORDER,

JOSEPH MAUNDERS, MANAGER & SECRETARY.

WEYMOUTH, MAY 1st, 1857.

JEFFERY, PRINTER, ST. MARY STREET, WEYMOUTH.

Channel Islands handbill, 1857 (*British Transport Historical Records*)

cause. No letters of allotment had been issued and in May Neel wrote anxiously to Saunders asking whether the Great Western would take up rescinded shares.

The steamer charter-party, back-dated to 13 April (the day on which the *Cygnus* and *Aquila* left Lowestoft), and the working agreement with the Great Western were eventually signed, at the Victoria Hotel, Weymouth, on 14 May. The main provisions of the latter were that the Packet Company would run at least two double crossings a week, to connect with the train services; that through rates and apportionment of receipts would apply as might be agreed; and—most important—that at the end of twelve months any loss on the steamers would be made good by the Great Western from their share of the receipts from through traffic, after deducting cartage and terminals. The original term of the agreement was eighteen months.

Through fares were less than the corresponding rail and sea fares booked separately, and the following examples illustrate the way in which the apportionment of receipts applied (second-class fares):

Journey	*Booked separately* *Rail*	*Steamer*	*Through Fare*	*Steamer proportion* *to G'sey*	*to J'sey*
London–G'sey or Jersey	20s (£1)	12s (60p)	21s (£1·05)	7s (35p)	8s 9d (44p)
Bristol–G'sey or Jersey	11s (55p)	12s (60p)	21s (£1·05)	10s 2d (51p)	12s (60p)

Four double crossings were made each week, to the *Express*'s more realistic three. Average passenger carryings appear to have been about twenty. The initial emphasis was on passengers rather than cargo and although by May the *County Chronicle* was reporting a 'healthy bustle' on Weymouth quay, where previously 'near stagnation' had prevailed, goods traffic was slow to develop. Receipts for the first five weeks were about £300 from goods and £678 from passengers. Passengers carried in the same period totalled 847, about one for every three travelling via Southamp-

GREAT WESTERN RAILWAY.

PARCEL RATES

BETWEEN

LONDON AND JERSEY OR GUERNSEY.

PARCELS are now conveyed to and from LONDON and JERSEY or GUERNSEY, *via* WEYMOUTH, at the following Rates, including Collection and Delivery:—

				s.	d.
Not exceeding		14 lbs.		1	6
Above 14 lbs. and not exceeding		28 lbs.		2	0
„ 28 lbs.	do.	56 lbs.		2	6
„ 56 lbs.	do.	84 lbs.		3	0
„ 84 lbs.	do.	112 lbs.		4	0
„ 112 lbs.				1*d.* per lb.	

RECEIVING OFFICES IN LONDON:

The Paddington Station;
Bull and Mouth, St. Martin's-le-Grand;
No. 351, Oxford Street, near the Pantheon;
No. 27, King Street, Cheapside;
No. 16, Fish Street Hill, opposite the Monument;
No. 264, Holborn;
No. 269, Strand, corner of Saint Clement's Church Yard;
No. 25, Regent Street, corner of Jermyn Street;
Nos. 62 & 63, Bridge Road, Lambeth;
No. 55, Parliament Street;
Nos. 43 & 44, Crutched Friars.

AND THE FOLLOWING AUXILIARY OFFICES:

Hatchett's White Horse Cellar, Piccadilly:
Slark's Office, 13, High Road, Knightsbridge;
Gloucester Warehouse, Oxford Street;
Kingston's Office, 11, Southampton Street, Fitzroy Square;
Peacock, Islington,
Bull Inn, Aldgate;
Four Swans, Bishopsgate Street;
Nag's Head, Borough;
Belle Sauvage, Ludgate Hill.

Parcels booked at the various Offices in the City up to Six o'Clock, p.m., will be dispatched by the Night Train, arriving at Weymouth on the following Morning. The Packets sail from Weymouth every Tuesday, Thursday, Friday, and Saturday, at Seven o'Clock, a.m., and from Jersey every Monday, Wednesday, Friday, and Saturday, at Half-past Six, a.m.

N.B.—The Public are strongly recommended to avail themselves of the above Offices, as the Great Western Railway Company have no control over the charge made upon, nor can they be responsible for, or insure the punctual dispatch of Goods or Parcels booked at any other places than those above named.

Residents in Jersey or Guernsey, on purchasing Goods, &c., in London, should be particular in ordering them to be addressed "*Per Great Western Railway Company,*" and forwarded through one of the above Offices.

***Paddington, May,* 1857.**

Schedule of parcel rates, 1857 (*British Transport Historical Records*) ton. As the season advanced the service settled down and traffic began to pick up, assisted by an opportune reduction in Weymouth harbour dues. 'Aquatic excursions', offering a week in Guernsey or Jersey at single fare for the return journey, and shilling-a-head trips round the bay, of the sort familiar to generations of holidaymakers, were well patronised.

Local interest in the steamers was lively; hardly a week passed without some press reference to them. The *County Chronicle* went so far as to commission its representative to make a special crossing, and printed a long article on the delights of the islands.[6] Although largely concerned with the Jersey scenery this also includes entertaining details of the actual journey which merit quotation.

An opening lament that no trains connected with the steamers, and that even from so near a starting point as Dorchester it was necessary to be in Weymouth overnight, is tempered with reflections on the 'unrivalled accommodations' of the Royal, Victoria and Golden Lion hotels, 'all within easy distance of the quays'. Alternatively, one might sleep on board, all the cargo having been shipped and cleared the previous night and the captain, stewards and stewardesses being all on board by 10 pm ready for a 7 am start.

Once at sea our correspondent was—need it be said—impressed by the *Aquila*'s 'smoothness of motion'. Since his other abiding impressions included 'the heat of the steam, the smell of the paint . . . and the odour of boiled cabbage' that may have been as well. Anyway, the time passed pleasantly enough and they soon reached Guernsey. There, passengers and cargo, including a horse, 'box and all', were landed in a 'broad-bottomed boat like a floating battery'.[7] And then *Aquila* was off for Jersey.

Her arrival there was to the accompaniment of a colourful hubbub on the quayside. Our correspondent goes on to describe it:

> Scarcely had we got alongside the quay near the inner basin, the flood tide bearing us thus far without stoppage, than touts were everywhere . . . touters on touters appeared from the hotels and

> boarding houses of St Helier's and flying squadrons of street and shore porters, thrusting one another aside and crushing back from the edge of the quay with painful difficulty as they gesticulated and touched their badges in pantomime and endeavoured to catch your eye . . .

You were, he continued:

> . . . more likely to be carried ashore as part of your own baggage than to make any more dignified debut in St. Helier's . . . you have caught the eye of the first dozen; one takes possession of your right leg, another of your left, a third undermines your last prop, your walking stick, a fourth has your hat, if it happens to have fallen off, if not, your portmanteau. The fight for your body is prodigious. Kicking is useless, and milder forms of remonstrance are favours. If you look sharp after your property and continue immoveable the porterage nuisance gives way to the next light division—the inn touters, who, aided by dismounted cabmen, now rush in . . .

A diverting performance it must have been, if you knew your own mind and were fit. At least you were left in no doubt that Jersey's principal industry—as it is today—was a very live issue even in the 1850s. But we must return to Weymouth.

At the company's first general meeting, on 1 July 1857, the provisional directors were all confirmed with the exception of Henry Tupper, the disenchanted Guernseyman, and encouraged by the improved traffic prospects the company decided to buy the *Aquila* and *Cygnus*. Despite the surveyor's favourable report, performance had been rather disappointing and both needed new boilers. It was therefore decided to offer only £13,000 for the two. Before this offer could be conveyed to the owners the *Cygnus* was in trouble. Outward bound from Weymouth she limped into Guernsey with a collapsed furnace crown in one boiler; and on the return trip the following day, as though to prove the point, the other boiler failed similarly.

The owners rejected the purchase offer out of hand and also refused to meet the repair bill. The company therefore threatened to build a steamer of their own and invited tenders for 'a first class iron paddle steamer to do 18 knots, to be ready by 1st March

1858'. It is hard to see how one vessel alone—even an 18-knotter—could have maintained an adequate service, and the gesture was probably only bluff. All the same, the hire costs would clearly lead to bankruptcy if allowed to continue.

To make matters worse, just at this juncture the *Express* returned to Southampton for docking and until November the rival service was conducted by the *Wonder*, reputed to be of exceptional speed—a choice that may have been made with the intention of trying to break the Packet Company once and for all. A satisfactory substitute for the *Cygnus* could not be found and the company had to pin their faith to the *Aquila*. In addition, at least one crossing was made by a hired schooner.

The *Cygnus* returned to service at the end of August. In her absence the *Aquila* had fortunately proved completely reliable, maintaining a thrice-weekly service, turn and turn about with the *Wonder*. *The Star* newspaper, presumably alluding to the latter vessel, remarked on the failure of the London & South Western attempt to 'blockade' Weymouth.[8] After the misfortune to the *Cygnus*, the fourth weekly sailing was not resumed. It had in any case been the least useful, coinciding with South Western sailings (out on Friday, home on Saturday).

In October 1857, while still continuing to accept tenders and toying with the idea of two new ships instead of one, the company decided to argue no further over a purchase price for the *Aquila* and *Cygnus* but to find the full £18,000 if necessary. In the event, on the basis of an independent valuation, the price was agreed at £14,000. The change of ownership took place on 21 November and the idea of new vessels was dropped.

Improvidence—and a Providential Wreck

By the end of the first year's operations nearly 9,000 passengers had been booked, from whom receipts amounted to £6,632. Goods receipts during the same period were £5,179, bringing the total to £11,811. Expenditure, however, was £19,575, resulting in a deficit far exceeding the railway's mileage proportion. Such a situation, hardly foreseen in the agreement, was one in which the company might have been expected to exercise economy; instead, they ill-advisedly launched an additional service, to Cherbourg, in co-operation with the Western Railway of France, and spent £9,500 on a third steamer for the purpose.

This third steamer was the *Brighton*, renowned for her speed and latterly in service between Jersey and Shoreham under the management of Messrs Maples & Morris, the marine agents of the London Brighton & South Coast Railway.[9] Transferred to Packet Company ownership on 23 July 1858 she left Shoreham for Weymouth on the 26th, under the command of Captain Prowse, and on arrival proceeded to cruise in the bay while shareholders and their friends were wined and dined on board. A few days later, pending the opening of the French service, she was placed on the Channel Islands run, with satisfactory results.

An agreement for the working of the Cherbourg traffic was signed on 6 August, with provisions generally similar to those under which the islands were served. Crossings started in September 1858, three times weekly in each direction; once weekly the steamer called at Alderney. From October, Cherbourg mails were carried and when, in March 1859, an Alderney mail was added, that island enjoyed a direct postal service for the first time in its history.

Alas! It cost £70 to make the double trip, and Cherbourg and Alderney traffic together averaged only about £13. The gamble hadn't come off.

An already shaky situation was now severely aggravated, and the company were forced to seek financial assistance. This came in the form of a private loan from Elias Neel and the other Jersey directors, secured against mortgages on the three steamers. Neither the Great Western nor the Western Railway of France wished to continue the Cherbourg service and at the end of June 1859, when 111 double trips had been made and losses totalled well over £6,000, it was suspended, never to be resumed. The weekly Alderney service did reappear in the timetable the following summer, but only briefly. The *Brighton* was put up for sale.

In little more than two years South Western competition and

its own weakness had brought the Packet Company to the brink of bankruptcy. At this lowest ebb in its fortunes Neel resigned the chair, to be succeeded by Abraham Bishop, a Guernsey linen-draper. When Bishop took office, at the July meeting, things could scarcely have looked worse; but two months later a chance occurrence changed the outlook completely. The South Western's Weymouth boat was wrecked.

At 6.45 on the morning of 20 September 1859 the *Express* left Jersey for Guernsey and Weymouth, under the command of Captain Mabb. Rounding the Corbière, Mabb hugged the land so closely that regular passengers on board remarked on the fact, and a little after 7 o'clock struck submerged rocks known as the Grunes Houillières. The *Express* was badly holed. Mabb attempted to return to St Helier but with the ship completely flooded forward and down by the bow was obliged to run her aground on the rocks, about 100yd from the shore. There were some 160 passengers on board, an unusually large number most of whom were bound for Guernsey races. Three of them panicked and fell into the sea before the boats were lowered but the rest, and three racehorses, were got safely to land. The *Express* herself was a total loss. Within a fortnight, pounding seas had put her beyond all hope of salvage.

In October a court of inquiry considered the case but, presented with conflicting evidence, failed to reach a conclusion. Mabb's error of judgement thus escaped the censure it probably deserved.[10]

The South Western service continued for a while, performed sometimes by the *Wonder*, sometimes by the *South Western*, but at the end of December the *County Chronicle* reported the 'sudden withdrawal' of the company's Weymouth boats. The South Western's own press announcements read 'sailings suspended for the present' but the suspension proved to be permanent. The last sailing actually took place on or about 15 December.

This unforeseen turn of events brought sorely needed relief to the Packet Company, for Weymouth's share of the available traffic was not enough to support two separate services. With Southampton already enjoying an almost unassailable supremacy, intervention at Weymouth must have been of little direct benefit to the South Western, but it had certainly jeopardised the prospects of the Packet Company. Had chance not intervened the unequal competition must surely have ended differently; even, perhaps, in Weymouth's final eclipse as a packet port.

Notes to this chapter are on page 221

CHAPTER THREE

PRECARIOUS PROGRESS, AND STEAMERS TO FRANCE (1860-89)

A FRESH START

THE South Western's withdrawal left the Packet Company in possession but almost exhausted. The local press still made what it could of any small news item calculated to show the Weymouth route in a good light but the cold truth was that Weymouth's boats were badly 'in the red' while Southampton's were paying 5 per cent.[1] Each year, so far, working costs had absorbed all the Great Western's share of the receipts and still not been balanced. But all was not yet lost and to preserve what it could of the wreckage the Great Western now offered further assistance—an annual subsidy of £2,000 on top of the existing commitment in return for closer control. A new agreement on those lines was signed in August 1860.

Bishop was not satisfied with this and wanted the service taken over altogether. He also contended that three steamers were needed, to provide a reserve. In that, of course, he was right, as witness the recent failure of the *Cygnus*, so the *Brighton* was withdrawn from sale. The Great Western refused to take over but offered instead to guarantee 6 per cent for five years on additional capital of £9,000, if that sum could be raised. It was raised without trouble in 3,000 preference shares, by converting the 984 unallotted original shares and issuing 2,016 new ones. This latest development produced bitter complaint from the more vociferous ordinary shareholders, who saw their chance of a dividend now gone for ever.

The first benefit from the South Western's withdrawal concerned the mails. The Post Office contract called for three a week via Southampton, but from February 1858 that provision had been virtually doubled by the carrying of an 'auxiliary mail' on alternate days by the company's Weymouth boat. After the loss of the *Express* Southampton sailings had been increased to four, but Jersey still campaigned for a Weymouth mail. At the end of 1860 the postmaster general was petitioned to restore it and in January 1861, when the South Western gave notice to revert to the stipulated number, took the opportunity to do so. The reinstated Weymouth mail was carried once weekly until May and then increased to three times a week for the summer (May to October). It was not subject to contract but continued on the same basis until January 1870, when it was again withdrawn.

During that time the Post Office contributed about £80 a month to receipts but unfortunately the cachet of being able to style the vessels 'mail steamer', for the first time since the short-lived Alderney service, did not impress the travelling public. The South Western route remained the more popular, for reasons which are not far to seek.

Leaving Jersey at 7 am, a passenger via Southampton could normally expect to be in London by 10 pm. But via Weymouth, although the boat's departure was actually earlier, at 6.45, he did not reach London until 11 pm or later. If the boat came in late passengers missed the last up train of the day and had to spend the night in Weymouth. In a similar situation the South Western invariably put on a special. In the other direction the comparison was even less favourable. Weymouth passengers certainly enjoyed the advantage of a daylight crossing but this too, as the *County Chronicle*'s correspondent had discovered, involved the inconvenience of being in Weymouth overnight. Only those to and from the west of England, and the timid, who counted the short crossing more than the tiresome train journey, preferred Weymouth. Similar difficulties affected the more perishable kinds of imported produce. Indeed, as far as the predominantly narrow-gauge northern parts of the system were concerned the Great

Page 53: The *Ibex* in trouble: *(above)* beached in St Aubin's Bay, Jersey, after striking the *Noirmontaise*, April 1897; *(below)* beached in St Sampson's Harbour, Guernsey, after salvage, August 1900

Page 54: *(above)* TSS *Roebuck* at sea, c 1900; *(below)* TSS *Reindeer* alongside Weymouth landing stage, c 1900

Western was itself better served via Southampton and Basingstoke than by its own circuitous route through Swindon, involving a break of gauge.

Only for the Jersey potato traffic could the Weymouth boats compete on satisfactory terms. This they did with increasing success, and by 1861 two special potato trains a week were being run during the season. It was largely thanks to the Jersey potato that at the company's sixth annual meeting, in 1862, the directors were able to report a credit balance on current working. By the ninth meeting, three years later, an £8,000 reduction in the original mortgage debt had been achieved, though outstanding liabilities still precluded any ordinary dividend. From October 1865 the company benefited indirectly from the opening of the harbour tramway (see chapter 9). This eliminated the double handling involved in road cartage between the quay and the station and the saving in terminals was credited to the steamer deficit.

When the preference shares expired, in 1866, the annual dividend subsidy was increased to £900, ensuring a flat 2 per cent for all shareholders. In addition £2,000 continued to be set aside annually towards mortgage repayment, an impost which the Great Western accepted with reluctance as the only alternative to closing down. Unaided the Packet Company had no hope of reducing the debt and in 1867 again considered the sale of the *Brighton* as a means of doing so.

The lengths to which the Great Western were prepared to go to keep the steamers running were well illustrated two years later when, for the first time, they had something in hand after meeting the deficit. As the reduced working loss reflected abnormally heavy expenditure on steamer repairs during 1867 and 1868 the Packet Company at once laid claim to the balance, and the Great Western acquiesced. Stretching the agreement they handed over an extra £1,600 while the Packet Company, for their part, bent it to suit themselves by appropriating the £2,000 allowance to running expenses!

STEAM VESSELS ACT, 1871

At this juncture the Great Western decided to go to Parliament for powers to operate their own steamers, a step which appears to have been embarked upon with some reluctance. On amalgamating with the South Wales Railway, in 1863, the company had inherited in respect of the Milford steamers an agreement something like the Weymouth one, with the firm of Ford & Jackson. According to general manager James Grierson, during his evidence in committee, the application to Parliament was prompted primarily by dissatisfaction with the Milford arrangements and the realisation that the only feasible alternative was for the company to seek their own powers.[2]

The possibility of improvement at Weymouth as well was borne in mind, however. The current Channel Islands agreement was due to expire in 1871 and, in anticipation of the bill being passed, negotiations were already in progress for Great Western steamers to use the new government breakwater at Portland, instead of Weymouth harbour. It was also hoped, if these negotiations were successful, to extend the service from Jersey to St Malo and to establish another, direct to Cherbourg.

Neither of these latter ideas was new, as may be recalled. The St Malo extension had been suggested by Captain Stevens as early as 1836 and there had been two previous attempts to establish a Weymouth–Cherbourg service: by the Commercial Company in 1839 and twenty years later by the Packet Company. Both had failed.

Nor, indeed, was Cherbourg a new objective even for the Great Western. In 1866 Daniel Gooch, with a vision not given to lesser men—or, more prosaically, with a wonderful optimism—had seen Weymouth–Cherbourg in a wider context, as part of a through route between America and France. Writing to M Julien, manager of the Western Railway of France, he suggested that a joint service might with advantage be run via Milford Haven—ie, by steamer from Queenstown to Milford, thence by train to Portland, by steamer again to Cherbourg, and so to Paris. This route is 140 miles shorter than the then usual alternative via Dublin, Holyhead, London, Dover and Calais, but whether a corresponding saving in time would have resulted is doubtful. It was a most interesting idea all the same, anticipating by more than forty years the Great Western's other trans-Atlantic bid when for a time Cunarders called at Fishguard. But for various reasons Cherbourg was unable to accommodate scheduled sailings and the plan came to nothing.

Past experience was thus discouraging. However, an apparently successful Cherbourg service (passenger and cargo) had been operated since 1869 by the London & South Western, and many people in the west of England were in favour of a permanent link with the western side of France. In due course the desired powers were granted. The Great Western Railway (Steam Vessels) Act, of 13 July 1871,[3] authorised the company to own and work steamers between Weymouth and/or Portland and the Channel Islands, Cherbourg and St Malo, as well as between Milford Haven and Cork and Waterford.

The proposal now was to take over the Milford services, build new steamers to operate them, and then utilise some of the redundant ones at Weymouth. Inevitably this would take time so there was no immediate development, and on expiry the Packet Company's agreement was again extended.

CRISIS IN JERSEY

In February 1873 crisis loomed afresh. Following the failure the previous year of a new harbour scheme at St Helier a leading Jersey bank, the Jersey Mercantile, suspended payment. The Jersey directors, who held the mortgages, were also directors of the bank and in March gave notice of foreclosure. Then, in April, by which time successive extensions had prolonged the old agreement by eighteen months, the Great Western served the prescribed notice of termination; and what the outcome now might be none could say.

More than thirteen years had passed since the South Western's withdrawal and the Great Western had done little more than stave off complete collapse. In a report laid before the board in June 1873[4] Grierson reviewed those years, and concluded that so far Channel Islands traffic had gained the company nothing. He recommended that support should nevertheless continue.

This recommendation was still under consideration when the monetary crisis in Jersey suddenly worsened. The Packet Company's own bankers, the Jersey Joint Stock Bank—chairman none other than Elias Neel—were creditors to the Mercantile Bank for £36,000, and on 3 July 1873 they too suspended payment. Many Packet Company shareholders faced ruin.

In October, with the agreement fast expiring, the company again pleaded for the Great Western to take over. Again they were met with refusal, but accepting Grierson's advice the board decided to continue much as before, extending the old agreement from month to month. To enable the mortgages to be redeemed fresh ones, to the value of £15,000, were entered into by the Great Western in the names of F. G. Saunders and T. Merriman Ward—respectively secretary and registrar.

POTATO TRAFFIC

The Great Western's continued reluctance to take the service over probably reflected its own financial state at the time. The renewed spate of 'mania' in the early sixties had involved the company in much expensive litigation and for some years the most stringent economy had to be observed. One result of this critical period that particularly affected Weymouth's trade was the postponement of gauge conversion. Most of the potato traffic, the port's principal cargo, went to the Midlands and north of England and thus, like much of the company's south–north traffic, was bedevilled by the break of gauge. The conversion of the Weymouth line, in June 1874, was a turning point for the port and the following year special potato boats were required as well as the special trains. The big increase in this traffic which took place from that time owed much also to the personal efforts of one John Wimble, who in 1868 had taken over the managership of the Packet Company after six years as Jersey agent. His experience as agent had given him a valuable insight into the trade and he knew most of the growers.[5]

In order to secure the maximum benefit from this improved prospect the Great Western in 1876 engineered a special potato agreement, supplementary to the ordinary one. Under this the Packet Company were to charter three extra boats in season, and run them as necessary, while the Great Western provided the extra trains. Ostensibly to cover the cost of these trains, special potato terminals were established. These were actually arbitrary rates of 8s a ton for Bristol traffic, 15s to Birmingham and 20s to places north of Wolverhampton (40p, 75p and £1), against the normal terminals of a few pence a ton. The intention, of course, was to reduce the Great Western mileage allowance, which the Packet Company's deficit continued to devour, and profit instead from the terminals, which were deducted from the gross receipts before the mileage apportionment was made. No ordinary shipping company would have agreed to such terms but the Packet Company were in no position to argue.

FRENCH AMBITIONS

Meanwhile the Great Western still cherished French ambitions. Early in 1872 they had, as expected, taken over the New Milford–Waterford service and Jackson's four paddle steamers, and subsequent delivery of replacements had made all four more or less redundant. The proposed transfer to Weymouth might therefore be put into effect and, towards the end of 1875, the company approached the London & South Western with a view to possible joint working between Portland, the Channel Islands and France. The South Western had been party to the 1871 discussions on the use of Portland breakwater but since then their own Cherbourg service had been in some difficulty. This latest overture was declined, without thanks.

The next move came from the Western Railway of France,

which in December 1875 approached the Great Western, whereupon the board authorised the reopening of negotiations and appointed a French agent. Numerous obstacles were soon encountered. Sanction was required from the French minister of works, because of French government interests at Cherbourg; dredging and other works were required; and the French already had a zoning agreement with the Brighton railway in respect of the Newhaven–Dieppe service which had to be safeguarded.

At home, too, there were difficulties. The Great Western had in mind a three-sided arrangement, embracing the Packet Company as well as the Western Railway of France. They proposed to transfer the Milford steamers *Great Western* and *South of Ireland* to the Packet Company and in return take shares to their value, thus strengthening both the Weymouth fleet and the ties between the two companies. Equipped with this additional tonnage the Packet Company would have been required to improve the Channel Islands service and also run daily to Cherbourg. They were not enthusiastic. The extra Channel Islands commitment was acceptable enough but Cherbourg was not—1859 was still a sore memory—and the question of their participation was not pursued. Discussion with the French proceeded only slowly and by the end of 1876 had made little progress.

IMPROVED FACILITIES

Another problem thrown into focus in the course of the negotiations was the lack of accommodation at Weymouth. The quay was hopelessly narrow and, so far from being able to handle a French service, was hard pressed to cope with existing traffic. In September 1876 came the first of several steps towards improvement. In the light of that season's experience the Packet Company asked Weymouth Corporation to provide a wooden landing stage, or platform, pointing out in support of the request that a cargo requiring twelve hours for discharge at Weymouth could be dealt with in only five at Littlehampton, where there was such a platform, with a crane.

The corporation were sympathetic but, as usual, had no reserve for harbour purposes. The Great Western therefore undertook to meet the cost of construction by advancing £1,000, which would be recovered by withholding potato dues for as long as might be necessary; the corporation undertook to do the work, and consented to the installation of a steam crane; and the Packet Company, as mere users, nodded assent. An agreement on these lines was signed in April 1877 and the stage was completed in time for the coming season. It was 200ft long × 22ft wide, and at a convenient height for rail wagons. By extending partly over the harbour it provided a small but useful increase in working space and, with all its limitations, immediately proved its worth. The *County Chronicle* was soon reporting record cargoes, involving up to five special boats and 400 tons in one day, and the traffic began to make a substantial contribution to Channel Islands receipts. In 1876, after paying the Packet Company's deficiency and other allowances, the Great Western was left with a mere £13, but by 1880 the corresponding figure had risen to over £7,000. The corporation fared even better, the tonnage landed enabling them to clear their debt, including interest at 5 per cent, by May 1879. Only the unhappy Packet Company failed to benefit, their share all going on repairs. In 1876 the *Brighton* was found to require hull and mechanical renewal estimated to cost £7,000. Salvation, so nearly at hand, was snatched from the company's grasp yet again. The Great Western offered to advance the money against a further mortgage and bring in either the *Great Western* or the *South of Ireland* on charter while the *Brighton* was out of service, but to their credit the company managed for once without assistance.

PADDINGTON FOR PARIS

Cherbourg negotiations continued throughout 1877 but still to little purpose. It had long been the aim to start the service on 1 May 1878, in time for the Paris Universal Exhibition due to take place that month, but that hope had begun to fade. The French company, unable because of government restrictions to participate in their running, wanted the steamers to be the responsibility of a third party, independent of either railway; the two sides were slow to agree on financial terms; and the French government was unco-operative over the improvement of Cherbourg harbour. However, by January 1878 the clouds seemed to be clearing. The French resigned themselves to Great Western management of the steamers, and Admiral Haswell, the marine superintendent, was instructed to prepare the *Great Western* and *South of Ireland* for sea. For 'book' transfer to Weymouth each was valued at £14,000. In March a deputation led by Sir Alexander Wood, the deputy chairman, visited Weymouth to explain the company's requirements. The corporation welcomed the new service and promised to dredge the harbour, extend the cargo stage and permit the use of a locomotive on the tramway instead of horses (see chapter 9). But Grierson was pessimistic, maintaining that the timing of the tides at Cherbourg would make a tidal service very inconvenient for passengers and difficult to reconcile with the existing train times, and that the service would never pay.

Haswell was therefore despatched to Cherbourg to see for himself and report back. He found that all was far from well. The proposed berth was difficult to approach, with insufficient water at low tide, the bottom was unsuited to a vessel lying aground and there were no proper facilities ashore. At the last minute the Great Western therefore withdrew, much to the French company's annoyance, until such time as Cherbourg was better prepared.

By July a tiny temporary landing stage had appeared. Only 18ft long—shorter than the steamers' paddle-boxes—it was just enough to enable a start to be made. On 15 July an official Great Western party, including Gooch and Grierson, crossed to Cherbourg on the *South of Ireland* to complete arrangements and the public service began on 1 August, seven years after the granting of parliamentary powers and nearly twelve after Gooch had first mooted the idea. Philip Mesny, magistrate of the court of

Alderney, asked for that island to be made a port of call, as it had been in 1859, but his plea went unheeded.

The schedule was designed to provide a daylight passage either way, with the 1859 timing of 15 hours overall between Weymouth and Paris:

London, Paddington	dep	9.00 am	Paris (St Lazare)	dep	12 mdnt
Weymouth	arr	2.15 pm	Cherbourg	arr	7.50 am
Weymouth steamer	dep	2.45 pm	Cherbourg steamer	dep	8.20 am
Cherbourg	arr	9.15 pm	Weymouth	arr	2.50 pm
Cherbourg train	dep	9.55 pm	Weymouth train	dep	3.20 pm
Paris (St Lazare)	arr	5.30 am	London, Paddington	arr	8.55 pm

Free conveyance by bus between the steamer and the station was provided at both Weymouth and Cherbourg. The first-class fare between London and Paris was 50s 4d single, 88s 6d return (£2·51 and £4·42); for three first-class tickets state cabins were obtainable.

The five-minute interval between the departure of the outward boat and the arrival of the inward was distinctly optimistic and a mere half hour to disembark and get from the quay to the station must have caused some anxious moments, even when the steamer was on time. On the first day the *Great Western* left Weymouth five minutes late, with about forty passengers, and the *South of Ireland* came in about an hour later.

The working agreement, providing for through rates between stations not covered by the Brighton company's agreement, was sealed in October. It was to be effective for five years (from 1 June) and thereafter by six-month extensions. The *Great Western* and *South of Ireland* were regarded as stop-gaps pending the provision of a 'proper first-class service'. Similarly, Weymouth was regarded as only a temporary base, pending the provision of a pontoon for berthing alongside the breakwater at Portland.

By the end of the year the service had accumulated a substantial deficit. Passenger traffic was negligible, despite a small reduction in the steamer fares,[6] and much potential cargo was being lost at Cherbourg because of the hopeless working conditions. As passenger traffic was so light the fixed daylight schedule was pointless when its abandonment would enable the boat to use the outer harbour, where the South Western boat berthed, and sail by night, which was better suited to the available trade. This change was adopted in February 1879, the sailing times now being about 11.30 pm from Weymouth[7] and during the evening, according to tide, from Cherbourg. Some improvement in tonnage resulted—horticultural and dairy produce, wine, etc—but in July it was officially noted that Weymouth could still accommodate an increase 'which there must be if the service is to pay'.[8] And on the passenger side the advertised claim that the service afforded 'a convenient, attractive and economical route to Normandy, the West and South of France, Paris and Spain' was now meaningless, particularly as far as traffic *from* the continent was concerned. If all went well, and the boat left Cherbourg at about 7 pm, one arrived in Weymouth at 1 am to await the 5.15 am up train. But when the tide was bad the unfortunate third-class passenger did not reach London until 4 o'clock in the afternoon and even then had to change at Swindon as the 9 am up was first and second class only beyond that point. Local press reports that most Cherbourg traffic was 'now going via Weymouth instead of Southampton' must be dismissed as wishful thinking.

It was soon apparent that a third vessel was required as stand-by. The agreement included provision for chartering but instead there developed what Gooch described as a 'loose sort of agreement' with the Packet Company. In February 1879, for instance, the *Brighton* made three runs to Cherbourg and the *Great Western* one to the islands.

CHANNEL ISLANDS INVESTIGATION

In January 1879, before negotiating a fresh Channel Islands agreement, the Great Western appointed an investigation committee of three directors, who reported in favour of continuing the service but against the continuance of the £2,000 annual subsidy. Grierson also recommended that the service should continue, particularly as one of the main obstacles to increased through traffic was still the Weymouth train service, which it lay in their own power to improve.[9] Furthermore, as many Jersey people were shareholders their patronage seemed assured. Actually, the Weymouth train service was by now a rather sour joke in the islands,[10] so much so that, whatever Grierson thought, there were many among the local merchants who regularly sent goods to England by the South Western's boats even though they did hold shares in the Packet Company.

The new agreement, drawn up on the basis of these recommendations, considerably revised the financial relationship between the two companies. The £2,000 subsidy was withdrawn but replaced by an annual payment of £700 for depreciation, in addition to the £900 dividend payment; the Great Western also waived all further mortgage interest. The debt, £15,000 when the railway took it over, had been reduced by this time to something under £9,000, a creditable achievement in all the circumstances. In addition the Great Western acquired a still closer control, particularly where heavy expenditure was involved.

The ties between the companies were further strengthened at the same time by the addition to the Packet Company's articles of association of a clause permitting charter of its vessels to the Great Western or the Western Railway of France, thus regularising the previous 'loose agreement'. The *Cygnus* appears to have been regarded as a joint stand-by boat until May. Then she broke down in mid-channel and had to be towed home and the *Vulture*, another of the redundant Waterford steamers, arrived for the summer. At the end of the year the *Aquila* made three trips to Cherbourg.

The next year witnessed the extension of the cargo stage, agreed to in 1878 but postponed because of the uncertainty then prevailing. It was completed in June 1880 and from then on its increased length, some 380ft, was available to Channel Islands and Cherbourg steamers alike. Shortly afterwards additional cranes were installed and towards the end of the year the corporation at last managed to dredge the harbour. These improvements were followed by two or three years of steady business and an unaccustomed freedom from crises. Thanks to the potato agreement the Great Western enjoyed a gross working profit on the Channel Islands traffic until 1882, when repairs to the steamers once again absorbed most of their mileage proportion. They thereupon decreed that future expenditure must be limited to what was necessary to meet Board of Trade requirements. The possibility of terminating the Channel Islands service altogether was considered but left in abeyance pending a decision on the whole question of accommodation at Weymouth and Portland.

PLANS FOR PORTLAND

In April 1883, with the expiry of the Cherbourg agreement imminent, Captain T. S. Lecky, Haswell's successor as marine superintendent, was directed to report. In company with M Pierre Delaitre, of the Western Railway of France, he made a tour of inspection of Weymouth, Portland and Cherbourg. Weymouth he uncompromisingly condemned. Steamer movements continued to be delayed by shallow water; the harbour's narrowness made it difficult for ships to swing, even when others were first moved to make more room; there was no slip or graving dock, necessitating hull repairs being taken elsewhere, involving trouble and expense; even a gridiron was impracticable, owing to the small tidal range.[11] Ashore there was hardly room to move and no covered accommodation. All stores for the steamers had to be drawn from Swindon as required, and spare gear was even carried about in the ships themselves, needlessly increasing draught, because there was nowhere else to keep it. What was worse, he could suggest no remedy.

Weymouth had, of course, been regarded from the beginning as only a temporary substitute for Portland and, even though the protracted discussions on the use of the breakwater had come to nothing, it was Portland that Lecky still saw as providing all the answers. There was plenty of space, plenty of water; and if existing facilities were less than perfect that was no insurmountable difficulty. One suggested scheme was the construction of a simple pier, projecting from an existing Admiralty wharf, to give the steamers enough shelter to work; but this plan, though 'infinitely superior to Weymouth', remained 'only a bad second' to a much more ambitious alternative.

In the south-west corner of what is now Portland harbour is a stretch of flat tidal land known as The Mere. There, suggested Lecky, were 'all the elements for the formation of a commodious wet dock'—easy access, good shelter, convenient proximity to the Portland branch railway and as much room as could foreseeably be required. Provided that trial borings and other preliminaries proved satisfactory an expenditure of £50,000 and two years work were estimated to cover everything: dredging, two piers 250ft × 150ft, cranes, sidings, patent slip, factory (repair shops) and so on.[12]

Although the report related specifically to the Cherbourg service much of it was equally relevant to the Channel Islands. From now on, indeed, although the Packet Company remained nominally independent, the two services were inseparably linked and both were governed by the same two considerations—out-of-date ships and Weymouth's inadequacy.

In the light of Lecky's report a renewed approach was made to the government regarding the possible use of Portland, the Cherbourg agreement in the meantime being prolonged on a 'six-months-notice' basis. At the end of 1883 trial borings were being made at The Mere, and the Board of Customs gave provisional approval for a harbour there. But after that the scheme just faded out.

One possible reason was that more thorough consideration produced a total estimate of £108,000, more than double Lecky's optimistic guess. A more cogent one was further uncertainty created by the loss in the small hours of Christmas Day 1883 of the best of the Cherbourg steamers, the *South of Ireland*. The night was dark and foggy and as the ship approached the Dorset coast the captain, William Pearn, misjudged his landfall. Before he realised his error he was aground on the rocks of Worbarrow Bay, east of Lulworth.

The *Aquila*, a launch and two barges were sent from Weymouth to assist, but could do nothing beyond removing passengers, crew and portable gear. During the next few days about two-thirds of the cargo was unloaded but the weather was unco-operative and on 3 January 1884, before further salvage could take place or pumping begin, the ship floated free and sank, becoming a total loss. The subsequent enquiry held Captain Pearn responsible; his certificate was suspended for three months and he was dismissed from the company's service.

Lecky had proposed the construction of a completely new vessel for the service, the intention being to pair her with the *South of Ireland*, leaving the *Great Western* to serve as relief boat. This plan was now upset, but a specification had been prepared and it was still intended to go ahead with her building. To replace the *South of Ireland* it was therefore proposed to charter; this proved impracticable, however, and in April the paddle steamer *Gael* was bought. Before being sent to Weymouth the *Gael* was taken in hand by Laird Bros of Birkenhead, for various alterations, and in the meantime the *Brighton*, on charter from the Packet Company since January, remained on the service for a further month.

In February 1884, all Portland plans having been shelved, Gooch and Saunders visited Weymouth again. The company's requirements, based on the proposed new tonnage, included further dredging and widening, doubling the length of the cargo stage, extending the quay eastwards and equipping it with three rail tracks, and doubling the tramway throughout, with clearance for passenger stock. A plan drawn up by W. G. Owen, the company's chief engineer, showed berths for two 280ft screw steamers and one 245ft paddle steamer, and a new bridge over the harbour, a little to the westward of the existing one and high enough to provide adequate tramway clearance.[13] At about the same time R. P. Brereton, formerly chief assistant to Brunel and now the company's consulting engineer, produced plans for a

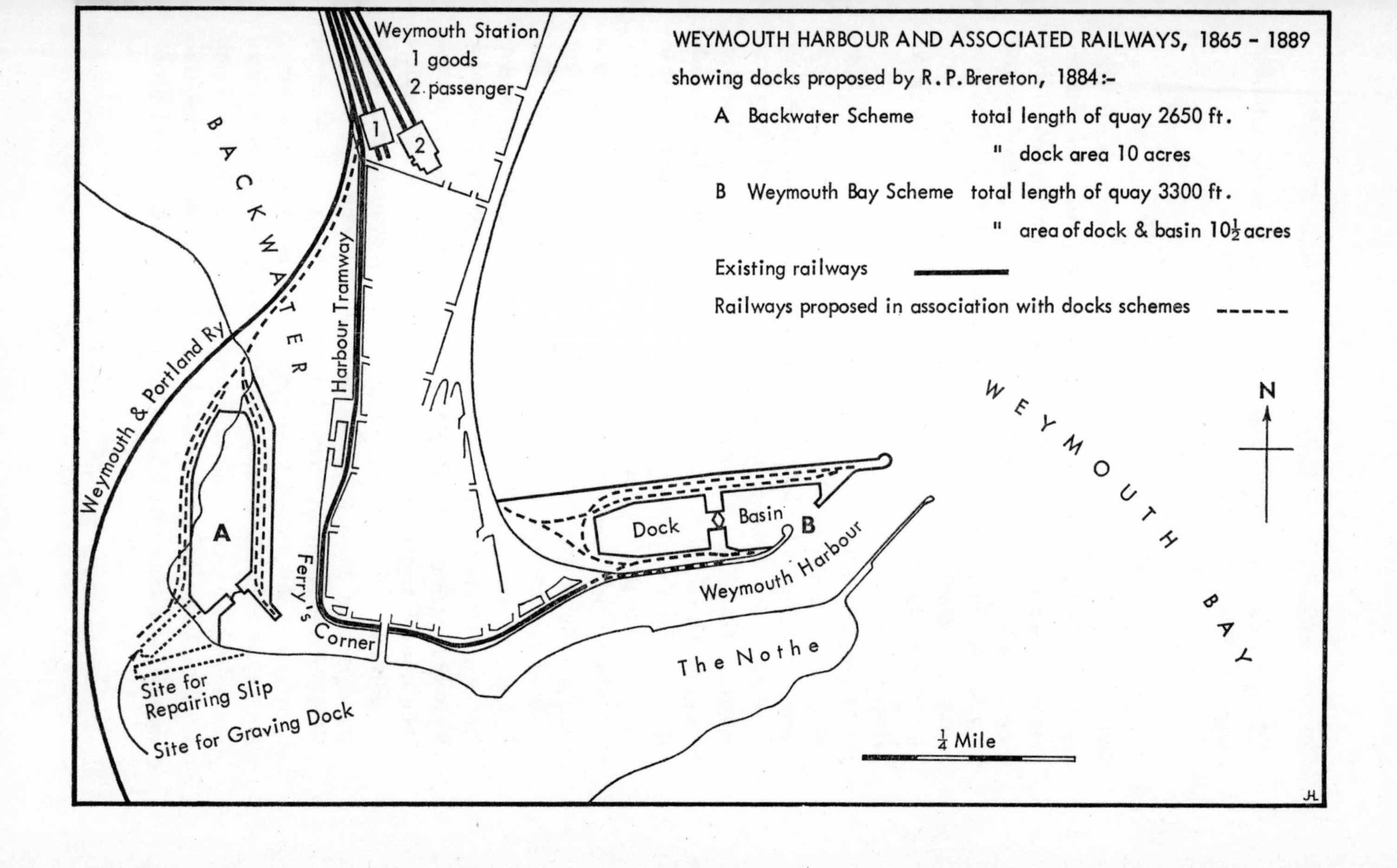
WEYMOUTH HARBOUR AND ASSOCIATED RAILWAYS, 1865 - 1889
showing docks proposed by R. P. Brereton, 1884:-
A Backwater Scheme total length of quay 2650 ft.
" dock area 10 acres
B Weymouth Bay Scheme total length of quay 3300 ft.
" area of dock & basin 10½ acres
Existing railways
Railways proposed in association with docks schemes
Weymouth Station
1 goods
2 passenger
BACKWATER
Harbour Tramway
Weymouth & Portland Ry
A
Ferry's Corner
Site for Repairing Slip
Site for Graving Dock
Dock
Basin
B
Weymouth Harbour
The Nothe
WEYMOUTH BAY
N
¼ Mile
JL

10 acre dock in the Backwater, or alternatively in the southern corner of Weymouth Bay, adjacent to the pier.

COLLAPSE OF CHERBOURG

Time drifted by and then, in January 1885, there was further trouble with the steamers. The *Gael* broke down and was replaced by the *Vulture*. The latter, however, was so run-down that she made only one trip before being in turn replaced by the *Aquila*. As some time was expected to elapse before the *Gael* was ready, the company were obliged to charter after all and early in March the *Aquila* handed over to the screw steamer *St Andrew*.[14]

Meanwhile in February the French crowned all by suddenly proposing to terminate the service altogether at the end of September, because of the continued unsatisfactory results. They later asked for the date to be brought forward and the Great Western, unwilling to continue alone, agreed to close down on 30 June. The *Great Western* and *St Andrew* remained to the end; the *Gael* did not return and the *Vulture*, a liability at the best of times, went to the scrap heap.

Harbour problems may have been partly to blame for this abrupt collapse but the real trouble, culminating in the recent spate of breakdowns, was the slow and inefficient steamers. The replacement envisaged by Lecky showed no sign of materialising and sole Great Western control had never been liked anyway. Relations between the two companies had consequently always been uneasy. In spite of the availability of an improbable range of through fares (did any adventurous Frenchman ever book through from Paris to Cork, or Limerick?) one may wonder whether the Great Western themselves ever quite believed in Cherbourg, at least for passengers. Their approach was never more than half-hearted and they continued throughout to allow through bookings via competing Anglo-continental routes. From 1881 to 1884 the company's share of the gross receipts from through traffic averaged £21,000 a year, 92 per cent of which

Page 71: *(above)* SS *Melmore*; note deck crane sheeted over and jib removed; *(below)* TSS *Roebuck* on the Kaines, Jersey, July 1911

Page 72: *(above)* Channel Islands boat train on arrival at Weymouth Quay, c 1906; note passengers alighting by portable steps and the wide gaps between carriages, owing to the use of special tramway couplings; *(below)* Weymouth cargo stage, c 1910; the potato season in full swing

was from goods and parcels, but, after deduction to meet a substantial deficit on the steamers (shared equally between the two companies) and terminal expenses, the average contribution to rail receipts was a modest £8,200.

THE FINAL BLOW

With Cherbourg a dead letter, the Channel Islands steamers paddled on alone and ever more expensively, their fate too hanging in the balance. Only the *Brighton* was in reasonable condition and even she might cynically have been regarded merely as the least decrepit of the three. Replacement was long overdue, but so far from having any reserve for that purpose, the company was still not out of debt. At intervals the Great Western continued to discuss various possibilities with Weymouth Corporation, and in December 1886 Gooch met the chairman and other representatives of the Packet Company. That meeting removed one doubt at least—either the service would be run entirely by the Great Western or it would close down. Railway subsidy for new ships was out of the question.

Within weeks of that decision came the final blow. On 29 January 1887, at 12.10 am, the *Brighton* cast off her moorings at Weymouth and headed south, under the command of Captain Thomas Painter. It proved to be her last crossing. At 6.30, approaching Guernsey in thick fog, Painter checked his position by dead reckoning. Some minutes later he did so again, but 'almost immediately afterwards'—to quote from the report of the official inquiry—'rocks were observed on all sides'. 'Full astern' was at once given, but 'before the way could be taken off her she struck'. Filling fast, within twenty minutes she had gone down into deep water. All on board, twenty-four crew and twenty-three passengers, had meanwhile taken to the boats. When the fog lifted they found that they were among the Brayes, an area of rocks off the northern tip of the island, but the exact spot where the ship struck was never determined. In due course all were landed safely at Bordeaux harbour, near St Sampson's. The court of inquiry, held in March, found Painter guilty of negligence and suspended his certificate for six months.[15]

Amid all their other troubles the Packet Company might hitherto have drawn some comfort from their thirty-year safety record. Now even that had gone. Nor could they now continue without practical assistance, and for the ensuing summer season (and again in 1888 and 1889) the service was maintained by chartering the *Great Western.*

EPILOGUE

This direct intervention by the railway seemed to settle any lingering doubts and by the summer of 1887 it had become common knowledge that they were preparing to take over. The protracted negotiations with Weymouth Corporation now assumed fresh purpose, and culminated in August 1888 in agreement for the carrying out of extensive harbour works. A month later three new twin-screw steamers were laid down in readiness for the takeover. That, however, constitutes another chapter in the story, and suffice it here to say that in April 1889 the Great Western served the Packet Company with formal notice terminating the agreement with effect from 30 June. This time there was no reprieve.

Three days before that date the *Aquila* and *Cygnus* were sold, for what *The Star* called a 'nominal sum'. *Aquila* made her last crossing from Jersey to Weymouth on Friday 28 June and *Cygnus* followed her home the next day.[16] For practical purposes the Weymouth & Channel Islands Steam Packet Company was dead.

Only the final settlement of accounts with the Great Western and the formal liquidation of the company remained to be attended to. Surplus assets at 30 June 1889 were valued at £25,193 (less liquidation expenses). In July the thirty-third and last ordinary general meeting was held, but the shareholders failed to agree as to how the assets should be distributed. The question was therefore settled by a decision in Chancery, in accordance with which the holders of the 2,917 paid-up original shares received £7 a share. Ten years previously shares had been bought at auction for as little as 17s (85p). In August 1889, at the Lyric Hall in Jersey, an extraordinary general meeting considered the final resolution: that the company be wound up.[17] Only twenty-five shareholders still cared enough to attend and of those ten did not vote. Those who did vote were five 'against' and ten 'for'. John Wimble was appointed liquidator.

Eighteen months later, on 19 February 1891, after all expenses had been paid, a final dividend of 19s a share (95p) was declared on all shares (2,917 original plus 1,631 additional) and the books were closed. All in all, things might have been worse.

What concluding assessment can be made of this ill-starred and rather ramshackle concern, which never quite made ends meet and for which better times were so often just round the next corner? The most that could be said from the point of view of the ordinary shareholder was that in the best years the Great Western's aid had enabled accounts to be balanced and that, at any rate from 1866, the 2 per cent 'dole' had provided a minimal dividend. True, Micklethwait and Ogilvy had not specifically guaranteed any dividend, but even in promising to make good all loss they had taken too rosy a view of traffic prospects and failed to foresee the seriousness of London & South Western competition, especially in the early days.

The Great Western's assistance was always liberal, if slightly grudging, but subsidy was never more than a palliative for a chronic lack of capital. Even when expenditure had been kept below receipts the surplus had always been drained off by the mortgage. Had Micklethwait and Ogilvy lived until 1 June 1887 they would at least have seen the discharge of the debt but their original pledge was never fully redeemed.

From the Great Western's own point of view the situation was hardly better. Why had they sustained for so long an undertaking that brought them so little? From which, indeed, so little had accrued to anybody except the mortgagees and a possible handful who had picked up shares at rock-bottom?

The official answer was that there was worthwhile indirect benefit—a certain degree of prestige and a presumed increase in Weymouth's ordinary traffic because the town was a packet station. There was some profit from conveying the steamer coal in the Packet Company's wagons from the Ruabon Coal Company[18] to Weymouth and, latterly, there was profit also from potatoes.

It would probably be nearer the truth to suggest that the company was prepared to accept minimal returns—or even stand a loss, within limits—just to ensure that the Channel Islands did not become an exclusively London & South Western preserve. If rather negative, this objective was in keeping with the company's prevailing outlook. The broad gauge 'encumbrance', as Sir Alexander Wood called it, and the knowledge that it must eventually go, were long a drag on enterprise.

The Weymouth timetable illustrates the point. From 1857 to 1889 the 'boat' trains remained practically unchanged, and the degree to which they inconvenienced Channel Islands travelling varied only with sailing times and the resultant 'connections'. Except for a limited resumption in the summer of 1870, probably induced by the loss of the *Normandy* on the night crossing from Southampton the previous March, daylight sailings and the need to spend the previous night in Weymouth came to an end in 1868. The usual sailing time from then on was 11 or 11.30 pm in summer and midnight in winter. The latest that passengers could leave Paddington was by the New Milford boat train—ie 5.15 pm—which detached a Weymouth portion at Swindon. In January 1882 departure time was put back to 5.45 but even then, in winter at least, the five-hour journey left an hour or more to waste in Weymouth.

London-bound passengers, until the summer of 1870, left the islands in the early morning—Jersey at about 6.30 and Guernsey about three hours later—and could ordinarily expect to catch the 5.20 pm up train and reach Paddington by a little after 11. In November 1870, however, departure from Jersey was altered to mid-morning, with no corresponding alteration to the last train.

The overnight stop in Weymouth, so recently eliminated from the outward journey, thus became a matter of course when homeward bound—a retrograde step not remedied until 1873, and then only during the summer months. A further alteration in departure time, to late afternoon or early evening, then brought passengers into Weymouth in the small hours when, after being roused for baggage examination, they could cool their heels while awaiting the departure of the 5.15 am train (arrival at Paddington 10.45).[19] During the summer of 1883 there was a return to a a 6.30 am Jersey sailing, saving fifty minutes to Paddington, but for some reason this was soon dropped again in favour of 5 pm. With little variation the 1870 winter arrangements, including the overnight stop, remained unchanged to the end.

At no time was any precise connection attempted and at no time was 14½ hours bettered between London and Jersey. In the reverse direction the overall time after 1873 was rarely better than 17¾ hours in summer—appreciably slower than in 1857—while in winter the overnight stop stretched this out to over 24 hours. With Bristol a notable exception, connections to other parts of the country than London were just as bad.

It is thus not surprising that, except for the special potato arrangements, twice-weekly sailings in winter and thrice in summer sufficed for all traffic from 1859 to 1882. In the latter year daily sailings were introduced for the summer months (usually July to September) and this then became the regular summer service.

Compare the situation at Southampton. The mail service ran three times a week and in addition there was a 'secondary' service, performed by older vessels and based on the docks. Though slower than the mail service these sailings were often at special cheap fares. The usual pattern was a mid-week extra to both islands and another on Saturday to Jersey only. From time to time one island or the other was also served intermediately by the St Malo boat giving, in all, four or five Channel Islands sailings a week practically throughout the sixties.[20] In October 1864 the mail service itself was transferred from the Royal Pier to the docks and the 8.30 pm train from Waterloo was extended to run alongside the steamer.

From 1870 the mail service was daily, from Mondays to Fridays, in summer, with an extra sailing direct to Jersey on Saturdays, and the sailings were progressively augmented until by May 1880 Southampton could boast a daily service summer and winter, six days a week. Overall times between London and the islands were not very much better than the *best* via Weymouth but were much more consistent, at about fourteen hours in each direction. Side by side with this steady extension of facilities there had been an equally steady improvement in the class of vessel employed, culminating in 1877 in the introduction of screw steamers.

Against such opposition the Packet Company's resources were woefully inadequate. An efficient service demanded more than financial guarantees, but even a more co-operative practical approach by the Great Western could hardly have achieved much more than the denial of a South Western monopoly. Nevertheless, perseverance through thirty difficult years had enabled the Great Western to keep a foot in the door. From 1888, with the appointment of Nathan Burlinson as superintendent of the line, there began what MacDermot so aptly termed 'the great awakening'. A fresh spirit was abroad, which in the next ten years was to put Weymouth on the cross-channel map with an entirely new authority.

Notes to this chapter are on page 222

CHAPTER FOUR

THE RACE TO JERSEY (1889-99)

THE GREAT WESTERN TAKES OVER

THE Great Western's Channel Islands service started on Monday 1 July 1889, immediately following the termination of the Packet Company's agreement; but the fact so simply stated emerged only after much uncertainty, and to trace the full course of events it is necessary to go back to 1887.

The previous thirty years had proved that natural advantages and a railway did not guarantee success. Three things more were required: modern ships; a properly integrated service; and adequate terminal facilities, with deep water and direct passenger transfer between ship and train. The first two of these the Great Western could themselves provide. The third depended on the co-operation of Weymouth Corporation.

The generally run-down state of the harbour when the service reopened, in 1857, was even then of long standing. For years expenditure had been no more than a reluctant minimum. Dredging had never been adequate and though there had been pier improvements from time to time these had been of no benefit to trade since the pier was not used by commercial traffic. The one commercial improvement since the steamers started, the erection of the cargo stage, had been initiated by the Great Western. However, the threat of removal to Portland had aroused the corporation's concern and at the end of 1886, after further talks with the railway, they promoted a parliamentary bill for the execution of various works, including harbour improvement. In due course this became the Weymouth & Melcombe Regis Corporation Act of 1887.[1]

Meanwhile, in July 1887, a Great Western deputation including Captain Lecky and W. Lancaster Owen, engineer in charge of new works, visited Weymouth. They inspected the harbour and quays and afterwards met the local harbour committee.[2] Discussion having produced a measure of verbal agreement it was left to the borough surveyor and Owen to produce a plan for submission to Paddington.

This was done, and formal agreement was in sight when the whole scheme came very near to foundering; on the turn of a penny, so to speak. The penny in question was a pier toll which, under their act of 1854,[3] the corporation were empowered to charge in respect of each passenger landing from or embarking on steam vessels at the pier, and on every piece of baggage landed or shipped there. They were also empowered to require that all landing and embarkation should take place at the pier, but had never been able to exercise that power in respect of cross-channel traffic as the pier did not meet the requirements of the Board of Customs for baggage examination. The effect had been to exempt the Packet Company and the Cherbourg service from payment of tolls.

Now, of course, if the corporation were to provide facilities at the pier their powers could be given effect. The Great Western reacted strongly, refusing to pay more than a small commuted sum and even that only under protest. In May 1888 the argument reached deadlock and the Great Western gave notice to withdraw the service on expiry of the current agreement with the Packet Company. Fortunately common sense prevailed. An agreed compromise provided for the levying of the penny on each passenger but not on baggage, and the talks went on.[4]

An agreement between the railway and the corporation was signed on 15 August 1888. Under it the corporation agreed to:

1 Dredge the harbour as required, and maintain a minimum depth of 12ft
2 Purchase and demolish property on the south side of the harbour opposite the custom house, to permit swinging

3 Erect a landing stage with all necessary passenger accommodation, including a rail platform and direct rail access
4 Complete all the foregoing by 30 June 1889

The Great Western for their part agreed to:

1 Establish on or before 1 July 1889 an improved steamer service, and to maintain it at least bi-weekly with steamers of specified minimum tonnage
2 In the event of transferring to Portland or otherwise ceasing to carry on traffic at any time before 1 July 1896 to pay the cost of the works in proportion to the unexpired term of the agreement

They were also empowered to increase the clearance under the town bridge arch to permit the passage of carriage stock over the tramway, and to extend the tramway as necessary, at their own expense (about £2,600).

A contract for three new twin-screw steamers, at a cost of £25,000 each, had already been placed with Laird Bros the previous month. Their building proceeded slowly, partly because of labour troubles in Lairds' yard. Oddly enough the Great Western board does not appear to have been imbued with any great sense of urgency either, for only six days before the first launch was expected to take place Lairds were anxiously enquiring what the ship's name was to be. The launch took place on the appointed date (29 January 1889) without ceremony, owing to the inclement season and the amount of work still required for completion. The ship was christened *Lynx*; the names chosen for the others were *Antelope* and *Gazelle*.

The second ship, the *Antelope*, was not launched until 4 May and it seems suddenly to have dawned at Paddington that with less than two months to go the agreed date could not be met. Shades of 1857! Later that month Henry Lambert, Grierson's successor as general manager, conferred with Burlinson, Lecky and other officers on innumerable urgent details.[5] It was now doubtful whether either the second boat or the tramway would be ready in time. To meet the first eventuality Lecky proposed to use the *Pembroke*, one of the Milford boats, and to have either the *Gael* or *Great Western* as stand-by. With regard to the tramway the existing bus service would be maintained for as long as might be necessary.

The meeting also considered the appointment of a deputy marine superintendent to take charge at Weymouth. The post had not been advertised but Henry William Hemmings, commodore captain of the Brighton Company's fleet at Newhaven, had applied for it on his own initiative. He was in due course appointed at his existing salary of £250 a year. As he came from a 'foreign' company it was considered desirable for the Weymouth clerk to have a thorough knowledge of Great Western routine and Lecky recommended Mr Percy Boyle, his 'very trustworthy junior clerk' at Milford. Boyle was given the post at a salary of £70 a year. In the course of time he rose to become Hemmings's successor and was for long an influential figure in the town and in Channel Islands shipping. Wimble was appointed district traffic superintendent for the islands and various other members of the Packet Company's staff were also given the opportunity of transferring to the Great Western.

Meanwhile the new shore facilities at Weymouth were nearing completion. The merest shadow of those envisaged in 1884—just enough to meet requirements—they consisted of a landing stage and a wooden baggage examination shed. The stage was of cast-iron piling, with a wooden deck, 200ft long × 50ft wide, half of which projected beyond the existing quay wall. The baggage hall, 173ft long, included sundry offices and a refreshment room. The tramway was extended by 475ft, the last 220ft being on the pier, giving accommodation alongside the stage for a train of four bogie carriages. A siding at the west end of the cargo stage was set aside for the transfer of steamer coal from rail wagons to barges, from which the actual coaling could be done with a minimum of dirt and inconvenience. No cargo was to be dealt with at the new stage; after disembarking passengers there the steamers were required to move up harbour to the old cargo berths, and when outward bound to follow a similar procedure in reverse.

On the south side of the harbour, space was cleared by demolition for a workshop,[6] and the existing Packet Company offices in Weymouth, Guernsey and Jersey were taken over. It was observed, incidentally, that the Jersey office, No 9 Bond Street, though 'commodious and convenient' and admirable for its old owners, was not sufficiently prominent for the Great Western and that some better site should be sought. It still serves as British Rail's Jersey office to this day.

By June 1889 the new establishment was ready; but no new ships. Delivery of the *Lynx* had been further delayed by faults in the draughting and ventilation system. It was therefore decided to postpone full implementation of the service until 1 August, and for July it was advertised as being performed by 'one of the well known fast iron paddle steamers'.

Failure by either party to be ready by 1 July involved a penalty of £20 a day, but as it happened the corporation were also behindhand. Lecky saw his opportunity and informed them that as the new works were not ready [!] the company, during July, would use smaller boats, which could swing without risk. In the event, with much dredging remaining to be done, it was thought imprudent to use the *Pembroke* and the service was maintained for a month by the *Gael* and *Great Western* which were, of course, not fast at all, but old and slow.

The *Lynx* finally arrived at New Milford on 6 July, showing abundant signs of rushed completion. The whole ship was filthy and rust was already showing through the hull paintwork. Yet further delay therefore ensued while she was put into a fit state to receive the public.

The public were not disappointed. On 21 July, on the ship's arrival at Weymouth, a now elated Lecky wrote to J. D. Higgins, the secretary:

> The Chairman may be interested in knowing that the people of Weymouth from the Mayor and Corporation downwards pronounce the 'Lynx' to be a magnificent vessel and much in excess

of their most sanguine anticipations, in fact one and all they are delighted with her.

Yesterday evening at nine o'clock the ship was lit throughout by Electricity and the public were admitted by ticket. These tickets were sent to the Mayor and Corporation, the Town Clerk, Principal Merchants and residents.

In all she was visited between the hours of 9 and 11 by nine hundred and odd persons who joined in a chorus of universal approval, many of them coming to me and expressing in person their feelings of admiration and surprise.

P.S. We may expect a very favourable notice in the local press.

The *Antelope* arrived at Milford on 25 July and from there went direct to Jersey. On the 29th Lecky reported:

We intend commencing the new boat service on Sunday next at 2 am [4 August] from Weymouth and Monday 8 am from Jersey. To avoid swinging they [the corporation] are going to tow the vessel out stern first and in stern first every afternoon as soon as passengers are landed . . . at their expense, until the swinging berth is ready.

So on Saturday 3 August 1889, a month and two days late and without ceremony, the full timetable was put into operation, replacing the compromise that had been dictated during July by the use of paddle steamers. The old and new schedules were as follows:

		W&CISP CO	GWR	
Paddington	dep	5.45 pm	9.15 pm	
Weymouth (town)	arr	10.38 pm	1.48 am	
(quay)	dep	11.15 pm	2.10 am	
Guernsey	arr	5.15 am	about 8.00 am*	7.05 am‡
Jersey	arr	8.15 am	10.00 am	9.25 am
Jersey	dep	5.00 pm	8.00 am	
Guernsey	dep	7.20 pm	about 10.00 am	10.20 am
Weymouth (quay)	arr	2.00 am	5.00 pm	3.15 pm
(town)	dep	5.20 am	5.05 pm	4.10 pm
Paddington	arr	10.45 am	11.25 pm	8.40 pm

* During July, with *Gael* and *Great Western*. As advertised these times were clearly intended to hide the company's embarrassment at not having the new steamers ready; in fact they were somewhat less than honest since neither *Gael* nor *Great Western* could have maintained them.

‡ From 4 August, with *Lynx*, *Antelope* and *Gazelle*.

GREAT WESTERN RAILWAY

NEW AND IMPROVED SERVICE

TO AND FROM THE

CHANNEL ISLANDS

VIA WEYMOUTH,

BY

THE EXPRESS STEAMERS,

"ANTELOPE," "GAZELLE," AND "LYNX,"

AND

THROUGH TRAINS IN CONNECTION.

DAILY (SUNDAYS EXCEPTED).

SHORTEST SEA PASSAGE.

QUICKEST AND BEST ROUTE.

WEYMOUTH TO GUERNSEY	GUERNSEY TO JERSEY
IN ABOUT 4¼ HOURS.	IN ABOUT 1¼ HOURS.

THE SERVICE BETWEEN

WEYMOUTH AND THE ISLANDS OF GUERNSEY & JERSEY

IS NOW CONDUCTED BY MEANS OF THE COMPANY'S OWN STEAMERS.

These Steamers have been specially built for this service upon the most approved principle, possess all the requisite qualifications of first-class ships, and are fitted with the Electric light and all the latest improvements and conveniences.

NEW EXPRESS TRAINS

ARE RUNNING BETWEEN

LONDON AND WEYMOUTH,

in connection with the Steamers, and direct connections have been established to and from all parts of the Great Western Line.

These Trains work to and from the Landing Stage at Weymouth and enable **Passengers** to pass direct from the Train to the Steamer, and vice versa.

Channel Islands handbill, 1889 (*British Transport Historical Records*)

The 9.15 down was an established West Wales train (the New Milford mail) to which Weymouth carriages were now attached as far as Swindon; from there the working was a new one. The 4.10 up was an entirely new train, put on for the steamer service.

The effect of the new boats was immediate. For the years 1884–8 the number of passengers arriving in Jersey during the five summer months, May to September, had averaged 13,000–14,000 via Southampton but via Weymouth only 5,000–6,000. In April 1889, in time for the summer holiday traffic, the South Western's Channel Islands fleet had been augmented by the *Dora*, fresh from the builder's yard, and the Southampton figures for May to July that year showed a marginal increase compared with the same months in 1888, those for Weymouth a slight decrease. But for August and September there was a sharp swing towards the Weymouth route, which for the latter month actually showed the higher figure:

	1888		*1889*	
	Via Southampton	*Via Weymouth*	*Via Southampton*	*Via Weymouth*
May–July inc	6,735	2,408	6,807	2,359
August	4,063	1,984	3,653	3,103
September	2,867	1,163	2,136	2,314
Total	13,665	5,555	12,596	7,776

Some of this success must be attributed to novelty attraction, but the high speed of the new steamers and a proper train service were very real improvements. For the first time since the thirties, 'short sea passage' was more than a hollow boast. The third steamer, the *Gazelle* (launched on 13 June) joined the service in September and it was decided that daily sailings, initially contemplated only for the summer months, should continue through the winter.

Through carriages to the landing stage did not appear in the timetable until October but they actually started early in August, probably when the *Lynx* and *Antelope* took over the sailings and certainly within the next few days (see chapter 9). Both 'boat' trains continued for some years to serve Weymouth town as well, the town portion being detached or attached at Weymouth Junction; for these operations four minutes were added to the journey time. A peculiarity of the working was that only the Channel Islands carriages ran through from Paddington. The Weymouth *town* portion was attached at Swindon, where any Weymouth passengers from Paddington or Reading had to change carriages.[7]

The October timetable also cut the Weymouth–Guernsey passage to 4½ hours in each direction, bringing the overall time, in the outward direction at least, to less than twelve hours, for the first time:

Paddington	dep	9.15 pm	Jersey	dep	8.00 am
Weymouth (quay)	arr	2.05 am	Guernsey	dep	10.00 am
	dep	2.15 am	Weymouth (quay)	arr	2.30 pm
Guernsey	arr	6.45 am		dep	3.45 pm
Jersey	arr	9.00 am	Paddington	arr	8.40 pm

Weymouth now showed a clear advantage of anything up to two hours over Southampton, and in practice the advertised times were frequently improved still further, mainly by curtailing the Guernsey call. On one passage the *Gazelle* left Weymouth 15 min late but reached Guernsey 15 min early, in 4 hours dead, and after staying only 20 min pressed on for Jersey. Arrival there was at 8.20 am—11 hr 5 min from Paddington and a full 3 hours quicker than via Southampton. By the winter months the Weymouth route was carrying roughly three passengers to Southampton's two, thanks partly to the added attraction of the shorter crossing at that time of the year and partly to reaction to crowded conditions on the Southampton route. The local press approved 'the great advantages of the commodious waiting and baggage room' and never failed to report a particularly good run.

THE SOUTH WESTERN RESPONDS

The South Western rose to the challenge. With modern ships, having efficient high-pressure compound machinery, and only antique paddlers to beat, they had maintained a casual supremacy: but no longer. In July 1889 the company's general manager was already preparing counter moves and in November came the first of these, the introduction of a new fast train timed to leave Southampton as soon as possible after the arrival of the steamer. Starting from the docks, alongside the steamer, the new train extended to homeward passengers the facility enjoyed in the other direction since 1864. At the same time three twin-screw 18 knot steamers were ordered, at a total estimated cost of £185,000—nearly two and a half times the cost of the *Lynx*, *Antelope* and *Gazelle*.[8]

As old adversaries the Great Western and South Western managements were fully equal to this extension of their rivalry into a fresh field. 'Shortest Sea Passage. Quickest and Best Route' declared the Great Western. 'The short and direct route to the Channel Islands' came the answer from Waterloo, and extolled the virtues of the South Western's 'Swift and Powerful Mail Steam Ships'. In January 1890 the South Western proclaimed their solicitude for their most important island customer, the summer holidaymaker, by dressing their timetable in a new cover, showing small illustrations of island beauty spots.

The competition caught the public imagination. In an early issue of the *Great Western Railway Magazine*[9] there appears a short article entitled 'On Board a Jersey Boat', which describes how at St Peter Port

> There was a great hurry and bustle to get the cargo for Guernsey unloaded and take on cargo for Jersey, on account of the S.S. Dora, from Southampton, preparing to leave for Jersey. This boat gained ten minutes' start of us and it was questionable whether we would catch her and reach Jersey first . . . Our competitor had got a long way in front but we were going fast and the distance became less and less between the respective boats. Excitement ran high as to which would reach their destination first.

Page 89: *(above)* TSS *Pembroke* as a cargo steamer, c 1921; *(below)* TSS *Ibex* in her final form, c 1921

Page 90: *(above)* TSS *St Julien* as built, with two funnels and after docking bridge; the photograph is thought to have been taken on the occasion of her introductory cruise to The Needles, May 1925; *(below)* TSSs *Great Western* (1902) and *St Julien* at Weymouth, August 1929; note ornamentation on stern. The *St Julien* is shown as running between 1928 and 1937

> As we came up off the Corbière, the Lynx was running parallel with the Dora, and cheer after cheer went up from the passengers on each vessel. We entered into St. Helier's amid great enthusiasm.

The success of the Weymouth boats was the more remarkable for having been achieved in the face of a succession of minor troubles. The stokeholds were insufferably hot, so firemen could not be persuaded to stay; the *Antelope* burst a feed pipe; the *Lynx* damaged a propeller; and both went aground in Weymouth more than once owing to inadequate dredging. There was also complaint of many small defects in the accommodation, some comparing them unfavourably with the South Western vessels or even with the *Cygnus* and *Aquila*.

The arrival of the *Gazelle* made things a little easier—until all three developed steering gear trouble, fortunately not serious. Nor did the dismal catalogue end with the year. In February 1890 the *Antelope* was aground again at Weymouth, and in June she was holed through striking the Cavale rock, off Guernsey. This put her out of commission for a week and the *Gael* had to be recalled to act as relief. There must have seemed no end to it.

One considerable advantage the South Western still held. For so long had the superiority of their vessels been accepted in the islands as a matter of course that in both St Helier and St Peter Port they enjoyed the pick of the available berths. In Guernsey the Great Western were not too badly placed, but in Jersey, where the South Western had a good berth at the Victoria Pier, with stagings at different levels so that vessels could work at any state of the tide, the Weymouth steamers had only the granite wall of the Albert Pier. Lying there they were liable to damage from the wall and furthermore, as the depth of water was inadequate, to frequent shifting about to remain afloat. At spring tides this could still involve the embarkation of passengers from open boats.

In June 1890 members of the Great Western traffic committee made a tour of inspection.[10] At Weymouth they found that much dredging was still required, a year after the stipulated date and, after taking a look at Portland as well, crossed in the *Lynx* to the islands, to try to arrange better facilities there.

MEASURE FOR MEASURE

In spite of the fact that improvement was still sorely needed in all three harbours—Weymouth, Guernsey and Jersey—and in spite of the ships' teething troubles, the early results were encouraging. Wiser for their experience the company were already looking ahead again and in August 1890 placed a new contract with Lairds for an additional boat, larger and faster, and 'embodying all the points found deficient in the present vessels', at a price of £57,000. This was the famous *Ibex*, over the years to become perhaps the most successful and most popular of all the Channel Islands steamers, by either route.

Meanwhile, in July, the first of the South Western's new steamers, the *Frederica*, had entered service. At that company's August half-yearly meeting the deputy chairman, the Hon H. W. Campbell, told shareholders that it had been found necessary to improve the steam packet service to the islands and build three new steamers 'of enlarged capacity and increased speed'. He went on:

> Of course you are aware that the Great Western Company are competing with us very keenly for the Channel Islands traffic, and if we are to keep, as I hope we shall keep, our legitimate share of that traffic, it is quite necessary to improve our boat service . . . and I think these boats are likely to give every satisfaction to those who want to cross the Channel to the Channel Islands.[11]

For the months of August to December 1889, compared with the same period in 1888, the South Western's Channel Islands receipts had shown a drop of over £8,500—22 per cent—attributable to Great Western competition.[12]

The *Frederica*'s sister ships, *Lydia* and *Stella*, followed in September and October 1890 respectively. They were too late to have much bearing on that summer's traffic but the three together did succeed in regaining some lost ground. The timetable described them as the 'Largest, Fastest and most Comfortable in the Channel Service' and announced sweeping cuts in Southampton times. Faster trains combined with the new ships to bring the time between Waterloo and Jersey down to 10¼ hours outward and 11½ hours home. This was an even more spectacular improvement than the Great Western's the previous year. In practice, moreover, as at Weymouth, scheduled timings were cut whenever possible. By the end of the year South Western confidence was quite restored.

At Weymouth bad luck still stalked, and concurrently with the South Western's advance Great Western endeavours received a slight setback through yet another mishap. On 5 September 1890, homeward bound, the *Lynx* was run down by a German tanker, the *Oevelgonne*, bound from New York to Hamburg. The *Gazelle* was already under repair and no spare vessel was available at Milford. So for a fortnight the company chartered the Isle of Man Steam Packet Co's paddle steamer *Snaefell*, a second and final reversion to that mode of propulsion. The *Lynx* was taken in hand for repair at Southampton, by Day Summers & Co. The *Oevelgonne* failed to stop after the collision and two months later, when she put into Plymouth for repairs, was promptly arrested.

At Birkenhead, construction of the *Ibex* went slowly ahead, while the day of her arrival at Weymouth was anxiously awaited. The Southampton accelerations had reduced the advantage gained by the *Lynx*, *Antelope* and *Gazelle* to a nine days' wonder, and in January 1891 T. I. Allen, assistant to Burlinson, Wimble, Captains Lecky and Hemmings and other officers met at Weymouth in a state of some agitation to consider how their new champion might most effectively be engaged. Wimble summed up the situation:

> What we have to contend with is a most serious competition with the South Western people. They make it apparent in everything they do. They advertise in all the papers, and, when any of the boats makes a good run it is in all the papers—*Frederica* left

Jersey 8.0 a.m. Passengers arrived London 6 o'clock, 6.30 or 6.40 as the case may be. What we have to show is that we can do it better. We can get the London passengers through in the same time as that. They run a special train immediately after the boat's arrival[13].

Primarily the additional vessel was required as a relief but the introduction of one far ahead of the others in both size and speed, as the *Ibex* would be, was bound to involve unbalanced working. After much discussion it was proposed to use her for a thrice-weekly daylight service, leaving Weymouth at 1.30 pm and returning from Jersey direct at 10.30 am on the intervening days. The management attached such importance to this holiday service that there was even talk of gracing it with Swindon's latest novelty, the corridor train. The *County Chronicle* for 4 June 1891 records the train's presence at Weymouth on trial:

IMPROVED RAILWAY CARRIAGES. In view of the very increased traffic which the G.W. Rly. Co. are likely to develop this summer by the construction of a steamer which will make daylight passages between Weymouth and the Channel Islands and the acceleration of the train service to and from London, some new carriages have been built for the 'boat train'. These have been on view at Weymouth station, and are altogether a new departure. The carriages are known as corridor carriages; that is, there is a corridor for walking the whole length of the train, but of course the various classes are divided and shut off. In every class is a separate smoking compartment, as also a compartment for the exclusive use of ladies, with lavatory accommodation for both sexes at each end of the 'coach'. Each compartment is brilliantly illuminated with a two-light gas burner, decorated with mirrors and photographic views of local interest, and most comfortably upholstered. Every care seems to have been taken to ensure comfort and convenience, and the corridor carriages cannot fail to be appreciated. The guard who travels with the train has entire control of the three classes of carriages. The coaches were sent to Weymouth in order to see if they could be used on the tramway and the trial was in every respect most satisfactory.

All to no purpose, however: difficulties in the supply of steel plate, through industrial unrest, delayed the *Ibex*'s launch until

6 June, and it was the end of August before she was delivered. On arrival at Milford the ship was immediately despatched to Jersey and Guernsey for exhibition before going to Weymouth. On board she carried an official party, headed by Viscount Emlyn, deputy chairman, and in each island was open to the public by ticket, issued to 'respectable people'. The *Ibex* finally reached Weymouth on 7 September, crossing from Guernsey with invited guests in a new record time of 3 hr 35 min.[14] On berthing she discharged rockets, attracting an admiring crowd, and during the evening was again open for inspection by ticket. In view of the lateness in the season she then merely took her place on the ordinary schedule with the other three, and the daylight service did not materialise. Neither did the corridor boat train.[15]

Such change as there was in the boat train that summer was comparatively minor. The up train, now billed as the Channel Islands Express, was re-timed to leave the quay at 4.30 pm and run independently as far as Swindon, where it joined the Weymouth town portion. This allowed to some extent for delay in Guernsey caused by ever-increasing produce shipments.

The only other development during 1891 was an arrangement (it was not a formal contract) for some mails to be carried via Weymouth. This was effective from 1 April and supplementary to the main contract at Southampton. It drew a subsidy of £200 a year (Southampton's contract was worth £6,500) in respect of the mails from the north and west of England, and Wales. The *Gazelle* was reported at the time as having arrived 'for the first time flying the Royal Mail colours'.

At the end of the year Lecky wrote to Frederick Saunders, the company's one-time secretary and now Gooch's successor as chairman, 'With a passenger service consisting of three vessels of the Ibex type we would, I believe, carry all before us . . . a summer day-service would be certain to attract more passengers and I hope the Directors will sanction a trial next season'.

The proposal had not actually reached the stage of board sanction when put forward for that summer, and still did not do so. In fact, the introduction of even a trial daylight service did not take place for another three years. During that time, however, the company continued to consolidate their position, constantly cutting times and improving efficiency, while the South Western, having partly retaken the initiative, hung on grimly. There was no respite for either.

In June 1892 the Great Western followed the South Western's lead of 1889 in putting on a special train to leave the landing stage at the earliest possible moment after the arrival of the steamer, 'for Trowbridge and Swindon, in connection with Express trains to Bristol, London and the North'. London passengers normally connected at Swindon with the 2.15 pm from Plymouth (Millbay). This was due at Paddington at 8.25 and, in conjunction with an 8.30 am start from Jersey, introduced for the summer season two years previously, gave a homeward timing in line with the outward—ie, of just under twelve hours.

If expedient, the special ran right through. A very fast run was recorded on 2 June, for example, when the *Ibex*, after an 18 min delay in Guernsey, crossed to Weymouth in 3¾ hours. The train was away by just after 3 pm and by one minute past seven, 10½ hours after leaving Jersey, passengers were in London. And that despite the length of the rail journey. However fast they did the sea crossing, on land the Great Western were badly handicapped, as all Weymouth traffic was of necessity routed over the old Wilts Somerset & Weymouth line via Trowbridge and Swindon. The Stert 'cut-off' was yet to be, and nowhere was the 'Great Way Round' jibe more justified.

Reference has already been made to delays in Guernsey to load fruit, and a significant advance in the summer of 1894 was born indirectly of that traffic. In 1890 and 1891 it had been catered for by chartering an outside boat (the *Gipsy* in 1890 and the *Lady of the Isles* in 1891). In 1892 and 1893, with the fourth railway boat available, charter had been dispensed with, the traffic being handled instead by the *Lynx*. For the fruit boat to take passengers as well, enabling the Jersey boat to omit the Guernsey call altogether, was a logical next step. This arrangement was now put into effect, and brought Jersey to within 10¾ hours of Paddington.

In the reverse direction the time was brought down to 10¼ hours. At the same time 'mid-week' tickets between Weymouth and the islands, available for fourteen days, were offered at 25s return (saloon) and 17s 6d return (after cabin) (£1·25 and 87½p)—a reduction of approximately 25 per cent.

The bypassing of Guernsey called for an alternative inter-island service and to provide this the Jersey boat made a trip to Guernsey and back before returning to Weymouth. Opportunity was also taken to adopt more convenient times of inter-island sailing, the boat leaving Jersey at 11 am and Guernsey at 5 pm.

The South Western, similarly embarrassed by delays at Guernsey, countered in July 1894 by announcing that 'In order to prevent delay to Passengers at Guernsey and for the accommodation of shippers, fast cargo steamers will leave Southampton for Guernsey every week night at 11.30 p.m. returning from Guernsey to Southampton every week day morning at 11 a.m. until further notice'. This arrangement enabled them to retain their Guernsey call and at the same time to keep it within bounds. Timings via Southampton had remained unchanged since the introduction of the *Frederica*, *Lydia* and *Stella* but the homeward was now cut by a whole hour by putting the departure from Jersey back to 9 am without altering the time of arrival at Waterloo. Most of the saving, of course, was in Guernsey, where the call was now for passengers and mails only. And throughout the summer a relief boat train left Waterloo ten minutes ahead of the normal 9.45 pm.

The advertised claim that this 'Accelerated Improved Daily Steam Packet Service' saved three hours on the railway journey was an exaggeration, but at least it was less blatantly untrue than describing the Southampton route as the 'shortest sea passage' as South Western advertising had done for many years prior to 1889, on the pretext that the crossing began and ended at The Needles![16]

July 1895 saw the Great Western's long awaited daylight service, though only on Saturdays. A new train, leaving Paddington at 9.18 am, gave arrivals in Guernsey at 6.30 pm and Jersey at 8.30; a corresponding return service left Jersey on Mondays at 4 pm, calling at Guernsey two hours later and reaching Weymouth at 10.30. No connecting train was provided, but London passengers returning by the normal morning boat could still enjoy a worthwhile weekend in either island (Saturday evening to Monday morning).

This new facility was widely advertised and proved so popular that in 1896 the South Western instituted a Saturday daylight service via Southampton. Leaving Waterloo at 8.55 am passengers reached Guernsey at 5.30 pm and Jersey the usual two hours later. This was thirty-seven minutes quicker than the 1895 time via Weymouth, but a corresponding Great Western acceleration resulted in 1896 timings that were virtually identical by the two routes. In fact, the Great Western still kept one jump ahead by making the Monday return working a through service, leaving Jersey at 10.30 am and running direct to Weymouth. Passengers could now be in London the same evening (arrival time at Paddington, via the town station, 9.30) whereas the South Western's return working was advertised only from Jersey to Guernsey.

The cut and thrust had now ruled for seven years. On balance the South Western had so far had rather the better of it, thanks primarily to the shorter and quicker London train journey. Another advantage was that on night crossings interchange at Southampton permitted a more comfortable hour of boarding and a longer night's rest. In parts of the country other than London, notably the Midlands, the South Western's advantage was less marked, both Bristol and Swindon being well placed for connections to Weymouth. The Great Western was also handling a good share of the cargo traffic, to which such considerations as a good night's sleep did not apply.

The public took a lively interest in the proceedings, as one might expect, and in the islands the rivals' performances were a constant talking point. 'Which one will be going first?' was a question frequently to be heard when the boats were in Guernsey together, and doubtless the answer sometimes determined which got the extra passengers. In Jersey there was always interest on the St Helier waterfront to see which would arrive first. Weymouth's direct night boat and the regular Southampton boat were both due at 8 am, and the Saturday daylight sailings also ran very close.

Further Great Western acceleration of the night boats in 1896 added to the tension, as it was achieved by retiming the Paddington departure to 9.45, coinciding with that from Waterloo. The lead snatched back for the South Western by the *Frederica* and her sisters, and gradually worn down again by the Great Western, was now finally extinguished. By this summer of 1896 the best timings by either route were level, at 10¼ hours between London and Jersey and 10½ hours home. With the winter timetable, however, Weymouth reverted to 11¾ hours and 12½ hours respectively, whereas at Southampton there was little variation throughout the year. This was an important distinction, but in practice its effect was limited by poor timekeeping. The Great Western boat was not due in Jersey until an hour after its rival but late departure from Southampton—commonly twenty minutes or more—and the now familiar delay in Guernsey often meant that between the islands they were very much closer. There were even occasions when the Great Western was in first.

It was all very exciting; but however satisfying the contest may have been for the Jersiais and Guernesiais and their summer visitors, those responsible for running the services must occasionally have wondered just how much further it could go. Running the ships flat out resulted in excessive wear and tear; timekeeping had deteriorated; and the growth of traffic meant fewer opportunities for the 'prestige' run with an early arrival.

As Lecky had foreseen in 1891, Weymouth's best prospect lay in a summer daylight service and in 1896, encouraged by the success of the weekend experiment and with a full scale version in mind for the following year, the Great Western ordered two additional vessels, larger and faster than the *Ibex*. Lairds were again among the firms invited to tender but this time the contract

(£110,000) went to the Naval Construction & Armaments Co (now Vickers Armstrong) at Barrow-in-Furness.

The prospect of even larger vessels once again underlined the shortage of harbour accommodation, and in anticipation of their arrival various improvements were put in hand. At Weymouth the landing stage was extended to the westward by some 40ft; in Guernsey the Great Western berths were dredged; and in Jersey, in belated response to the traffic committee's representations in 1890, the States allocated the Great Western two berths at the recently completed New North Quay.

In that island, too, much-needed dredging was being undertaken on a considerable scale. The shallowness of St Helier harbour, long a cause of irritation and inconvenience to both companies, but particularly to the Great Western, has already been commented on. The difficulty was aggravated by the exceptional rise and fall of the tide—35ft or more at springs—and losing the tide meant four or five hours at anchor in the roads while passengers and mails were sent ashore in open boats—a constant anxiety in the event of delay.

AN ERROR OF JUDGEMENT

Just how necessary was the deepening of St Helier harbour was dramatically brought home to all concerned early in 1897, even as the work was in progress. The date was 16 April, Good Friday. The Waterloo boat train, delayed by heavy Easter holiday traffic, reached Southampton more than an hour late, and it was past 1 am when the outgoing mailboat, the *Frederica*, left the quayside. The Paddington boat train was little better and the *Ibex*, timed to leave Weymouth at 2.10 am, did not get away until 2.55. At 7.32 she berthed in Guernsey, just 15 min after the *Frederica*. Within half an hour she had disembarked 109 passengers, taken on 61, and discharged some of her cargo. Without waiting to discharge the rest she was on her way again and at 8.5 am backed through the pierheads and turned towards Jersey. The *Frederica*, having nearly 200 Guernsey passengers to disembark as well as 22 tons of cargo to be landed, took a little longer, and was 10 min behind.

The deadline for saving the tide at St Helier on this occasion was about 9.45 and both ships pressed on at something very close to top speed—18½ to 19 knots. The *Frederica* was slightly the faster of the two, and by the time an hour had passed, as both ships approached the Corbière, was within two or three lengths of the *Ibex*, lying on her starboard bow.

At this state of the tide both ships would usually have cleared that danger spot well out to sea but with an eye on the clock John Le Feuvre, captain of the *Ibex*, decided to take the Noirmontaise channel, inside the rocks of that name, and turned to port, towards the land and the advancing *Frederica*. There was just room for both to pass in safety but Le Feuvre, fearing a collision, changed his mind and turned seaward again. This manœuvre was intended to take him *outside* the Noirmontaise, but his judgement was slightly out and he ended up by striking as he passed. The *Frederica* passed through safely.

With seven propeller blades gone out of eight, and two compartments flooding through a 13ft gash, the *Ibex* put into Portelet Bay, with the *Frederica* standing by. Her Jersey passengers, numbering 261, were put ashore in boats from both ships, and continued to St Helier by the Jersey Railway—the only occasion, surely, on which visitors from England completed their journeys to Jersey as they had begun them, by train.

On the next tide, when the *Ibex* refloated, a tug attempted to take her in tow, but against the current, and in deteriorating weather, was unequal to the task. The ship therefore lay at anchor all night. At first light on Saturday, still slowly taking water, she was coaxed by the *Gazelle* into St Aubin's Bay and beached—a tricky operation reflecting much credit on Captain Hemmings, who directed it personally and was injured in the process. During low tide on Sunday the leak was plugged and that evening the *Ibex* was taken to St Helier by the *Gazelle* and two tugs. The Board of Trade inquiry, held the following month, placed no blame on Captain Allix, of the *Frederica*, but held Le Feuvre to have been negligent. His race against time and tide cost him a six-months suspension of his certificate.[17]

THE DAYLIGHT SERVICE

After temporary patching at St Helier the *Ibex* was permanently repaired at Barrow, where the two new ships were now approaching completion. As a temporary relief at Weymouth the *Pembroke* was transferred from the Milford–Waterford service. The *Ibex* returned to Weymouth in June, her return coinciding with the delivery of the first of the new ships, the *Roebuck* (launched 6 March 1897) and together, on 1 July, these two opened the daylight service. On the opening day, with London press representatives and other guests on board, the *Roebuck* crossed to Guernsey in a new record time of under 3½ hours.

The daylight service ran on six days a week, Mondays to Saturdays. Cargo was carried but only for Jersey, which enabled the Guernsey call to be cut to a minimum. The schedule was as follows:

Paddington	dep	8.50 am	Jersey	dep	8.30 am
Weymouth	arr	1.10 pm	Guernsey	arr	10.15 am
	dep	1.30 pm		dep	10.30 am
Guernsey	arr	5.00 pm	Weymouth	arr	about 2.30 pm
	dep	5.15 pm		dep	special
Jersey	arr	7.00 pm	Paddington	arr	about 7.15 pm

In the outward direction the daylight boat was duplicated by the existing night service. As separation of the Guernsey and Jersey traffic was no longer necessary the night boat reverted to the old arrangement, so restoring the morning service between Guernsey and Jersey. This was balanced by a new Jersey–Guernsey service in the afternoon, leaving at 5 pm and reaching Guernsey at 6.45. Remaining at Guernsey overnight the boat then completed the round trip by continuing to Weymouth the following morning with fruit and general cargo, arriving at about 4 pm. A balancing inter-island service, Jersey–Guernsey in the morning and back in the evening, was, of course, provided by the daylight boat.

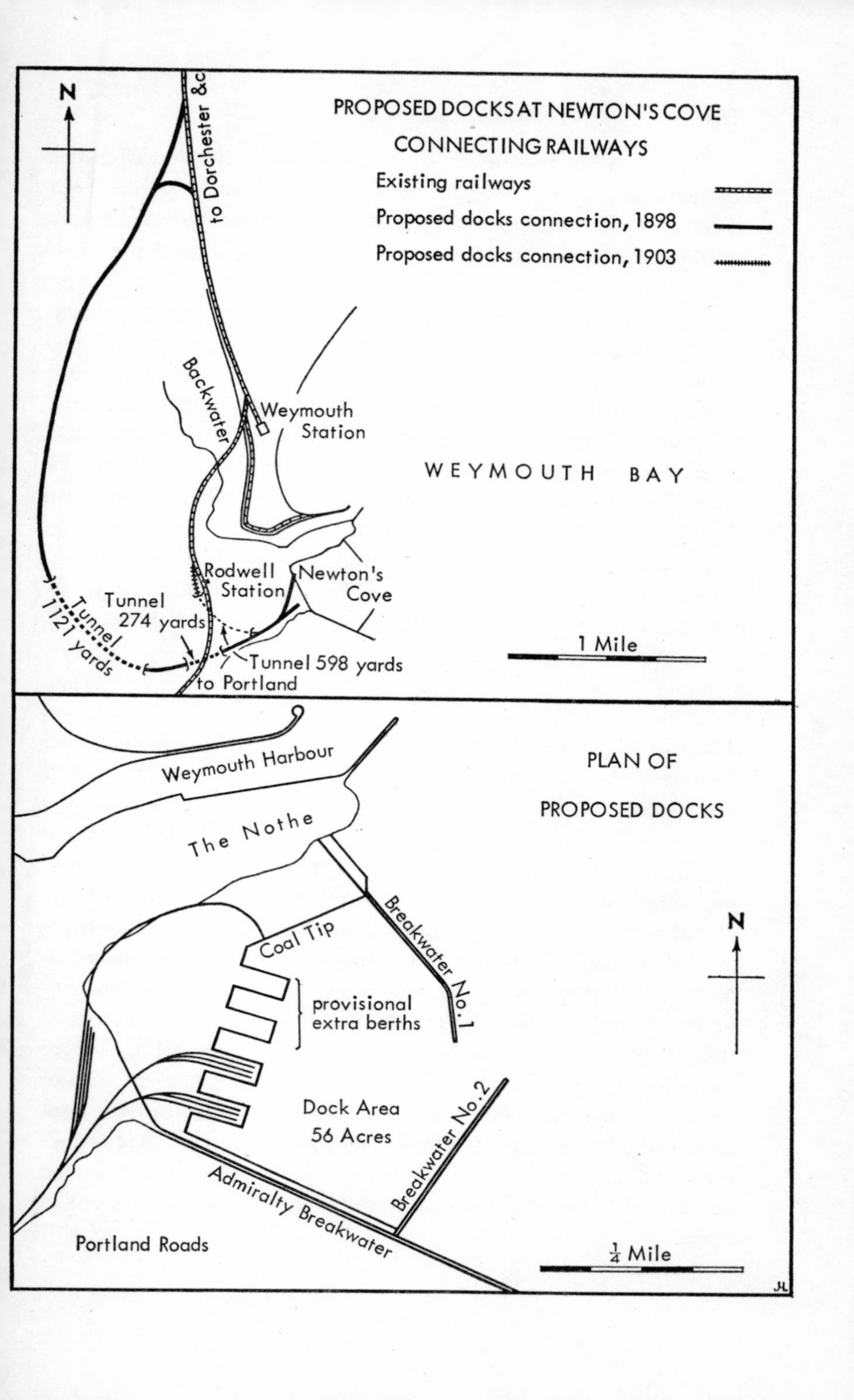

PROPOSED DOCKS AT NEWTON'S COVE
CONNECTING RAILWAYS
Existing railways
Proposed docks connection, 1898
Proposed docks connection, 1903
N
to Dorchester &c
Backwater
Weymouth Station
WEYMOUTH BAY
Rodwell Station
Newton's Cove
Tunnel 274 yards
Tunnel 1121 yards
Tunnel 598 yards
to Portland
1 Mile
PLAN OF
PROPOSED DOCKS
Weymouth Harbour
The Nothe
Coal Tip
Breakwater No.1
provisional extra berths
N
Dock Area 56 Acres
Breakwater No.2
Admiralty Breakwater
Portland Roads
¼ Mile
JL

Not to be entirely outdone the South Western increased their daylight sailings to three a week, leaving Southampton on Tuesdays and Thursdays as well as Saturdays, but with the return working still advertised only as far as Guernsey (and thence to Southampton with cargo).

As in 1889 and 1891 the new service was dogged at the outset by bad luck. On 10 July, with less than a fortnight's running to her credit, the *Roebuck* had to be withdrawn with a broken steampipe. The *Pembroke*, hardly back at Milford after deputising for the *Ibex*, was again sent to Weymouth and three days later the *Roebuck* was sent to Milford. She was still off service when her sister ship, the *Reindeer*, made her maiden crossing, on 3 August, and a further three weeks elapsed before the two were able to settle down to work together as intended. By then the holiday peak was passing. Nevertheless, for September, Jersey arrivals showed Weymouth slightly in the lead once more.

NEWTON'S COVE

The quite remarkable expansion of Great Western Channel Islands traffic that had taken place during the previous seven or eight years had been achieved against the handicap of what the *County Chronicle* described as the 'paralysing limits' of Weymouth harbour. In January 1896 Lecky, who had, of course, never had a good word to say for Weymouth, reminded the company's steamboat committee that the seven-year restrictive period imposed by the 1888 agreement, during which abandonment of Weymouth would have involved the payment of compensation, would shortly expire, and recommended the directors to think again about alternative accommodation. Possibilities before them were to go ahead with the 1883 Mere scheme, or that of 1884 in Weymouth Bay, or to construct berths within the new Admiralty breakwater at Portland. Construction of that breakwater, at a point known as Bincleaves and completing on the northern side the enclosure of Portland Roads, was then about to begin.

The last-mentioned appeared to be the best prospect, but the Admiralty objected. The company therefore decided instead to build a new harbour of their own in Newton's Cove, abutting on but *outside* the Admiralty breakwater. This the Admiralty accepted, and plans for such a harbour, with a new line of connecting railway, were drawn up accordingly. They were considered by the steamboat committee in August 1897, when J. C. Inglis, the then chief engineer, estimated the cost at £375,000, made up as follows:

	£
Harbour	200,000
Equipment	45,000
Railway	130,000

Against this could be expected a saving of some £3,000 a year in harbour and wharfage dues paid to Weymouth Corporation, and there was also the prospect of attracting other traffic—from France, for example.

Parliamentary powers for the scheme were sought, among others, in the Great Western Railway (New Works) Bill in the session of 1897–8. Weymouth Corporation, to whose harbour revenue the said £3,000 was a major contribution, decided to oppose the bill and petitioned Parliament against it. As they did not go to the length of briefing counsel to argue their case, however, their opposition was ineffectual and for practical purposes the Weymouth clauses were unopposed. The bill received the Royal Assent on 12 August 1898.[18]

The works authorised were the construction of two jetties, approximately 800ft long, with all necessary approach roads and other ancillaries, and two breakwaters enclosing a total water area of some fifty-six acres, of a minimum depth of 24ft. From a junction south of Upwey the new railway was to bear away in a southerly direction and then turn sharply eastwards to pass in a tunnel under the Portland branch near Castle Cove. The length of this line was a little under 4½ miles, to which various spurs and sidings added another ¾ mile.

As is well known, the close of the nineteenth century was a

time of thrusting expansion on the Great Western, and Newton's Cove was described as intended to develop the company's marine business in general. The scale of the proposed works, admitting vessels 'of all sizes at any hour of the tide', reflected the desire to attract something more than Channel Islands trade.

For the time being, however, that remained the only issue, while the question 'how much further can the contest go?' remained unanswered. The *Roebuck* and *Reindeer* had demonstrated that 3½ hours to Guernsey was not an impossible timing, but to maintain it with regularity in day-to-day service was another matter. In the summer of 1898 arrival in Jersey reverted to 7.30 pm—the first relaxation since the competition began—and the 1897 timings emerged as the peak. But the pace was still too hot and, at least during the greater part of the year, extravagant. Before 1898 was out the opposing general managers were talking about a truce.

By the beginning of 1899 settlement was in sight: at the end of March, for the South Western, came disaster. The occasion was once again the Easter holiday rush. On 30 March, the Thursday before Good Friday, each company ran an excursion daylight sailing, on the normal 'summer' schedule. The South Western boat, the *Stella*, commanded by Captain William Reeks, left Southampton at 11.25 am, ten minutes late. On passage she encountered fog—patchy, but too thick for casual dismissal. Good seamanship demanded caution but, mindful no doubt of the Weymouth boat, Reeks raced on at nearly 19 knots. Too late to check the *Stella*'s speed he was suddenly confronted with the Casquets, and at 4.10, on the rock called the Auquière, the *Stella* struck. In eight minutes she had gone, with the loss of over 100 lives.

HONOURS EVEN

'Truce' negotiations continued, with added urgency we may suppose. In June 1899 Sir Charles Owens, the South Western general manager, reported to his directors that he had been in touch

Page 107: *(above)* TSS *St Patrick* (1930); *(below)* TSS *Sambur* at Weymouth, April 1950

Page 108: *(above)* TSS *Roebuck* (1897); first-class dining saloon; *(below)* TSS *St Patrick* (1930); first-class dining saloon

with the Great Western 'with a view to curtailing the steamboat service to the Channel Islands by both companies and pooling the receipts'.[19] At about the same time his opposite number, J. L. Wilkinson (Lambert had resigned in 1896) advised the Great Western board what was in mind, and both boards authorised the continuation of the good work. Within the next few weeks agreement was reached; the proposals may be summarised as follows:

1. That from 1 October to 30 April in any year (or as might otherwise be mutually agreed) each company would run only three times a week, on alternate nights from England and alternate days from the islands
2. That from 1 May to 30 September in any year (or as might otherwise be mutually agreed) each company would run six times a week, from Southampton by night and from Weymouth by day, both companies running homeward by day
3. That each company's gross Channel Islands receipts, less certain agreed deductions, would be paid to a common fund, which would then be divided between them in the ratio of the corresponding receipts for 1897 and 1898
4. That the return tickets of either would be available by the route of the other.

Revised arrangements on these lines were put into effect with the winter timetable, on 1 October 1899, and embodied in a formal agreement between the two companies which was sealed on 20 December following.[20] The race was over, and though the future might be a little duller it would be quieter and certainly safer. Having brought the South Western to terms in the face of many obstacles the Great Western could well rest content.

The chapter poses a postscript: did the steamers engage in actual racing? Open sanction of such a practice would have been unthinkable, and officially the answer was always 'No'. Nevertheless, in the popular estimation the frequent close running unquestionably was racing. Already well aired in the island press, which condemned with equal readiness any kind of delay and anything that it chose to regard as risky, the issue gained a wider prominence at the inquiry into the stranding of the *Ibex*. Two witnesses at least said that to them, as passengers, the ships had definitely appeared to be racing, that 'one was trying to get ahead of the other'.

This, of course, was strenuously denied. Captain Le Feuvre was asked by counsel for the Board of Trade:

> Now, it has been suggested that you were racing with the *Frederica*. Is that the fact?
> I was not.

And later, cross-examined by counsel for the South Western:

> And were you not actually trying to cut him out, to get across his head so as to prevent him getting into harbour first?
> No, there was nothing about that. I did not try to cut him out, nor never have.

And Captain Allix, of the *Frederica*, when asked, also denied that he had had any intention of racing.

The court accepted that both had merely been racing the tide, not one another; but they also noted that, as only one ship could enter the harbour at a time, Le Feuvre's object had been to reach St Helier ahead of the *Frederica*, which smacks very much of 'a rose by any other name'.

The question also exercised the minds of learned counsel investigating the loss of the *Stella*.[21] Captain G. H. Lewis, assistant marine superintendent at Southampton, was asked:

> Had it ever been reported to you that these boats had raced one against the other?
> No Sir.
> Think, Captain Lewis?
> I am quite certain.
> Have you ever heard from any-one any suggestion of that kind?
> Well, I have heard people suppose such a thing.

Did it ever occur to you as necessary to take any notice of what people had supposed?
Certainly not.

He and other official witnesses also denied knowing that a Great Western boat had been running that same day to precisely the same times as the *Stella*, and professed indifference to what might be happening at Paddington or Weymouth. Their conscious care to disavow racing must have been quite transparent. Lewis's evasion when he was pressed again stretched credulity still further:

You know perfectly well, Sir, do you not, that your boats are running in constant competition with the boats of the Great Western Railway Company?
I know nothing of the sort, Sir.
And have never heard it suggested?
Not in competition with them.
Never heard it suggested until you came into Court to-day; you will not swear to that?
Yes, I think I can.
Very well, if it relieves you to swear it, do.

The court announced its opinion: although the accident had been caused by speed it was not prepared to say that excessive speed had been maintained for the purpose of beating the Great Western boat. 'Not proven', perhaps—but no one could offer another explanation of Reeks's intemperate haste. The Great Western captain had respected the weather conditions and the Weymouth boat—again the *Ibex*—did not reach Jersey until 12.28 am, five hours late, but safe. Commenting more generally, the court felt obliged to remark the tendency to 'reduce the length of the passage by increasing speed' with consequent additional risk, and that 'when different lines compete to the same ports rivalry will naturally exist'.

Within fairly narrow limits the times of sailing and arrival were dictated by the tides, but deliberately close scheduling could only be described as provocative. When two boats left Guernsey more or less together it was not unknown for the first away to 'dawdle a bit in the Russel so as to let the other come up close behind and so make a good race of it'. When clear of dangerous channels they would then edge closer, while passengers lining the rails shouted across at one another and those in the stern of the leader dangled derisive tow-ropes. Parallel tracks were often maintained far beyond the normal point of divergence, right up to the Casquets.[22] In speed there was little to choose between the rivals, but slight advantage often lay in luck or better knowledge of the local navigation. The captains would have been singularly lacking in imagination had they never taken such advantage, and entered into the spirit of the 'race'. As skilled and responsible men they could usually do so innocently enough, but the temptation to 'chance it' was there.

Both companies obviously knew what went on and neither silence nor denial could conceal the fact. The rivalry invites comparison with the much more famous races which at about the same time were engaging the east and west coast train routes to Scotland. Ships did not match the concentrated excitement of the 'eighty-eight' or the 'ninety-five', perhaps, but with the contestants in full view of each other for much of the distance run instead of taking wholly independent routes, as the racing trains did, the Race to Jersey bred its own brand of excitement. In one respect at least the cases were similar: neither side was sorry to call it a day.

Notes to this chapter are on page 223

CHAPTER FIVE

CONSOLIDATION, AND STEAMERS TO FRANCE AGAIN (1900-14)

POOLING produced substantial economies for both companies[1] and though the public might regret the passing of the lavish provision made for them during the nineties they still enjoyed a comfort, speed and convenience undreamed of ten years previously.[2] The transformation was, of course, especially noticeable at Weymouth but even a passenger on one of Southampton's newest ships, the *Vera* or *Alberta*, owed much to the competition and, indirectly, to the Great Western.

In comparison with the ten years up to 1899 the next fifteen were in some ways uneventful. Indeed, except during two wars, the timetable established by the agreement was to remain basically unaltered for almost sixty years. This next phase was nevertheless not devoid of interest. It brought a steady growth in traffic, both passenger and cargo, and if it lacked excitement there was no lack of variety: an extension of parliamentary powers; a further unsuccessful entry into the French market; the commencement, then suspension and finally the abandonment of the Newton's Cove harbour works; excursion traffic; and, as regards the steamers, one purchase, two sales, two conversions and three accidents.

WRECK OF THE IBEX

The first and most serious accident occurred when joint working was barely more than three months old. The date was 5 January 1900. The overnight boat from Weymouth was the *Ibex*, Captain Thomas Baudains. At about 6.20 am, approaching St Peter Port, Baudains picked up the leading lights for the Little Russel but instead of setting his course by them, as he should have done, elected to check his position by taking a bearing on the Casquets light. With the Casquets lying more or less astern the light was obscured by the wheelhouse. Course was therefore altered to port, to bring it into view. The bearing taken, the helmsman resumed his course, but in doing so over-corrected and ran too far to westward, so that the St Peter Port lights were lost. In the ensuing confusion the *Ibex* struck sidelong against a rock of the Platte Fougère reef (not far from where the *Brighton* had gone down in 1887) and ripped her starboard plating.

Already travelling at not far short of full speed, Baudains turned towards Herm in the hope of putting the *Ibex* on the beach, but as the water rose steam pressure rapidly dropped, obliging him to alter course for Guernsey again. He failed to make it. About fifteen minutes after first striking, the *Ibex* described a half-circle to starboard and settled on an even keel near the Gant Rock, about 2¾ miles north of St Peter Port, heading north-east and with her decks just awash at low tide. Passengers on board totalled thirty-three or thirty-four. It was thought initially that all had been saved, but a man's body was later found in the saloon by a diver. It turned out to be that of a naval rating, which probably accounts for the soundness with which he had slept through all the upheaval; and huddled under a blanket he had been missed when a check was made. One of the crew also lost his life, despite valiant efforts to save him. Some survivors were landed at St Sampson's, others at St Peter Port, those for Jersey later going forward in the *Antelope* which was sent from Weymouth for the purpose. Of the cargo, part was salvaged during the next few weeks as tides permitted but much was lost. Claims for loss and damage totalled some £6,000.

At the Board of Trade inquiry into the accident, held the following month, counsel for the company stated that the captains' instructions were to avoid all risks and, no doubt recalling that less than three years had elapsed since the Corbière incident, remarked further that 'since the agreement there was no question of racing'. This was revealing, since racing had, of course, never been officially admitted. On being judged to have navigated negligently, and having his certificate suspended for six months, Baudains resigned.[3]

The subsequent salvage of the *Ibex* is one of the best known episodes in cross-channel history. Removal of the wreck one way or another was essential, as it was a danger to navigation, and in March the company accepted the offer of the Northern Salvage Company, of Hamburg, to raise it for £15,000 on a 'no cure, no pay' basis.

The method chosen was to lift with the tide by cables passed underneath, buoyancy being derived from two pontoons and two hulks, one of each on either side. The work started at the end of May and became a major holiday 'sight' in Guernsey, two local tugs, the *Alert* and the *Assistance*, running regular excursions 'around the Scene of Operations' at a fare of 1s (5p). As the divers could work only at slack water it was not until 21 July, and at the third attempt, that the vessel was successfully raised. She was then carried stern first into St Peter Port and beached. Ten days later, with the holes plugged and her hull now watertight, she was moved to St Sampson's and from there, in due course, to Birkenhead for complete refitting at Laird's yard.[4]

Virtually a new ship, the *Ibex* returned to Weymouth on 21 April 1901 and resumed service two days later. The *County Chronicle* remarked that since what it called her 'resurrection' she looked 'smarter than ever', and incorporated many improvements. Well she might, since the total cost of the operation—lifting, towing and refitting—amounted to £47,250, about four-fifths of her original cost ten years previously. Whether the exercise had been worthwhile financially may well be doubted.

JOINT WORKING

Meanwhile the first year of joint working had come and gone, the brunt of Weymouth's contribution falling on the *Antelope* with the *Roebuck* and *Reindeer* brought in for the daylight service. As it turned out, this was the only year for which the summer timetable operated for the full period prescribed in the agreement. For the next two years it started on 1 July and from 1903, as holiday traffic continued to grow, on 1 June. The Weymouth boat then sailed by day during June, July and August and, to limit the need to enter St Helier after dark, by night during September.

From the summer of 1900 the steamer timings were further eased but the down train was accelerated by fifteen minutes. The opening that year of the 'cut-off' between Stert and Westbury reduced the distance between Paddington and Weymouth by a little over fourteen miles and the following summer the down train started to use the new route. This enabled it to be accelerated by a further fifteen minutes. The up special continued as before, however, so as to provide connections to other parts of the system. These were made at Yeovil (Pen Mill) for the west of England; at Trowbridge for Bristol and South Wales; and at Swindon for the Midlands.

In winter, when Weymouth alternated with Southampton, the original intention appears to have been for the sailing days to rotate, year by year, but except during 1900–1, when the days were reversed, the Weymouth pattern became established as Tuesdays, Thursdays and Saturdays, returning to the islands at 2.15 the following morning. (On Mondays, Wednesdays and Fridays, of course, passengers travelled via Southampton). As in summer, the timetable showed some initial uncertainty and a set pattern did not emerge until the beginning of 1902. Arrival in Jersey was then standardised at 9.30 am, making the journey from Paddington half an hour slower than during the previous four winters. Homeward, there was an increase in the overall time to a little over thirteen hours during the first two 'pooled' winters, but from October 1901 nearly an hour was cut from the up train by routing it via Lavington. Arrival at Paddington was now at 8.20 pm. It is interesting to note, however, that in winter the *down* train continued to run via Swindon; the winter routing was thus an exact reversal of the summer. On the resumption of the daylight service in 1921 (after its withdrawal during the

1914–18 war) both up and down trains ran via Lavington in summer but the overnight train—ie the down train in winter—clung to the old route until 1934.

Taken all round, there was now little to choose in quality of service between Weymouth and Southampton, and each had its adherents among regular travellers according to personal preference and circumstances. The close ties between the small island communities and the United Kingdom bred something of a 'family' atmosphere about the steamers, with crews and regular passengers, such as 'commercials' and children at boarding school, well known to one another. London passengers tended to prefer Southampton, especially in winter. The longer night's rest afforded by that route was appreciated by those going to the islands and an added advantage, in either direction, was the shorter and faster train journey, which saved some forty minutes overall. In fact, a winter passenger who took the trouble to make his own way from the quay to the town station could reach London more quickly by going to Waterloo even from Weymouth—at 7.40 pm, little later than when travelling via Southampton and forty minutes earlier than by the Paddington boat train. Bristol, Birmingham and the west generally were well served via Weymouth, and the popularity of the daylight service with holidaymakers was such that in summer the disparity between the two ports was only marginal. From June to September Weymouth's share of the traffic now averaged about 47 per cent.

The reduction in winter sailings following the agreement meant that, as passenger vessels, the *Lynx*, *Antelope* and *Gazelle* had become to a large extent redundant. They remained the mainstay of the winter service until 1903, enabling the larger and more expensive vessels, particularly the *Roebuck* and *Reindeer*, to be held in reserve for the daylight service, but increasingly they were utilised for the Guernsey perishables traffic (grapes, flowers and tomatoes). From about 1904 they dropped out of the passenger sailings altogether except for occasional spells as relief vessels.

When not required for the fruit traffic they were often at Plymouth, as tenders to calling ocean liners. The first of them to be so employed appears to have been the *Gazelle*, in 1900; the *Lynx* spent some time there in 1901 and all three took turns on that duty until the arrival of additional specially-built tenders in 1908. The *Antelope*, indeed, became for practical purposes a Plymouth steamer and after 1904 was seldom seen at Weymouth. Attendance on ocean liners was varied in season and on bank holidays by excursions to Looe, Fowey or Falmouth. When operating at Plymouth the Weymouth steamers remained under the jurisdiction of Captain Hemmings, to which extent Plymouth became a sort of 'outport' of Weymouth.

While the Lynx class were partially surplus to requirements, there was one addition to the Weymouth fleet. This was the *Melmore*, a small cargo steamer bought second-hand to reduce the company's dependence on charter for the Jersey potato traffic. The *Melmore*, which took up service on 13 May 1905, was the first Great Western vessel at Weymouth purely for cargo though the chartered potato steamers, with their funnels temporarily in Great Western colours, might loosely have been so regarded. With few exceptions these belonged to one firm, James Fisher & Sons, of Barrow-in-Furness, with whom the company had developed a regular association—actually it began in the days of the Packet Company—and each year three or four Fisher boats were a familiar part of the Weymouth scene from early May to mid July.

One other event of 1905 that may be mentioned in passing was an accident of a different kind. On 26 January, while lying alongside the fish jetty at Milford, the *Roebuck* caught fire. Interior damage was extensive and by the time the fire was out she had sunk under the weight of water pumped into her. Nine days elapsed before she was pumped out and refloated and it was June before she was back in service, fortunately in time for the summer season. Repairs were carried out at Barrow, at a cost of over £11,000.

The Guernsey fruit traffic continued to develop year by year and in May 1907 the general manager recommended that, to make better provision for it, one of the Lynx class should be converted into a cargo boat by removing the saloon and most of the other passenger accommodation. The choice fell on the *Gazelle*, which was taken in hand by Cammell Laird the following February at a cost of about £4,900. She returned to Weymouth in May, in time for the 1908 season.

Meanwhile the usefulness of the *Lynx* and *Antelope* had been extended in other directions. In 1906 they were chartered to a French growers' association to carry strawberries between Brest and Plymouth, a trade in which they continued to be engaged for the next few seasons; later that year, in July and August, the *Lynx* broke new ground in the excursion field when she was chartered to a Jersey syndicate to run holiday cruises round the island and trips to Sark and France; and finally, in July 1908, the Plymouth–Brest service was put on a regular footing, the *Antelope* or *Lynx* thenceforward running weekly, for passengers as well as cargo. Occasionally the *Ibex* or *Reindeer* was used instead.

STEAM VESSELS ACT 1909

A regular Plymouth–Brest service raised a new question, for although it provided a convenient outlet for steamers that were no longer fully employable at Weymouth it was, strictly speaking, *ultra vires*, as the 1871 act specified Weymouth and Portland as ports on the English side of the Channel and St Malo and Cherbourg on the French. As long as the *Antelope* was merely on charter any possible contretemps had been avoided, but the establishment of a permanent service outside the prescribed limits called for further parliamentary powers.

The necessary bill was deposited at the end of 1908. With the not very successful Cherbourg episode a long way behind them —and apparently forgotten—the company presented their case in a mood of high optimism. In evidence before a House of Lords select committee, general manager J. C. Inglis claimed that arising from the 'closer political entente' (the Entente Cordiale, concluded in 1904) future prospects for French traffic were excellent.[5] Indeed, with a permanent arrangement, the west coast of France promised to produce 'infinitely more than the Channel Islands'. The company therefore desired to be able to operate between Weymouth and Plymouth and all French ports between St Malo and Nantes, as well as Cherbourg. Other witnesses spoke of the need for improved communication between the Midlands and north of England and western France. There was opposition from independent shipping interests and also, to protect French trade handled at Barry docks, from the Barry Railway; but in due course, on 16 August 1909, the bill received the Royal Assent.[6]

WEYMOUTH TO NANTES

Outside the potato season, the *Melmore* seems hitherto to have been rather at a loose end. She was used whenever necessary for Jersey general cargo—rarely to Guernsey—but at other times had been at Milford as stand-by steamer for the Waterford service, at Plymouth, running between there and Jersey, or simply laid up. The extended parliamentary powers gave her fresh scope and on 4 September 1909, within three weeks of the passing of the act, she opened a weekly service for passengers and cargo between Weymouth and Nantes. This brought railway continental traffic into Weymouth for the first time since 1885. Handbills printed in French sported a map of the 'Chemin de Fer Great Western' and extolled the route's virtues for the quick conveyance of perishables. A considerable traffic was also hoped for in wine and brandy. Looking beyond these immediate expectations in the cargo field, the company announced that as traffic developed more frequent sailings and larger steamers would be provided, with increased passenger accommodation. The *County Chronicle* predicted that both passenger and cargo traffic would reach 'large dimensions'.

Departure from Weymouth was on Saturdays at 2.30 pm and the return from Nantes on Tuesday afternoons according to tide. In January 1910 the sailing days were changed to Wednesday

GREAT WESTERN RAILWAY.

New Steamship Service

BETWEEN

Weymouth and Nantes.

COMMENCING SEPTEMBER 4th, 1909,

THE GREAT WESTERN RAILWAY CO. WILL INAUGURATE

A REGULAR WEEKLY STEAMSHIP SERVICE

BETWEEN

WEYMOUTH AND NANTES

FOR THE CONVEYANCE OF PERISHABLE AND OTHER MERCHANDISE.

Accommodation will also be afforded for a limited number of passengers.

Departure from Weymouth will be every Saturday at 2.30 p.m. and from Nantes every Tuesday afternoon.

As the Goods and Passenger Traffic develops more frequent sailings and larger Steamers with increased accommodation will be provided.

For Rates of Freight and other information apply to T. H. RENDELL, Chief Goods Manager, Paddington Station, and for particulars as to Fares and Tourist Arrangements to J. MORRIS, Superintendent of the Line, Paddington Station.

JAMES C. INGLIS,
General Manager.

August, 1909.

Printed at the Company's Office, 66, Porchester Road, W.

Nantes handbill, 1909 (*author's collection*)

and Saturday respectively. Fares from Weymouth were 15s single —one halfpenny a mile—and 25s return (75p and £1·25), while from Paddington the corresponding rates were 27s (£1·35) and £2. In spite of these low charges passengers were few. In April and May 1910 the *Melmore* was replaced on some sailings by the *Lynx*, and on one of those occasions eighteen were carried; but frequently there were only three or four, and sometimes none. Passengers arriving at Weymouth rather out-numbered those leaving, but the only regular patronage seems to have come from sailors from Nantes joining or leaving French ships in the South Wales ports.[7]

French cargo got off to a good start, averaging 230 tons a trip for the first month. Unfortunately this initial flourish was not maintained and the figure was soon down to 40 or 50 tons. A proposal to equip the *Melmore* specially for the perishables trade by insulating the forehold and fitting ice-tanks was dropped. Exports were even more disappointing, averaging only 11 tons each trip and fluctuating wildly, from an occasional 70 or 80 tons down to a few hundredweight.

In July 1910 the service was transferred to Plymouth and increased to twice weekly. The timetable announced the establishment of a 'new service between Plymouth and Nantes in place of the service formerly run from Weymouth' but in reality the move was merely for the summer season, to relieve congestion at Weymouth. Most of the Plymouth–Nantes sailings were made by the *Lynx*, with occasional substitution of the *Melmore*, *Antelope* or *Ibex*. There was some improvement in tonnage but in October the weekly Weymouth sailings were resumed, by the *Melmore*.

REVISED AGREEMENT

An important Channel Islands development in 1910 was a revision of the pooling agreement with the London & South Western. This revision had its origin in the opening, in 1906, of the Great Western's short route to Exeter, which subjected South Western west-of-England traffic to intensified competition.[8] The outcome was that on 13 May 1910 the companies signed a comprehensive pooling agreement, covering all competitive traffic, and, although the Channel Islands agreement of 1899 was valid until 30 September 1914, opportunity was now taken to determine it as from 31 December 1909 and incorporate its provisions in the new one.[9]

Additionally the new agreement covered the zoning of French traffic, the South Western being henceforward limited to St Malo and ports to the east, and the Great Western to Brest and ports to the west. This involved the discontinuance of the South Western's Roscoff cargo service—a point of some importance to Weymouth at a later date, as will be seen—while as regards Cherbourg certain of the Great Western's existing rights were retained, including the liberty to run excursions at irregular intervals. These already ran once or twice a year; in 1910, for instance, there were two, one by the *Ibex* and one by the *Antelope*.

WRECK OF THE ROEBUCK

The following year witnessed yet another accident, the third to mar the comparatively short span covered by this chapter. As in 1905 the victim was the *Roebuck*. On the morning of 19 July 1911 she left St Helier for Weymouth under the command of Captain Le Feuvre with about 260 passengers. The weather at the time was described as 'hazy' but shortly afterwards it thickened and after about half an hour at sea the *Roebuck* ran on the Kaines, a group of rocks near St Brelade's. The result was bizarre. The *Roebuck* struck on the flood tide, but, as this particular hazard dries out by several feet at low water, the ebb found the unfortunate vessel perched high in the air, stuck fast between two adjacent reefs. An observer unfamiliar with Jersey's exceptional tidal conditions might have been forgiven for doubting his eyes!

There was no loss of life or cargo and the ship was successfully towed off on 28 July by the salvage vessel *Em. Z. Svitzer*, of the Svitzer Salvage Co, and beached in St Brelade's Bay. After temporary patching she was moved to St Helier and then to Southampton, where at the end of August she was taken in hand by Harland & Wolff. Repairs took three months and cost over £20,000, bringing the total accident bill since the Great Western took over the service to not far short of £100,000.

At the Board of Trade inquiry it was surmised that the vessel had been 'set in' towards the coast by some abnormal tide or current, for which Le Feuvre had not allowed. He was judged to have been at fault for setting too fine a course and running too fast in the prevailing conditions. Inevitably his certificate was suspended but, 'looking to his long unblemished character', for only three months.

This last observation was a little odd, as in truth Le Feuvre's record was already rather tarnished. The Weymouth masters received a bonus of £10 for each half-year free of accident or trouble but more often than not his was forfeited.[10] Also, of course, it was he who had been responsible for putting the *Ibex* on the Noirmontaise in 1897. The company now decided to dispense with his services but granted him an *ex gratia* pension of one guinea a week (£1·05).

NANTES SERVICE WITHDRAWN

The autumn of 1911 brought an end to the Nantes service. During the year it alternated, the *Melmore* running first from Plymouth for four months, with a call at Brest on the way home; then from Weymouth, calling at Plymouth on the way out; and finally, in June, going back to Plymouth again for the summer. Results continued to disappoint, despite these presumed efforts to improve them, and on 30 September sailings were discontinued, barely more than two years after they had begun. The last departure from Weymouth was on 6 June. Inglis's forecast of French traffic greatly exceeding that from the Channel Islands had proved wildly wrong, and in France the company had once again 'backed a loser'.

Certainly in retrospect Weymouth–Nantes seems a somewhat

Page 125: *(above)* The ultimate in Great Western steamers—TSS *St Patrick* (1947); at Weymouth, June 1949; *(below)* TSS *St Helier* leaving Weymouth for the last time, bound for Antwerp and the breakers' yard, in charge of the Dutch tug *Schouwenbank*, 17 December 1960

Page 126: Harbour works at Weymouth: *(above)* preliminary fill for the abortive Newton's Cove scheme, 1901–2; *(below)* reconstruction of Weymouth pier, January 1932

improbable route, and its lack of success not surprising. At 10 knots—*Melmore*'s best—the 352 mile trip round the Breton peninsula and up the River Loire was a slow and tedious business, occupying thirty-six hours or so, and although there was traffic to be had it was too small and too irregular to support a proper service. The route's main interest today is that it remains the longest ever attempted within the field of railway cross-channel operation and the only one to go beyond home trade limits (Brest to the Elbe). One man at least had no cause to regret the latter feature: for James Imrie, a comparatively junior Weymouth officer, came unexpected promotion, for he alone held a foreign-going master's certificate.[11]

The Brest service was also discontinued from 30 September. Since July 1910, when the company bought the Great Eastern Railway's *Chelmsford*—appropriately renamed *Bretonne*—the Weymouth steamers had played a reduced part in it, but a passing reference to its discontinuance ties an otherwise loose end.[12]

With the ending of the French services further changes were made in the disposition of the older vessels. At the end of the year the *Lynx* was taken in hand, by Grayson of Liverpool, for conversion to a cargo steamer on similar lines to the *Gazelle*; she returned to service in March 1912. The cost of the work was £13,112—more than twice the estimate—to which the installation of new boilers, by Rollo & Sons, added another £2,000. The company seem to have considered the money as well spent, however, and the *Lynx* was described as 'good for another twelve years'.

The *Melmore* was no longer required. She returned to Weymouth intermittently but in February 1912 was offered for sale at £5,000. In the event, the following June, she found a buyer at £4,200.

Finally the *Antelope*: the 1912 season found this vessel once again on charter, running French strawberries from Plougastel to Plymouth, but when that came to an end she was spare. In November 1912 the company were approached by brokers acting for foreign buyers and agreed to sell for £7,000. As in the case of the *Melmore*, however, they were obliged to come down, and in August 1913 a Greek firm bought the *Antelope* for a paltry £4,500. The *Bretonne* was also sold.

NEWTON'S COVE—THE REST OF THE STORY

To round off the story to date one more loose end remains to be tied: Newton's Cove. For fourteen years the new harbour had been an open question, sometimes to the fore but more often in the background, half forgotten. First steps towards putting the company's powers into effect were taken soon after the passing of the act: purchase of land for the connecting railway and certain preliminary works at the harbour site. The latter were undertaken in conjunction with W. Hill & Co, the contractors who had recently started construction of the northern Portland breakwater. Responsibility for part of that breakwater was assumed by the Great Western instead of the Admiralty.

Almost as soon as work began, however, the situation changed, by virtue of the agreement with the London & South Western. The need to expand Channel Islands facilities had not been the sole reason behind the new harbour but it had been the most urgent, and as a result of the agreement much of that urgency disappeared. Two further discouraging factors were cost and the company's concern at the large number of civil engineering works to which it was currently committed. So no more was embarked on than was necessary to discharge immediate obligations to the Admiralty.

The approach road and other works with which that department was concerned were completed by December 1902. Inglis then recommended that when construction continued it should extend to the full limit of deviation permitted by the act, and a revised plan was prepared showing additional sidings and two additional jetties. Concurrently provision was made for an extension of time. The period prescribed for purchase of the land would have expired in 1903 but the company's act of that year authorised a three-year extension; it also extended by five years, to August 1913, the period allowed for completion.[13]

In October 1903 the whole question was gone over again. Inglis reported to the board that the company had been approached on the possibility of services between Weymouth and Nantes (bi-weekly), Cherbourg (daily) and St Malo and Brest (seasonally). With French prospects apparently so good, and a better harbour also likely to result in increased Channel Islands traffic, he was confident that it was still expedient to go ahead. At the same time a way had to be found of cutting costs. Subject to obtaining the agreement of the South Western (joint lessees) it was therefore proposed to double the Portland branch as far as Rodwell and construct a short connecting line from there instead of the authorised line from Upwey, and to forgo the additional jetties. This latest revision was calculated to reduce the estimates, now standing at £638,000, to £259,000. It was approved by the board and by the Admiralty and early in 1904 construction was announced to start immediately.

A year later the 'immediate' start was still expected, but further work appears to have been confined to maintenance of existing construction. No positive step was ever taken towards doubling the Portland line and when a new bridge was built across Weymouth Backwater in 1908–9 it carried only the existing single track.

In evidence on the 1909 Steam Vessels Bill, Inglis ascribed the lack of progress to the difficult state of the money market and the company's commitments elsewhere. The latter was almost certainly a veiled reference to the other grand harbour scheme, at Fishguard, which had cost far more than expected. Expenditure at Weymouth had been considerable, too, though there was little enough to show for it. The total to date was stated to be about £70,000, of which £35,000 was accountable to the Admiralty breakwater.

For the next two years Newton's Cove was hardly mentioned. Then, in October 1911, the board approved the inclusion in the company's bill for the next session of provision for a further extension of time, beyond 1913. This was the more surprising as it coincided with the ending of the Brest and Nantes services, whose very indifferent results must surely have dispelled any lingering illusions regarding French traffic. That the question was still kept alive at all can only be taken as a measure of the company's dissatisfaction with existing arrangements. But prudence prevailed. All that could really be looked for now was the scheme's decent burial, and the relevant clauses were deleted.

In January 1912 Inglis was succeeded by a new general manager, Frank Potter, his former assistant. In July an official party led by the chairman, Viscount Churchill, and including Potter and Captain Hemmings, spent some hours at Weymouth inspecting the harbour site. That presumably settled the issue, for towards the end of the year Potter was directed to approach the Admiralty regarding the scheme's probable abandonment and that department's assumption of responsibility for as much as had been completed.[14]

The necessary powers for abandonment were included in the company's act of 1913.[15] That part of the Portland breakwater which had been vested in the company in accordance with the original act was transferred to the Admiralty, which also assumed certain rights of user in respect of the approach road and adjacent lands. Today few signs of railway activity remain: the approach road, spanned by an overbridge carrying a public footpath; a boundary stump or two; and a nearby public house called the Railway Dock.

In Dorset, as in the country at large, many unfulfilled railway schemes cropped up over the years. Newton's Cove was the last, and perhaps none was of greater interest. Nevertheless, it is difficult to believe that it was ever really practicable. Closely circumscribed by influential and capricious neighbours—the Admiralty on one side and the War Department (at the Nothe fort) on the other—and on a somewhat exposed corner of the coast, the harbour would at best have been a difficult and unreliable place to operate. The prolonged vacillation suggests that even at Paddington there was a decided lack of conviction.

Meanwhile the accommodation problem was still not solved. Only to the extent of a 100ft addition to the cargo stage, built by the corporation in 1905, were facilities at Weymouth any better in 1913 than in 1900. In fact, the new Admiralty breakwater actually interfered with the harbour's use, by deflecting across its mouth certain wave patterns that had previously run harmlessly ashore.[16] (This was later remedied by lengthening Weymouth's southern breakwater).

Concurrently with his approach to the Admiralty regarding the abandonment of Newton's Cove, Potter had also discussed the Great Western's future intentions with representatives of Weymouth Corporation.[17] On learning that the company had no immediate plans to leave Weymouth, provided that certain improvements were forthcoming, those gentlemen went so far as to suggest that the directors might consider taking over completely. This, however, Potter rejected, on the grounds that their harbour commitments were already adequate. So far had the outlook changed!

Despite the cramped conditions the total tonnage handled rose between 1900 and 1913 by a third, from 33,000 tons to over 44,000, and passengers passing through the port by half, from about 42,000 to over 63,000. Even more significant was the increase in the Great Western's share of the total Channel Islands traffic, as shown by regular payments to the South Western to preserve the 1897–8 proportional division of receipts as required by the 1899 agreement. From 1910 those payments were commuted to a fixed sum of £5,000, payable annually for the further five years that the original agreement would have run.

This continuous and successful expansion was greatly to the credit of the local management and staff, who accepted the situation as a challenge. With only one passenger berth and two for cargo the handling of so much traffic was truly remarkable. In the busy season double-banking of the steamers was taken for granted; passengers were regularly embarked at the cargo berths;

and the changing of berths was endless. But needs must run whom the Devil drives: to function at all the station had to function efficiently, and the reputation first earned in these years endured right through to nationalisation, and beyond.

Notes to this chapter are on page 224

CHAPTER SIX

PROBLEMS SURMOUNTED AND PROGRESS REDOUBLED (1914-40)

A MAKESHIFT FLEET AND U-BOATS IN THE CHANNEL

WITH the outbreak of the 1914–18 war all further advance was, for the time being, frustrated. There was, in fact, no aspect of railway operation more quickly affected than the cross-channel services, for while the trains ran much as usual, albeit under government control, many railway ships were soon requisitioned. At Weymouth there was a sort of 'general post', all the regular steamers except the *Ibex* being replaced within a few weeks by various 'foreigners'.

During August and September 1914 the *Roebuck*, *Reindeer* and *Ibex* all made special trips with troops between Weymouth and the islands, including Alderney, and between Jersey and Le Havre. On 18 August the *Reindeer* was transferred to Fishguard to run the Rosslare service in place of the regular steamers, which had already been requisitioned, and at the beginning of October both she and the *Roebuck* were themselves requisitioned, the first of the Weymouth steamers to go. On 23 October the *Lynx* and *Gazelle* also went. All four were equipped for minesweeping. In January 1915, to avoid confusion with HM ships already bearing the same names, *Roebuck* and *Lynx* became respectively *Roedean* and *Lynn*.

The *Reindeer*, *Lynx* and *Gazelle* went to the Mediterranean and stayed there for the rest of the war but the *Roebuck*'s war service lasted only three months. On 13 January 1915, at Scapa Flow, she dragged her anchor, got across the ram of HMS *Imperieuse* and was holed and sunk. It was hoped at first that she might be raised—for yet a third time!—but in June the Admiralty reported that she was a total loss. The sinking did achieve some lasting significance however. The *Roebuck* was the first railway steamer to be lost on war service and, as a result of the company's rejection of the compensation offered by the Admiralty, improved terms were negotiated which established the basis of such compensation generally.

At Weymouth the daylight service ran as advertised until the end of August 1914 but thereafter was not reintroduced until 1921. Instead, with only the *Ibex* available, the thrice-weekly alternation with Southampton continued to operate both summer and winter until further notice. Among the difficulties of maintaining the service with only one vessel was that of finding a relief to cover unavoidable absences for such things as boiler cleaning or annual survey. On several occasions a steamer was borrowed from another railway service but frequently, and invariably after 1916, absence of the *Ibex* meant suspension of the service. This happened three or four times a year, for anything up to a month or more. For about eighteen months the cargo service also depended on vessels borrowed from other railway companies. The borrowed steamers were as follows:

Passenger service:

Vera	from LSWR Channel Is service	Nov 1914 (4 trips)
		Feb 1915 (4 trips)
Galtee More	from LNWR Greenore service	June 1915 (7 trips)
Mellifont	from L&YR Drogheda service	June–Jul 1915 (9 trips)
Great Southern	from GWR Waterford service	July–Aug 1916 (4 trips)

Cargo service:

Bertha	from LSWR Southampton	26 Oct 1914–20 Feb 1915
Mersey	from L&YR Goole	21 Feb 1915–19 Aug 1915[1]
River Crake	from L&YR Goole	19 Aug 1915–30 Mar 1916

Like the 'regulars' in normal times, the borrowed railway steamers were augmented as necessary by outside charter. By the beginning of 1916, however, charter had become both difficult and expensive. It was therefore decided that to minimise it the *Pembroke*, latterly employed at Fishguard as a tender to ocean liners but laid up there since the beginning of the war, should be converted for cargo and transferred to Weymouth. She began her new role on 30 March 1916, replacing the *River Crake* and renewing the brief association established nineteen years previously when she acted as relief mail steamer.

On 24 September 1916, near Guernsey, the *Pembroke* was attacked by a U-boat with gunfire. As a result the Admiralty suggested that both she and the *Ibex* should be armed. Meanwhile daylight passages were prohibited, involving a rearrangement of the timetable. At the end of October the *Ibex* was sent to Plymouth for survey and when she returned it was with a 12-pounder gun at her stern. Normal service was resumed. The *Pembroke* was given defensive armament in January 1917, at Portland.

The countrywide reductions in train services effective from 1 January 1917 included the withdrawal of through trains to Weymouth Quay. Departure from Paddington then reverted to 5 pm, as in Packet Company days, and the London–Jersey journey to a tiresome 16½ hours. The following November there was a further deterioration in the service when, by agreement with the South Western, passenger sailings were reduced to twice weekly by each company's route.

During the latter half of the war there were at least two further incidents involving submarines. In May 1917, on passage between Weymouth and Guernsey, the *Ibex* narrowly missed being torpedoed. In another encounter, however, on the night of 18 April the following year, she became a celebrity when her own gun scored a hit. The submarine promptly submerged and was accepted as having been sunk. In appreciation of this achievement the Admiralty awarded £500 for distribution among the officers and crew.

In the spring of 1918 the *Ibex* was requisitioned at a few hours notice to serve as a transport between Dover and Calais. In her absence, some sort of service was maintained by the *Pembroke*, the Board of Trade granting an emergency certificate for forty passengers. The same thing happened early in 1919 when the *Ibex* spent twelve days trooping between Le Havre and Weymouth and then went straight to Plymouth for overhaul. For two months the entire service, both passenger and cargo, again devolved on the *Pembroke*.

The *Ibex*'s war effort was afterwards commemorated by the fixing of a brass tablet at the head of her saloon staircase:

> During the Great War, 1914–1919, this vessel maintained the Great Western Company's Passenger and Mail Service between Weymouth and the Channel Islands, and on three occasions was attacked by enemy submarines, one of which she sank by gun fire. The Government requisitioned the steamer at various times for the conveyance of troops to France.[2]

NORMAL SERVICE RESUMED

In 1919 there was a resumption of three sailings a week during the summer, with through carriages from (but not to) the quay. This was the limit of possible improvement until the Admiralty released the *Reindeer*, then refitting at Southampton. The two cargo steamers were refitting at Devonport, the *Gazelle* after war service which included the ramming of a submarine and a unique encounter with a Greek steamer which turned out to be the old *Antelope* under different colours. All three returned to service in 1920—the *Reindeer* in February, the *Lynx* in March and the *Gazelle* in April—and that summer it was possible to resume daily sailings.

An innovation in 1920 that was to remain a regular feature of operations at Weymouth for nearly forty years was the seasonal transfer of steamers from Fishguard. (Hitherto such movements had been made only to meet some specific emergency). During May the *Waterford* was used for the Guernsey fruit traffic and for the rest of the summer the *Great Southern*. Each year from 1921 to 1932 (except 1924, when it was the *Great Southern* again) the *Great Southern*'s sister ship, *Great Western*, was at Weymouth for most of the summer, and throughout those years the Channel Islands perishables traffic was independent of outside charter. The *Great Western* was also used as a relief mail steamer when required.

In October 1920, and again in the spring of 1921, the effort to get back to normal was impeded by coal strikes, causing restriction of the mail service and the suspension of cargo sailings, but July 1921 did see the reintroduction of the daylight service, with restaurant car trains; the 9.15 pm to the quay reappeared in September. The last reminder of the war, the restriction of sailings to two a week from November to February (plus two by the South Western) persisted for one more winter, provoking ill-informed criticism in the island press. The truth was that the traffic, always markedly seasonal, was now profitable for only about three months in the year. Fares, it is true, were 75 per cent above their pre-war level[3] but running costs had more than doubled. On the cargo side likewise, increased charges were more than offset by increased costs; dockers' wages, for instance, had increased by nearly four times since pre-war, from 5½d an hour to 1s 9d (2½p to 9p, approx).[4] The full winter timetable was restored in November 1922.

THE PROBLEM AFLOAT AND THE PROBLEM ASHORE

As the service expanded so did the traffic—up to a point. During the war cargo tonnage had been well maintained—slightly increased in fact— despite the run-down state of some of the vessels allocated to the service in 1917 and 1918. Passenger traffic, on the other hand, had inevitably suffered during the later stages, and by 1918 had fallen by 60 per cent compared with 1913. In 1920 both began once again to show an upward trend. Passengers, at 67,000, were fractionally up on the 1913 figure, while cargo increased by 18 per cent compared with the average of the previous seven years. Succeeding years showed no further advance, however; rather the reverse. Expansion was now frustrated precisely as it had been until 1889, by out-of-date steamers and the harbour's inadequacy. In the islands the company was accused of neglecting island interests in favour of Fishguard (the Southern, similarly, faced allegations of favouritism in respect of the French services).

In July 1923 a party of directors and principal officers, led by Viscount Churchill, embarked at Portland in the Fishguard steamer *St Andrew* on a Channel cruise, taking in both Guernsey and Jersey.[5] Towards the end of the year the company invited designs for new mail steamers and in March 1924 an order was placed for two, with geared turbines, to be built by John Brown at Clydebank at a total cost of £248,000. In October two new cargo steamers were ordered, from the Newcastle yard of Swan Hunter (£90,000).

So much for the problem afloat; the problem ashore remained. In 1920 an attempt was made to relieve congestion during the potato season by an arrangement with the Admiralty to discharge some ships at Portland, using navy labour, but the facility was little used. The following year the company made Weymouth Corporation a grant of £3,000 towards the cost of dredging (against some small concession in harbour dues) but, like the tentative use of Portland, this was merely a palliative that missed the core of the problem. Only total reconstruction would do.

Meanwhile various traffics were being refused for lack of space. There was a slight resumption of French perishable imports in 1923—mostly potatoes—but far more was on offer than could be handled. The cramped conditions also inflated costs in various ways. Lack of siding space necessitated much double handling and extra shunting, both at the quay and in Weymouth yard. It also wasted time; this had to be made up at night and under post-war wage agreements 'dark time' commanded enhanced rates. Because only four carriages could stand at the pier a full-length train interfered with cargo working, and the need for portable steps beyond the platform meant that men had to be taken off other work just to ensure passenger convenience and safety.[6] The feasibility of large-scale works now began to receive active consideration and by January 1925 a first draft plan had been prepared.

JERSEY IN 9¾ HOURS

In the spring and early summer of 1925, as the new steamers became available, there was almost a clean sweep of the old. The first to go was the *Lynx*. On 16 March she sailed with cargo for Jersey and from there went direct to Plymouth, to await disposal. The *Gazelle* finished work at the end of the month and was then laid up. On 14 April the *Ibex* came in for the last time and three days later the *Gazelle* sailed for Plymouth. On the 29th came the first replacement, the cargo vessel *Roebuck*. May brought further changes. The new mail steamer *St Julien*, commanded by Captain C. H. Langdon, late of the *Ibex*, and with many of the company's directors and principal officers on board, dropped anchor in the bay on the evening of the 4th; on the 7th, to widespread expressions of regret at the passing of what the *County Chronicle* called a 'dear old friend', the *Ibex* left to join the *Lynx* and *Gazelle* at Plymouth; and the 14th saw the arrival of the *Roebuck*'s sister ship, *Sambur*.

The *Roebuck* and *Sambur* were the first to be in service; the former crossed to Jersey on the night of 18–19 May while the latter's maiden trip was to Guernsey, on the night of the 23rd–24th. On the same date the *St Julien* took up the overnight mail service. The previous day a party of guests invited by Sir Felix Pole had cruised on board to the Isle of Wight and back and now, on her maiden crossing, her passengers included the lieutenant-governor of Jersey, senior Great Western officers and representatives of the island press—an auspicious enough introduction to everyday service. Guernsey was reached in a leisurely 5 hours; despite a late start there was no attempt to emulate the record 'maidens' of the nineties. In spite of the early hour, on a Sunday, a large crowd was gathered in welcome. One lady, a regular Great Western patron, expressed her pleasure by presenting the ship with a large floral horseshoe. Arrival in Jersey aroused equal interest, both pierheads being 'black with spectators'. There was, in the accustomed manner, an abundance of open-handed praise: 'sweeping, easy lines . . . amazingly roomy decks . . . vastly impressive [the turbine drive] . . . supremely fitted for her purpose . . . &c&c.'[7] And all of it was justified. She was a fine, solid ship.

The second mail steamer, the *St Helier*, was not delivered until 7 June. For a few days she took over from the *St Julien* (from the 17th) and on the 29th—a fortnight earlier than usual—the two together opened an accelerated daylight service:

Paddington	dep	9.30 am	Jersey	dep	8.30 am
Weymouth Quay	arr	12.55 pm	Guernsey	dep	11.00 am
	dep	1.15 pm	Weymouth Quay	arr	3.20 pm
Guernsey	arr	5.25 pm		dep	3.50 pm
Jersey	arr	7.15 pm	Paddington	arr	7.30 pm

On the same date, as counterpart to the new steamers, the company put on a new boat train, consisting of the first set of the 1925 articulated stock to enter public service. This too attracted much favourable comment.

Though the sea crossings did not match the fastest logged during the days of competition, cutting the time of the boat train to a bare three hours between Paddington and Weymouth Junction achieved—on paper at least—a shorter time overall, London–Guernsey–Jersey, than ever before *or since*. The new schedules showed savings of 90 minutes 'out' and 1 hour 'home' compared with previous post-war summers, and were respectively 2 hours and 1 hour quicker than Southampton could then show. It would be agreeable to be able to go further, and say that the boats always ran to time, but that, alas, was not so. Arrival in Weymouth was invariably punctual, but the outward schedule was perhaps a little ambitious; on occasion it was bettered, but more often arrival in Jersey was around 8 o'clock. The new service was none the less a success. During the four summer months (June to September) over 67,000 passengers passed through the port, more than ever before and equal to an increase of 47 per cent compared with the previous year, while the year's cargo tonnage, in and out, increased by 8 per cent.

With the arrival of the *Great Western* from Fishguard for the summer the last of the old cargo steamers, the *Pembroke*, could be dispensed with. She was withdrawn from service on 4 July 1925 and, after being laid up for a month, left under tow for Clydebank to be broken up. It was widely expected that the *Reindeer* would soon follow but she was overhauled and kept for the time being as a relief steamer—a precaution which, incidentally, did not prevent the company from being 'caught out' a few months later by a freak double mishap.

Entering Jersey on the morning of 10 March 1926, a Wednesday, the *St Helier* struck the pierhead and had to be taken out of service. The Thursday homeward sailing was cancelled and that night the service was taken up by the *Reindeer*, hurriedly got ready for sea. The following morning, entering Jersey, the *Reindeer* struck the pierhead and had to be taken out of service. The *St Julien*, being refitted at Plymouth, had meanwhile been recalled to Weymouth but for three days the company had to borrow the *Vera* from Southampton, offering passengers the unfamiliar experience, in peacetime, of travelling in an ex-South Western vessel flying the Great Western house flag. The *Reindeer* was back in service by the end of the month but the *St Helier* had to be sent to Clydebank for repairs and was away until May.

Her return coincided with the declaration of the General Strike. This inevitably disrupted traffic but its effects were mitigated at Weymouth by the fact that the *St Julien* and *St Helier* were oil-fired. The Southern was less fortunate and for about five weeks Southampton sailings were cancelled. During that time the entire passenger service, as well as much additional cargo, passed through Weymouth.

A notable innovation in 1926 was the Guernsey day excursion. On 25 August nearly 700 holidaymakers embarked in the *Reindeer* and enjoyed about four hours ashore. A week later the experiment was repeated and 'marine day trips' to the islands (usually to Guernsey but occasionally to Alderney or Jersey) afterwards took their place with those to Cherbourg as a regular feature of the summer programme. Some were combined with rail excursions from as far away as Bristol, Swindon or even Wolverhampton and one or two were run in the reverse direction.

THE PRESSURE MOUNTS

Next there was expansion in the cargo field. Between February and April 1927 the company handled over 2,000 tons of French broccoli, from Roscoff. In subsequent years the season was extended; the traffic grew rapidly and by 1931 had increased tenfold. This, of course, was the sort of traffic that had been looked for in vain in the past and, although it was not carried in railway ships, its handling and distribution by rail provided valuable business. In addition some 6,000–7,000 tons of French early potatoes a year, and some broccoli, were landed from various minor Breton ports—Lézardrieux, Tréguier and Paimpol. It is a curious point, incidentally, that lying to the east of Brest and to the west of St Malo these ports were in a sort of no-man's land as far as regular railway shipping was concerned, the 1910 agreement having zoned that part of the French north coast to neither the Great Western nor the South Western. Two independent shipping lines prominently concerned with the sea transport were Care Lines of Cardiff and Walford Lines of London, later linked for this purpose as Care-Walford Lines.

The peculiar virtue of the broccoli traffic was that it occurred in the early months of the year when pressure on space was least critical. Even so, it could be handled only by interpreting 'quayside' in the loosest sense, and many days during the season would find the 56lb crates stacked high across the public roadway between the pier and the cargo stage. Such encroachment would not have been tolerated at busier times of the year and today, of course, would be unthinkable whatever the season.

In January 1928 more French imports appeared, when a French shipping line, Compagnie Nantaise de Navigation à Vapeur, began to make Weymouth a regular port of call on its existing service to London from La Pallice, Nantes and Brest. Unlike the Roscoff traffic, which had been initiated by the

Page 143: *(above)* Henry William Hemmings, assistant marine superintendent, Weymouth, 1889–1915; *(left)* Percy Boyle, traffic and marine agent, Weymouth, 1916–35; *(below)* Channel Islands boat train leaving Weymouth Quay, 1921; engine No 1337, *Hook Norton*. Note tow-rope linked over smokebox door handle

Page 144: The tramway: *(above)* Channel Islands boat train negotiating Ferry's Corner in 1922, showing sharpness of curvature before realignment; engine No 1377; *(below)* three-link coupling as used on the tramway from 1889 to 1938

shipping companies concerned, this new association with Nantes appears to have been the result of Great Western enterprise, reviving the old connection of 1909–11. Initially the only cargo was broccoli but after a month or two a wider range began to come in—casein, hoopwood, fencing, brandy, eggs and fruit and vegetables according to season. Perishables for the London market arrived a day earlier by Great Western than when carried the whole distance by sea. Weymouth was also, as always, a useful port for the Midlands. This extension of French traffic, though not on the same scale as the broccoli, involved regular shipments at approximately weekly intervals throughout the year.

So pressure mounted; and while rebuilding plans were drawn and re-drawn one or two makeshift improvements were made. After the arrival of the *St Julien* and *St Helier* the single electric crane that had hitherto sufficed at the passenger stage was joined by a 6 ton steam crane, and in 1928 a similar one was placed on the buffers at the end of the cargo stage.

Much easily-handled traffic, such as flowers, was already discharged at the passenger stage by wooden chutes and the additional crane enabled that berth to be used for heavier cargo as well when not otherwise occupied. The broccoli boats used it regularly. Conversely the cargo stage remained indispensable for outgoing passenger movements. At peak weekends up to 4,000 passengers might pass through the port, requiring two sailings in each direction on the Saturday and a relief sailing from Jersey overnight, arriving at Weymouth in the small hours of Sunday. Sunday itself was often filled in by an excursion to Cherbourg or Guernsey.

A THIRD MAILBOAT

As well as a new pier a third modern mail steamer was now clearly needed. It had already been decided, in 1927, that the outlay involved in maintaining the *Reindeer* to Board of Trade standards could not be justified once her current certificates expired, and that she should be replaced by a steamer equally suitable for the Channel Islands and Irish services. In February

1928 she was withdrawn. The new steamer, however, had still not been ordered and a jump in holiday traffic that summer had to be met by pressing the *Great Western* into regular weekend passenger service, usually as Guernsey relief steamer. A slower ship than the *Reindeer* and built only five years later (1902) she was hardly ideal for the purpose and her employment did nothing to allay a fresh crop of complaints of inadequate accommodation on the Weymouth route.

Despite the complaints the question of a permanent replacement continued to hang fire—until chance intervened. In April 1929 the Fishguard steamer *St Patrick* was burnt out and this provided the opportunity to build the dual-purpose vessel already contemplated. Built by Alexander Stephen & Sons, Glasgow, and perpetuating the name *St Patrick*, she was launched on 15 January 1930 and arrived at Weymouth in March. On berthing, however, she damaged her rudder and three weeks delay ensued while she was sent to Southampton for the fitting of a replacement. Her first crossing was on 18 April. The *St Julien* having been borrowed since the previous September by Fishguard, to offset a temporary shortage of ships there, the *St Helier* remained on the run for an unbroken twenty-nine weeks—an exceptional performance. Although intended as much for the Channel Islands service as for the Irish, the *St Patrick* was, like the earlier Fishguard Saints, registered in the name of the Fishguard & Rosslare Railways & Harbours Company, a joint enterprise of the Great Western and the Irish Great Southern company.

In July 1930 a through service was introduced from the Midlands (peak Saturdays only) giving stations as far north as Shrewsbury a connection with the midday sailing. Since London traffic alone required three down trains and two up on Saturdays in July and August, Midlands passengers had to be content with the town station and make their own way to and from the quay. The Birmingham trains, which ran via Stratford-on-Avon and Stapleton Road, added to existing troubles by being notoriously bad timekeepers.

Pier reconstruction was formally agreed between the company

and Weymouth Corporation on 31 December 1930, after more than six years preparation. The existing pier was to be entirely rebuilt to accommodate two full-length rail tracks, modern cranes and additional quayside buildings. Only the old timber baggage shed was to be retained, the landing stage, on which it stood, being incorporated in the new structure. All the structural work, dredging and pier maintenance were the responsibility of the corporation (with the support of a twenty-year Great Western guarantee on the loan charges) while the Great Western undertook to provide and maintain the permanent way and crane tracks, cranes, capstans and fuel-oil pipes. The contract was placed with the Birmingham firm of Bolton & Lakin and work started in February 1931 under the general superintendence of a resident Great Western engineer.

A CASE OF OVER-CONFIDENCE

While work progressed, the port continued to function normally; French imports, indeed, scaled record heights. Otherwise the year passed uneventfully, and 1932 was well on the way to doing the same when on the evening of Friday 5 August, at the very peak of the holiday season, came the startling news that on her way to Jersey the *St Patrick* had gone aground off the Corbière.

As was usual at that time of the year the midday mail service had been duplicated, the normal scheduled run to both islands being taken by the *St Julien*, which sailed at 1.30 pm, while the *St Patrick* followed about ten minutes later, bound for Jersey direct to serve as homeward relief the following day. At Weymouth the weather was fine and clear but about an hour out it became foggy. The *St Patrick* maintained her course and speed and at 5.13 pm, by which time she had run some sixty-five miles, took a last wireless bearing on the Casquets. The fog being—so far—of the patchy sort that sometimes afflicts the Channel in summer, bearings thereafter were able to be taken from known landmarks during the brief clear intervals. Off Grosnez, at the northern tip of Jersey, it became thicker and continuous, but course and speed were still maintained. A little after 6 o'clock an indistinct fog signal was heard from the Corbière. Speed was reduced while a repetition was called for. Very shortly afterwards a tide eddy was seen on the port bow. There was no time for last-minute avoiding action before the ship struck amidships, on the port side. Though only a glancing blow it caused extensive damage and fifteen minutes later the *St Patrick* came to anchor with her boiler room and tunnel flooded.

At about half past eight, in response to wireless calls for assistance, the Jersey States tug *Duke of Normandy* arrived, followed shortly afterwards by the Southern Railway mail steamer *Isle of Sark*. The *St Julien*, which at the time had been anchored, fog-bound, off the Platte Fougère, waiting to enter Guernsey, arrived about an hour later. All the passengers, numbering about 300, were safely transferred to the *Isle of Sark* in that vessel's boats and a collection of other small craft that had gathered at the scene, and the *Isle of Sark* and *St Julien* then stood by all night.

On the Saturday morning both continued to St Helier, the *St Julien* after first towing the *St Patrick* as far as St Aubin's Bay. From there, the same evening, the tow was continued to St Helier by the Southern Railway steamer *Princess Ena*. Saturday's sailings were, of course, badly upset. Passengers returning in the *St Julien* did not reach Weymouth until 8.15 pm, 5 hours late, while nearly 700 who had been shut out of the *St Helier* at midday left, in the *St Julien*, at 1 am on Sunday. After lying in St Helier for a week the *St Patrick* was towed to Plymouth for docking and thence to Birkenhead, for permanent repairs.

The Board of Trade inquiry was held in November. It found that the accident had been caused by the default of the master, Captain Charles Sanderson, in having set too fine a course and in having maintained an excessive speed. Although bearings taken during the latter part of the crossing had been accurate, the associated distances had been largely guesswork, with the result that the vessel's position had been fixed inaccurately. Furthermore, it had not been checked by taking soundings. Sanderson was censured by the court and ordered to pay £100 towards the costs of the inquiry.[8]

It was a manifest case of over-confidence, of familiarity breeding contempt. Though nobody was hurt, and the *St Patrick* was repaired for something under £7,000, minds inevitably went back to 1899 and the *Stella*. The comparison was uncomfortably close; and but for the grace of God and a few feet it might have been closer.

THE NEW PIER

By the early summer of 1933 the new pier was sufficiently advanced to be used for some cargo working. The first vessel to discharge there appears to have been the *Roebuck*, with a cargo of Jersey potatoes, on 18 May. The official opening took place on Thursday 13 July. It was performed by HRH the Prince of Wales and the first vessel to use the new pier 'officially' was the *St Helier*, which ran a special excursion from the islands for Weymouth's 'Grand Civic Ceremonies'.[9]

Since 1933 there have been certain further improvements to the pier but substantially it is still as it was then. It is a quarter-mile long × 100ft wide and of reinforced concrete throughout. It provided three new berths, served by electric portal cranes with capacities from 30cwt to 5 tons, and two rail tracks each able to hold about fifty wagons or a full-length passenger train. Electric capstans were installed but never used; they were shortly removed. All shunting has always been by locomotives. New or extended buildings included a new refreshment room and various offices and stores. The total cost was something over £150,000 (as against the original estimate of £102,000).[10]

After the official opening, with the new berths in commission, the quay wall was extended westwards along the face of the old landing stage which was then filled in, making a more or less uniform construction throughout. At the same time the old steam crane was replaced by a 5 ton electric one, bringing the total number of new cranes to five. The bulk of the traffic was thereafter transferred from the cargo stage to the pier, the rebuilt passenger berth being brought into use in February 1934.

By a perversity of fate the extreme demands that had been made on space before reconstruction started were now sharply diminished. For example, in 1929 twenty-three cargoes of French potatoes had had to be discharged at Portland, and in each of the two succeeding years about a dozen, but in 1932 that particular trade was killed overnight by the presence of Colorado beetle and consequent prohibition of imports. Broccoli, for a different reason—the new Import Duties Act—plummeted from over 20,000 tons in 1931 to under half that figure in 1932, and by 1934, the first season for which the extra berths were available, was down to a little over 3,000 tons. The CNNV cargo service, though it lingered until 1939, failed to fulfil its early promise.

The reconstruction was, nevertheless, amply justified by the continuing needs of the Channel Islands traffic, and for three or four years each succeeding season was marked by some fresh improvement or increase. The first, in 1933, was the diversion of the Saturday Birmingham trains from the town station to the quay. Then, in 1934, they were re-routed via Oxford and Swindon, Bristol being given a separate service, with connections from South Wales and various northern towns. This also had to be accommodated at the quay. At the same time all outward timings were advanced by an hour, establishing the well remembered '8.30 boat train' from Paddington; correspondingly, arrival time in Jersey became 6.15 pm.

In October 1934 the company made the first substantial improvement for nearly forty years in Weymouth's *winter* schedule, putting a long overdue end to running via Swindon. Instead of leaving Paddington at 9.25 pm, passengers now enjoyed a winter Channel Islands Boat Express, leaving at 10.15 and running via Lavington. Thanks to the shorter distance the 2 am arrival at the quay was maintained, giving the best Paddington–Jersey winter timing since the direct boat of 1896, and to

Guernsey ($8\frac{3}{4}$ hours) winter's best ever. For the first time in many years, too, Weymouth was the quicker route all the year round.

EXCURSIONS AND CRUISES

There was also a widening of the excursion field. One innovation was the use of the mail steamers for trips to Cherbourg or Guernsey from other west country ports, such as Plymouth, Torquay and Dartmouth. The first two such trips, from Plymouth and Torquay respectively, were combined with circular sea and rail tours from Weymouth, passengers having the option of returning by rail the same day or two days later by sea, when the steamer got back from the cross-channel trip.[11] The response was disappointing, however; the rail journey between the west of England and Weymouth was always a discouraging experience and in subsequent years the 'circular tour' aspect was dropped.

Another idea, taking advantage of Weymouth's peculiar duality of role as port and holiday resort, was a 'Grand Coasting Cruise in the English Channel, with music, dancing and deck games'—6 hours aboard the mailboat for 6s (30p).[12] The 'music, dancing and deck games' fell a bit flat and were not repeated, but the idea itself was very successful. From 1935 afternoon and evening cruises, at 4s and 2s 6d respectively (20p and $12\frac{1}{2}$p) became a regular addition to the cross-channel excursions and from then until 1939 an average of over 5,500 passengers participated each season. Course was usually set towards Bournemouth Bay or Lyme Bay, according to the weather.

The finishing touch to the pre-1939 timetable was given in September 1936, with the commencement of the winter service. The boat express now had a restaurant car both ways and the up train, instead of becoming part of the 4.15 pm from Weymouth town at Weymouth Junction, as hitherto, ran through on the summer schedule, saving 40 minutes to Paddington.

The summer and winter schedules established in 1936 remained in force for three more years, and for three more years the general level of traffic continued to creep upwards. Then, for a second time, progress was halted by war.

SERVICE SUSPENDED

The 1939 daylight service, booked to run until 23 September, was immediately discontinued. Further changes quickly followed. The last boat trains ran on 5 September (the down train arriving at the quay at 2.20 am on the 6th). By the end of the first week of the war Weymouth had been designated a contraband control station. At 4 pm on Saturday 9 September the *St Helier* came in with a handful of returning holidaymakers—114, compared with the 800–900 dealt with on a normal Saturday in early September—and four hours later the *St Julien* followed, light. Passenger sailings were then suspended, leaving the islands served until further notice by the Southampton steamer *Isle of Sark*.

On the 12th the *St Julien* left for Avonmouth 'OHMS'. After two trooping trips to St Nazaire she sailed on 5 October from Avonmouth to Southampton. There she was converted to a hospital carrier, afterwards running in that capacity between Newhaven and Dieppe and, in May 1940, Boulogne and Southampton.

The *St Helier* remained at Weymouth, laid up, until 19 September and was then sent to Fishguard to replace the requisitioned *St Andrew* on the Rosslare service. She remained so employed until 16 November when she was herself requisitioned; from then until the following May she served as a government transport between Southampton and Cherbourg.

Meanwhile, at Weymouth, Channel Islands cargo sailings were being maintained by the *Roebuck* and *Sambur*, sharing both the quay and the services of the company's shore staff with the ten or twelve small vessels of the contraband control fleet. These more or less routine activities continued uneventfully until 20 May 1940 when they were interrupted by the arrival of the Southern Railway mail steamers *Canterbury* and *Maid of Orleans* with Belgian refugees, embarked at Cherbourg. These unlooked-for passengers, numbering over 2,000, left the quay in three special trains. During the next nine days some seventy Belgian trawlers arrived with further refugees, about 1,000 of whom were likewise conveyed in special trains from the quay.

DISTINCTION AT DUNKIRK

Concurrently both the Weymouth mail steamers were distinguishing themselves in the Dunkirk evacuation. With the equally honourable part played by their Fishguard counterparts, *St Andrew* and *St David*, their exploits have been fully and graphically described in the official publication *Dunkirk and the Great Western*. Suffice it here, therefore, to summarise. Between 24 and 31 May the *St Julien* crossed the Channel several times bringing wounded from Dunkirk to Newhaven and on 10 June made a further successful trip, this time from Cherbourg. The *St Helier*'s achievement was quite outstanding. Between 22 May and 2 June she made no fewer than eight crossings, one from Folkestone to Calais and back and seven between Dunkirk and Dover. Though damaged in two collisions she was lucky in being spared anything worse, and by skilled and most courageous seamanship succeeded in bringing away about 1,500 refugees and 10,200 allied troops. Her master, Captain R. R. Pitman, and first and second officers were each awarded the DSC while her quartermaster received the DSM.

The *Roebuck* also played a part. On 29 May, at the proverbial 'moment's notice', she was requisitioned and ordered to Dover. Two days later she was sent to the small Belgian resort of La Panne but, being unable to embark troops there, was ordered instead to Dunkirk. She returned successfully to Dover with over 600, including wounded, and by 5 June was back at Weymouth, none the worse. Her comparatively modest contribution was attributable to the fact that having at that time not been degaussed she would have been needlessly hazarded by having to make further trips.

On 6–8 June the *Roebuck* managed one more run to Guernsey,

bringing back some 380 tons of tomatoes, before the war called again. The following day the *Sambur* came in, similarly laden, and both were then ordered to stand by for Admiralty service. On the 12th they were sent to St Valéry-en-Caux to assist in evacuating the beleaguered 51st (Highland) Division. Her Dunkirk damage hastily repaired, at Southampton, the *St Helier* had been given a similar assignment, but finding the place already in German hands had returned to Southampton. When the *Roebuck* and *Sambur* arrived twenty-four hours later, however, they were misled into approaching close inshore. Confronted by heavy gunfire they sustained both damage and casualties before making good a lucky escape. This time they did not return to Weymouth but remained on Admiralty service for the rest of the war.

The *St Helier* continued her cross-channel sorties at high pressure. On returning to Southampton from St Valéry she was sent to St Malo with French troops for repatriation and returned with British and French refugees. A second St Malo mission followed, more hazardous than the first; in the course of this she successfully embarked some 2,500 British and French troops and brought them safely to Southampton. The next day, 18 June, she was off again, this time for La Pallice. The situation on her arrival was anything but propitious for embarking troops, however, and after some uncertainty the *St Helier* sailed for home. She survived air attack, the uncomfortable proximity of a German submarine and a severe storm, which burnt out her degaussing equipment, before finally anchoring safely in Plymouth Sound on the 21st. And there, for the present, we must leave her.

Weymouth, during the first three weeks of June, was a focal point for large-scale troop movements associated with events in France. The particular interest of this is that many of the vessels involved were requisitioned railway steamers serving as government transports. They included the *Canterbury*, already mentioned, and several other names familiar in peacetime on Irish or continental routes: *Duke of Argyll* (LMSR), *Brittany* and *St Briac* (Southern) and the LNER's *Amsterdam*, *Antwerp*, *Archangel*, *Felixstowe* and *Vienna*. A note of near-normality amidst these strangers was struck on 6 June by the arrival of the *Isle of Sark,* diverted en route to Southampton from the Channel Islands.

Between 20 and 30 June 1940 there followed further waves of refugees, this time from the islands. The assorted vessels bringing them included some of the railway steamers just mentioned and also more than a dozen others equally out of place at Weymouth: *Duke of York* and *Rye* (LMSR), *Malines* (LNER), *Biarritz, Deal, Dinard, Fratton, Haslemere, Maidstone, Minster, Ringwood, Tonbridge, Whitstable* and *Worthing* (Southern) and the Belgian Marine mail steamer *Prinses Astrid.*

Among all this special traffic the Harwich steamer *Sheringham,* deputising for the *Roebuck* and *Sambur,* interspersed a few Guernsey cargo sailings. On 26 June the *Sheringham* was joined by the *Felixstowe,* lately engaged with troops and refugees; but the *Felixstowe* never sailed. On 1 July she was loading cargo for Jersey when it was learnt that the islands had been occupied by the Germans. The curtain had finally fallen, and within a few weeks the Weymouth marine establishment was disbanded until further notice.

Five years were to pass before normal business was resumed. In little more than a further two the Great Western itself had passed, and in retrospect the 1930s may be seen as a culmination. Between 1932 and 1938 (the last full year) ordinary passenger traffic increased by nearly 10 per cent, excursion bookings by 55 per cent and Channel Islands perishables by 50 per cent. The French broccoli traffic, though it never fully recovered from its setback in 1932, averaged some 3,700 tons each season, which it was never to do again. The year 1938 itself broke several records: ordinary passengers (including inter-island), 133,195; excursion passengers, 22,370; tomatoes imported, 4,624,612 boxes; and Guernsey flowers 307,604 boxes.

It was a time to remember.

Notes to this chapter are on page 225

CHAPTER SEVEN

UNDER NEW MANAGEMENT (1945-65)

TRANSITION

DURING the five years suspension of normal business, Weymouth harbour was occupied by the military, whose activities are outside present concern. One item does merit a passing mention, however. As a major invasion base the harbour had to be prepared for the handling of essential cross-channel shipping and in 1943 a port construction and repair group of the Royal Engineers built a terminal for use by the Southern Railway's train ferries. This consisted of a wooden pile pier, springing from a convenient knuckle about 400ft west of the cargo stage and curving round to run parallel to the quay wall, so enabling a ferry berthed alongside the stage to lie stern-on to the pierhead. *Shepperton Ferry* and *Hampton Ferry* would have been noteworthy additions to the list of visiting railway steamers given in the previous chapter but they were not required. The terminal was never used and in 1945, as soon as the war was over, it was dismantled, leaving no trace behind.

The invasion preparations were also instrumental in the re-establishment at Weymouth, on a small scale, of the company's Docks Department, Mr W. G. Salmon being appointed from Cardiff in March 1943 as quay superintendent for liaison with the military authorities. Mr Salmon was the last Great Western manager at Weymouth and it was under his guidance that normal business was resumed.

The first steamer to return was the *Sambur*, on 14 September 1945. Four days later she reopened a limited Channel Islands service, sailing twice weekly to Jersey and calling at Guernsey outward and homeward alternately. The *Roebuck* joined her in October. The later war service of these two vessels can be disposed of quite briefly. In December 1940, on completion of damage repairs, they were sent to Sheerness to serve as balloon barrage vessels on convoy duties in the Channel. During 1942 both were renamed: in August *Roebuck* became *Roebuck II*, to avoid confusion with HMS *Roebuck*, and in November *Sambur* became *Toreador*. On disbandment of the balloon barrage unit, in May 1943, both were laid up at Southampton until the following year, when they were equipped for duty with army units preparing the Mulberry harbours.[1] After the invasion of France they served with dredging units of the Royal Engineers and, on being returned to the company, they resumed their proper names and were refitted for normal service at Cardiff.

Refitting of the mail steamers took rather longer, and although the Southern Railway had started Channel Islands passenger sailings on a restricted scale within a few weeks of the islands' liberation (on 25 June 1945) it was not until the following year that the Great Western was able to join in. Until then the *Roebuck* and *Sambur* maintained a mixed service, for cargo, mails and up to twelve passengers. Starting in June 1946, to assist in the post-war rehabilitation of that island and at the request of the authorities there, the Guernsey service included a weekly call at Alderney. This was the first time that Alderney had been served by the Great Western steamers—apart from excursions and War Department specials—since 1860. The arrangement lasted until 30 March 1947, by which time the number of calls made was about forty.

The mail service was reopened on the night of 15–16 June 1946 by the gallant *St Helier*, whose later war service, like that of the cargo steamers, requires a passing reference to keep the story up to date. On reaching Plymouth from La Pallice in June 1940 she was sent to Liverpool for repairs and, after a spell at Gourock ferrying prisoners-of-war to the Isle of Man, joined the navy. As HMS *St Helier* she was employed for some time at Dartmouth, as a depot ship for MTBs, and in June 1942 was

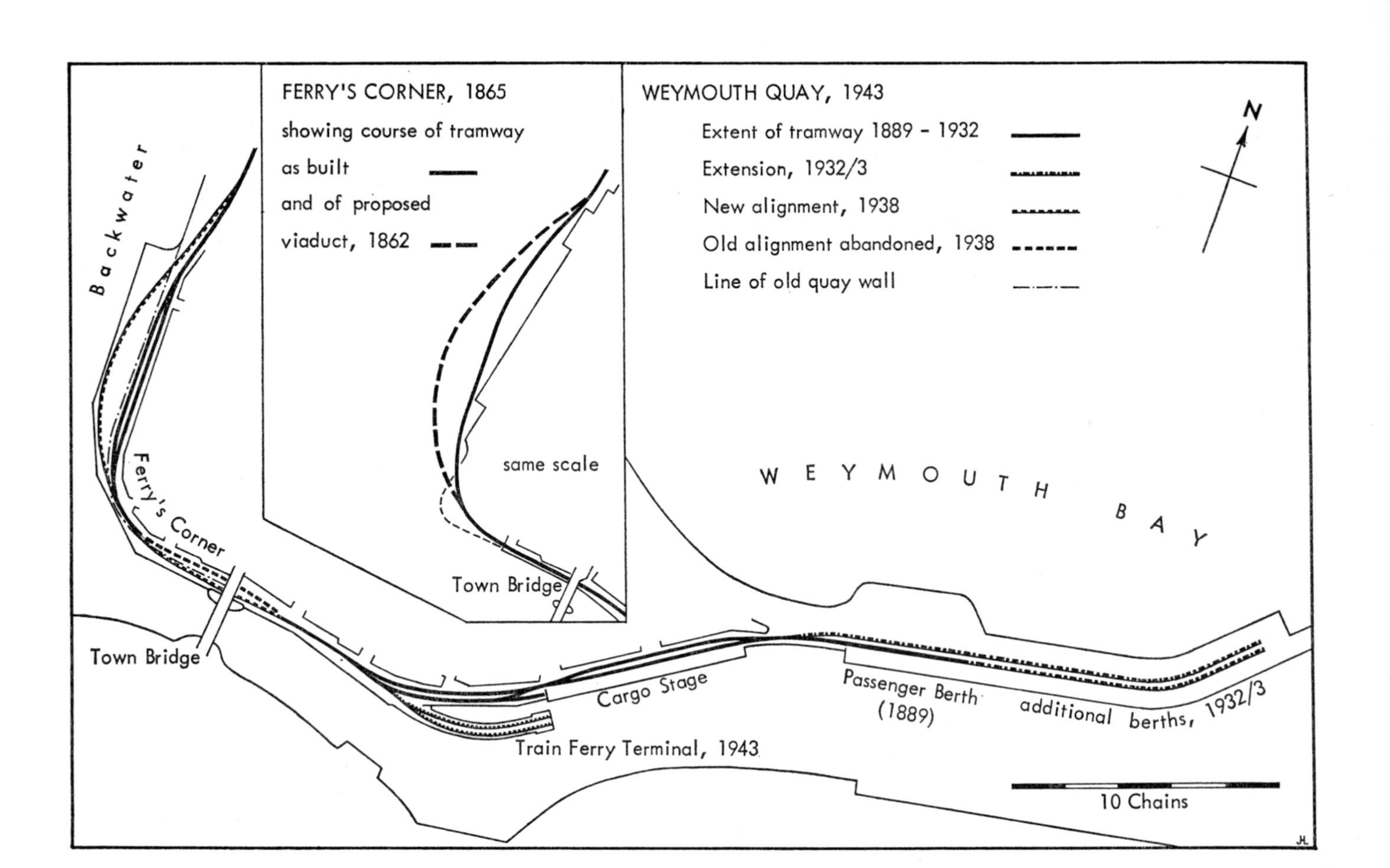

FERRY'S CORNER, 1865
showing course of tramway
as built
and of proposed
viaduct, 1862
same scale
Town Bridge
WEYMOUTH QUAY, 1943
Extent of tramway 1889 - 1932
Extension, 1932/3
New alignment, 1938
Old alignment abandoned, 1938
Line of old quay wall
N
WEYMOUTH BAY
Backwater
Ferry's Corner
Town Bridge
Cargo Stage
Passenger Berth
(1889)
additional berths, 1932/3
Train Ferry Terminal, 1943
10 Chains
JL

taken in hand for conversion to an assault landing ship (LSI(H)) in preparation for the Normandy landings.[2]

On returning to her normal activities, after an 'austerity' refit, she was given what the *Great Western Railway Magazine* described as 'a right royal welcome', other ships in Weymouth harbour dressing overall and the Home Fleet, at Portland, saluting in recognition of her distinguished record. To commemorate that record she now carried two plaques. One, in the form of a silver maple leaf on an ebonised wooden base, was inscribed:

> Normandy, June 6 1944. Presented to the officers and men of H.M.S. St Helier by Captain George Malcolm as a token of appreciation for kindness and comradeship shown to Canadian soldiers on D-Day.

The other, consisting simply of a piece of oak carved with the single word 'Dunkirk', was bestowed unofficially during her naval service.[3] It betokened a sort of vicarious pride for, although under naval orders at Dunkirk, the ship had, of course, been manned by her civilian crew.

The *St Julien*, which had served throughout the war as a hospital carrier, in northern waters until 1943, then in the Mediterranean for about ten months and finally with the invasion fleet, was meanwhile at Penarth, refitting. She returned to Weymouth at the end of November.

The third mail steamer, *St Patrick*, did not return. The only Weymouth steamer to remain on the company's service during the war she was, ironically, the only one lost. After trooping in October 1939 she reverted to her accustomed winter route, Fishguard–Rosslare. During 1940 and 1941 she was attacked more than once by German aircraft and on 13 June 1941—Friday the thirteenth—as she approached Fishguard at the end of her overnight crossing, was dive-bombed and sunk. Thirty passengers and crew were lost, including the master, Captain James Faraday.[4] For some years after the war she continued to be represented at Weymouth by one of her lifeboats, which the company—and later British Railways—used as a harbour launch.

A replacement was laid down in April 1946, alongside a sister ship to replace the Fishguard steamer *St David*, sunk in 1944. The yard concerned was one long associated with Great Western steamers: Cammell Laird of Birkenhead. The first of the two, reviving the name *St David*, was launched on 6 February 1947, followed on 20 May by a new *St Patrick*. As the latter entered the water she flew at her masthead the war-scarred pennant of her namesake, which had been restored to the company after being washed ashore on the Pembrokeshire coast.

That summer the 'winter' service which had operated during the previous twelve months (three times weekly, by night) was replaced by a daily daylight service, with buffet car expresses to and from the quay. Timings were slower than in 1939 but, thanks to post-war affluence and restrictions on foreign travel which enhanced the attractions of the Channel Islands as holiday resorts, this last year of the Great Western's independent existence was distinguished by a spectacular increase in summer traffic. Passengers, at 122,000, were more than double the 1946 figure and about 9 per cent up on 1938, the best pre-war year. The year also saw the completion of both new ships. The *St David*, intended to run from Fishguard, spent a few weeks there and was then sent to Weymouth (3 September) to provide experience in the navigation of larger vessels in the island harbours pending the arrival of the *St Patrick*. She was the last steamer to enter service under Great Western management. The *St Patrick*'s maiden crossing did not take place until the night of 3–4 February 1948, and by then the company had passed into history.

INTEGRATION WITH THE SOUTHERN

In company with most other railway steamers those at Weymouth were transferred to the British Transport Commission on 1 January 1948. At first their management remained at Paddington (Railway Executive, Western Region) but on 1 November 1948 it was transferred to the Southern Region and vested in the docks and marine manager at Southampton. The *St Patrick* was not affected. Like her namesake and the *St David* she was registered in the name of the Fishguard & Rosslare company, which was outside the nationalised undertaking, and her management remained with the Western Region. For the time being the shore establishment at Weymouth also remained a Western Region responsibility, but in July 1949 that too was taken over by the Southern.

Nominally at least the Weymouth and Southampton services were now one. Weymouth funnels were painted Southern buff instead of Great Western red and the local scene was occasionally varied by a visit from one or other of the Southampton steamers. Beyond such superficial changes, however, the service retained its pre-war character. This was true of both ports alike, and it was soon apparent that there was a widening gap between pre-war performance and post-war needs. Between 1951 and 1955 passenger traffic between the United Kingdom and the Channel Islands increased by 45 per cent, but by sea the increase was only 12 per cent. The benefit of the post-war boom was being reaped almost entirely by the airlines.

QUEST FOR SURVIVAL

Air competition itself was not new. Scheduled flights to Jersey had begun as early as 1933. But before the war air's impact on seaborne traffic had been only marginal. In 1938 passengers carried by Jersey Airways, in which the railway companies held an interest, just topped 34,000, about 10 per cent of the total. But by 1951 air travel accounted for 36 per cent; and by 1955 the figure was 51 per cent. To put it another way, in five years the actual volume of air traffic more than doubled, and more people were now flying to and from the islands than travelling by sea.

The ships themselves were carrying about 25 per cent more passengers than in 1938 and in summer were invariably overcrowded. There was, in fact, too much traffic to be handled without large-scale participation by the airlines, but the overcrowding, and the fact that apart from the *St Patrick* the ships on both routes were out of date, gave the airlines a gratuitous boost. With both routes running at a loss, concentration on one or the other must come sooner or later and the traditional rivalry between the two, quiescent since the 1899 agreement, became a quest for survival.

Neither could be regarded as the obvious choice. Southampton was nearer to London and, although the proportion was declining, it still took nearly three-fifths of the seaborne passengers. On the other hand overcrowding was worse than at Weymouth where, when traffic was heaviest, the service was by day; a degree of discomfort that can be tolerated by day soon becomes intolerable at night. The short crossing was cheaper to run and permitted a quicker turn-round, and Weymouth's harbour and wharfage dues were lower; but formidable disadvantages were the lack of space and restricted access by both rail and road. The question remained open, and rumour flourished.

Early in 1956, after meetings with island officials, the Southern Region announced that the two oldest steamers, the *St Helier* and *St Julien*, were to be replaced 'at the earliest possible moment'. Formal Transport Commission approval followed in November and the building of two new cargo vessels (to be based on Southampton) was announced at the same time. The total estimated cost was more than £3,500,000. Orders were placed at the end of 1957, with J. Samuel White, of Cowes, for the mail steamers and with Brooke Marine, Lowestoft, for the cargo vessels.

Meanwhile—a pleasant reflection for the historically minded—the pattern established in 1899 prevailed for long enough to embrace Weymouth's centenary. As the *St Julien* sailed on 17 April 1957 her master, Captain Victor Newton, was sent a congratulatory telegram by the divisional shipping manager, recalling the first sailing of the *Cygnus*, and on arrival in Jersey she entered harbour dressed overall. Appropriately the event had been marked by a Great Western ship, setting a seal on the passing scene.

The prospect of larger ships reopened the old question of

adequate berthing. In April 1958, following the Admiralty's announcement of its intention to close the naval base, the Transport Commission considered using Portland as additional cargo accommodation, but on investigation the idea proved to be impracticable, as it always had in the past. They therefore fell back on Weymouth and prevailed upon the corporation to invest £40,000 in extending the mailboat berth. The commission guaranteed the loan charges to the extent that the higher dues payable on the new ships might fail to cover them. Negotiations for more extensive reconstruction continued.

Pending the outcome of these negotiations uncertainty remained, but the pattern of change was becoming clearer. From 1 January 1959, on the retirement of the divisional shipping manager at Southampton, the Weymouth manager was made responsible for railway shipping at both ports; the summer timetable, traditionally of longer duration at Southampton than at Weymouth, was now the other way about; and winter sailings from Southampton were cut to once weekly in each direction (following a cut to twice weekly by each route in November 1958). At Weymouth twice-weekly sailings were maintained and retention of the *St Patrick*, which hitherto had returned to Fishguard at the end of each summer, gave a higher standard of accommodation. On 17 December 1959 she was transferred from the Fishguard & Rosslare company to the Transport Commission and became a permanent member of the Weymouth fleet.

PADDINGTON BOWS OUT

Timings, too, were improved by switching the Weymouth boat trains to Waterloo. To the regret of all 'Western' men the Paddington Channel Islands Boat Express ran for the last time on 26 September 1959. For the time being, passengers were accommodated on the 6 pm from Paddington, as they had been in winter since 1950, but from 3 November they travelled from Waterloo, the 9.15 pm to Southampton Docks being extended to Weymouth on the appropriate nights (Tuesdays and Fridays).

At the same time there was further integration of the shipping services themselves. Instead of spending the weekend lying in Jersey the Weymouth mailboat now continued to St Malo, a port long associated with Southampton. The first season of this combined working, the homeward leg of which brought Weymouth a trickle of French traffic, was shared by the *St Patrick* and the Southampton-based *Normannia*, enabling the *St Julien* and *St Helier* to be laid up for the winter.

AN ACT OF FAITH

Construction of the new steamers was by now well advanced and the first of them was launched on 29 January 1960, with the name *Caesarea*. The name of the other, still taking shape on the next slipway, was announced at the same time as *Sarnia*. Both these names—the Roman ones for the islands of Jersey and Guernsey—had historical associations with the Southampton service.

At the launching the then chairman of Southern Region, Sir Philip Warter, alluding to recent severe losses on the Channel Islands passenger service, described the decision to invest heavily in its future as 'an act of faith'. A similar 'act of faith' was now required of Weymouth Corporation, whose approval for further harbour works was still awaited. Not for the first time essential development was feared by some to conflict with the town's holiday trade and only at the proverbial eleventh hour, and by a narrow margin, were the objectors outvoted. The new works programme was sanctioned in February 1960. Its principal provisions were the laying of a third rail track on the pier—first proposed in 1884!—and additional sidings on the tramway, and the replacement of all existing single-storey buildings on the pier by two-storey ones to create open space for the mechanised handling of cargo.

The expected BTC announcement came in June: from the summer of 1961 the Channel Islands passenger fleet would consist of only three ships, the *Caesarea*, *Sarnia* and *St Patrick*, and it would operate from Weymouth. Predictably Southampton rose in arms and in September the proposal went before the South Eastern Area TUCC. Objections were heard from Southampton Corporation, the local chamber of commerce and the Guernsey Tomato Marketing Board. None carried much conviction. Southampton's case was largely a reflection of the historical rivalry between the two routes while Guernsey's only concern was that additional traffic at Weymouth should not prejudice the rapid handling of tomato shipments. The commission's case rested on Weymouth's familiar natural advantages and an estimated annual saving of £209,000. Most of the saving was to come from reducing the fleet to three ships and that was feasible only on the short route. Moreover, Weymouth's money-making sideline, day excursions, would be able to continue.[5] TUCC approval, announced in October, was more or less a foregone conclusion.

September 1960 marked the end of the road for the *St Helier* and *St Julien*. The *St Helier* finished work on the 14th, an event noticed by both radio and television as well as the local press. Her last public service was nothing more memorable than a Torquay–Guernsey day trip and on returning to Weymouth she was banished to a buoy in Portland harbour to await disposal. The *St Julien* continued for another fortnight, making the last daylight sailing of the year, on Saturday 24 September, and returning the following Tuesday. Before she left Guernsey for the last time, dressed overall and flying the international code signal 'Thank you. Goodbye', her master, Captain J. P. Goodchild, presented her name pennant for preservation in the Castle Cornet Museum. She was then laid up 'open to offers', leaving the winter service in the hands of the *St Patrick*, as in 1959–60. At the same time Southampton's *Isle of Guernsey* was designated reserve vessel for both routes and the last remaining Isle, *Isle of Sark*, was sold for breaking up.

At Cowes the *Sarnia*, launched on 6 September, was now fitting out and on 12 November the *Caesarea* arrived at Weymouth. Four days later about 200 press and other guests were conveyed to Weymouth quay by Pullman train and entertained to lunch on board while the ship cruised up channel to Southampton. Next came similar publicity in the islands. The press responded handsomely, with all the stock clichés: 'small luxury liner'; 'up-to-the-minute ship'; 'the last word in mailboats'; and so on and so forth. In contrast to this gala première the ship's maiden crossing, on the night of 2–3 December, passed unnoticed. On being relieved by the *Caesarea*, the *St Patrick* was taken in hand at Cardiff for a £90,000 refit to bring her accommodation as nearly as possible into line with that of the new ships. She returned to Weymouth in April.

The first stages of the major reconstruction programme were put in hand in December. To ensure completion by May 1961, when the concentrated service was due to open, the contractors were given complete occupation of the pier, necessitating some rearrangement of port working. The extension of the mailboat berth, which had been in progress for the previous twelve months, was completed in February and the other works, including the third rail track, by May. All was ready on time.[6]

A SERVICE FOR THE SIXTIES

The timetable introduced on Saturday 13 May 1961 involved the most extensive shake-up since the 1899 agreement, and savings of up to fifty minutes between Waterloo and Jersey made the new times, if not the equal of pre-war, at least the best since the war:

Waterloo	dep 8.10 am	Jersey	dep 9.00 am
Weymouth Quay	arr 11.40 am	Guernsey	dep 11.15 am
	dep 12.30 pm	Weymouth Quay	arr 3.15 pm
Guernsey	arr 4.30 pm		dep 4.00 pm
Jersey	arr 6.45 pm	Waterloo	arr 7.35 pm

This basic timetable operated on Sundays as well during July and August. At weekends there were additional sailings overnight in each direction and on Saturdays two afternoon arrivals, at 2.15 and 3.30. It was, of course, principally the extra sailings, and the large number of extra passengers that concentration must throw on Weymouth, that distinguished the new timetable from any previous one. The pint-sized port, which so often in the past had accommodated a quart of traffic, was now expected to manage two quarts. A notable innovation, most of the better-class patronage having already been lost to the airlines, was the abandonment of class distinction on board. Fares for the one-class accommodation, described officially as 'semi-luxury', were fixed at a point *below* the old second class (only £5.15.6 return from London, mid-week) (£5·77).

The service opened without the *Sarnia*, which was still in the final stages of completion. For five weeks weekend sailings and excursions were run by the reserve steamer *Isle of Guernsey*. This was no doubt unavoidable but a ship half the *Sarnia*'s size and thirty years old understandably provoked strong criticism from passengers expecting to sail in a brand-new one, especially after the glowing publicity.

The *Sarnia* arrived in June. On the 13th she repeated the *Caesarea*'s press cruise of the previous November, but in the reverse direction, and then made a brief trip to Guernsey to show the flag. Her commercial service began on the 17th. The principal sailings now fell to the new ships, leaving the *St Patrick* to handle the extras and excursions. The *Isle of Guernsey* followed the *Isle of Sark* to the breakers' yard.

Performance even now left much to be desired, particularly on peak Saturdays, when as many as 2,500 passengers might be crammed through the port in not much more than two hours. This concentration of traffic produced the unprecedented sight of four boat trains marshalled at the quay together, due away at 2.45, 3 o'clock and 4 o'clock for Waterloo and at 4.15 for Birmingham and Cardiff. In between these departures stock had to be worked down to the quay for a final Waterloo train at 4.30. Timekeeping was not easy, and whatever Weymouth's merits for the steamer service the Operating Department viewed the new order with a good deal of disfavour.

If the second boat[7] was late in the last passengers were often not ashore until after the 4.15 had gone. Those for the Western

Region then had to take the 5.50 from the town station and those for Birmingham to travel via Waterloo and Euston, reaching New Street at about half past midnight and probably vowing that next time they would fly. The demand for night sailings, on the other hand, had been over-estimated. Even in August, relief trains run in connection with these were lightly loaded, particularly on Saturdays.

There was no shortage of critical comment. 'Southern' men, resenting the abandonment of Southampton, lost no time in saying 'told you so', and it had to be admitted that this first season's working had revealed some ragged edges. Nevertheless, when the time came for totting up the summer figures three ships were found to have carried 11 per cent more passengers than had been carried by six during the corresponding period in 1960.

Changes made in 1962 included extension of the daylight service and easier timings, to try to improve punctuality; and the timetable notes included a caveat that Birmingham passengers on Saturdays should travel by the first boat if they wanted to be sure of catching the 4.15. There was a marked improvement in punctuality and smoothness of working and a further small rise in the figures, but results could still have been better. In winter the position had hardly improved at all. Over 87 per cent of the traffic was squeezed into the five summer months so from November 1962 winter boat trains were dispensed with. Instead, passengers were taken by bus to the town station where those for London joined the 3.50, about the slowest train of the day. Only if numbers warranted it was there a through working from the quay, a three-coach special running ahead of the scheduled train. Down, the 9.15 was still advertised but did not normally run, passengers being carried on the 9.20 to Bournemouth which on mailboat nights included through carriages to Weymouth Quay. And from 1 January 1963, to offset a continuing deficit, there was an increase in fares.

About the only part of the picture that was fully up to expectations was the excursion traffic, general use of the *St Patrick* resulting in substantially increased carryings. The greater irony, therefore, that this success was short-lived. During the summer of 1963, following withdrawal of the Southampton steamer *Brittany*, the *St Patrick* was diverted to the Jersey–St Malo service. She was still able to return to Weymouth at weekends for the scheduled Channel Islands sailings but the excursion programme was cut by more than half. And in the autumn more cuts were announced. Winter sailings (November to February) would in future be only twice a week and, worst of all, the passenger fleet was to be permanently reduced from three ships to two. Despite a further small improvement in traffic that summer the *St Patrick* was not earning enough to offset the long winter lay-up, so was to be transferred to Southampton. In the circumstances the cut in sailings, though disappointing, was not unexpected, but the news about the *St Patrick* came as something of a bombshell. Excursions would now have to be abandoned altogether, presumably, and there would be no reserve vessel to fall back on in case of emergency. There was a growing conviction that 'they' were deliberately trying to close the service.

Actually, the decision to transfer the *St Patrick* was probably influenced by another factor. The BRB were anxious to discontinue Southampton's services to Le Havre and St Malo, which had been written off as irretrievable loss-makers; the steamers currently allocated to those routes, *Normannia* and *Falaise*, were earmarked for more profitable employment elsewhere, and the *St Patrick*'s transfer would release them at once instead of at some unknown date when the TUCC might approve the closures. Be that as it may, in October the transfer took place; and in the new year, despite strong protest from the islands, sailings were down to twice a week.

WEYMOUTH–ST MALO

At Southampton the *St Patrick* duly took up the Le Havre service and in May 1964, when that was discontinued, was transferred to St Malo. The latter service now became indirectly the means of providing Weymouth with a minimal excursion programme after all. Southampton–St Malo sailings were made twice a week (from June to September) and it was now arranged that on alternate Tuesdays, in between those sailings, the *St Patrick* would cross overnight to Weymouth and fit in a day trip to Guernsey before returning to St Malo the following night. Nine such trips were fitted into the programme in this way, the number of passengers carried totalling nearly 10,000. For a makeshift arrangement this was not unsatisfactory. Perhaps the most interesting aspect of this 'associated running', however, was that it gave Weymouth a regular passenger service to France after a lapse of more than fifty years—albeit, at once a fortnight, not quite what the Great Western had had in mind for St Malo in 1871! A boat train was provided in each direction, the up train leaving Weymouth Quay at 6 am and the down leaving Waterloo at 9.15 pm.

The inclusion of the Guernsey trips was looked upon officially as a last-ditch attempt to improve St Malo's prospects. This it failed to do. Even with the Weymouth sailings included, the number of passengers carried (42,400) was actually smaller than in 1963. In January 1965 the BRB announced that, subject to TUCC consent, there would be no St Malo sailings that summer—and no more excursions.

The proposal went before the TUCC in March. Among the objectors was Weymouth Corporation, whose concern was not so much for St Malo as for the last remnant of the excursion programme. The TUCC was not impressed, however, and closure consent soon followed. The episode had lasted for just 18 weeks and 18 sailings, 9 in each direction. No wonder that at the time of the inquiry St Malo was referred to as Weymouth's least-known service!

The *Sambur* having been sold, earlier in the year (see page 188), the *St Patrick*'s departure meant that the Great Western fleet was represented at Weymouth only by the *Roebuck*, which thus achieved the distinction of being the last of the company's steamers to serve the port. In July 1965 the *Roebuck* was sold and her going brings the account of Great Western shipping at

Weymouth to a close. The Channel Islands service today is the subject of a brief postscript in chapter 10, but additional notes on individual steamers and a chapter on the tramway may appropriately be given first.

Notes to this chapter are on page 225

CHAPTER EIGHT

THE GREAT WESTERN'S WEYMOUTH FLEET

THESE notes supplement the references to individual steamers in the preceding chapters. They are not intended as comprehensive descriptions—which, in many cases, may be found in the technical journals—but they do include much that has not been published previously or is otherwise little known. The steamers are dealt with in order of their first appearance at Weymouth. For measurements see appendix 1.

AQUILA and *CYGNUS*

Although not identical these two steamers were for practical purposes sister ships. They had clipper bows, the *Cygnus* with a fiddle head and the *Aquila* with a shield, and twin funnels placed aft of the paddle-boxes. While operating for the North of Europe company the *Cygnus* acquired a nodding acquaintance with royalty, when an official party sailed in her to Denmark for the opening of the Royal Danish Railway and entertained the Danish king on board.[1]

From time to time the Packet Company made various alterations and improvements. An extensive refit of the *Aquila* in 1860 caught the eye of the *County Chronicle*, which reported on it at some length:

> . . . a liberal amount of painting and decoration . . . new boilers and furnaces . . . the ladies' saloon is tastefully fitted up, and not less so the main saloon. Here the apparatus for the ablution of the gentlemen passengers demands a slight notice. Around one end the basons [*sic*] are so arranged, that when there is no further need of them, seats stuffed with some soft material, and covered with a rich fabric, fall down over the whole, furnishing a com-

> fortable lounge. A new figure head has been given her in the shape of a well executed figure of an eagle, with wings extended, and upon which a considerable quantity of gold leaf has not been wasted.

The register records the official date of the change of head as 10 August 1860.

In 1868 *The Comet* reported the fitting of an enlarged bridge, with stanchions for awnings, and better fore cabin accommodation; and a 'great addition' in 1873 was the erection of an 'ornamental' deckhouse aft. A similar deckhouse was built on the *Cygnus* at about the same time and in 1867 the latter vessel was fitted with new cylinders, while undergoing routine boiler renewal. There was a further change in the *Cygnus*'s appearance in 1883, when she was extensively replated and given new iron paddle-boxes, of a distinctive pattern, in place of the old wooden ones.

On the termination of the agreement, in 1889, both ships were sold to Alfred Tolhurst, a Gravesend tug owner, who resold immediately afterwards. The *Aquila* was then bought by Onesimus Dorey, of Guernsey (Plymouth, Channel Islands & Brittany Steamship Co). There were several subsequent changes of ownership and two of name—first to *Alexandra* and then to *Ruby*—and she was broken up in 1899. The *Cygnus* was bought by T. Holden, of Southport, and used for a short time between Liverpool and the Isle of Man. In 1891 she was bought by David MacBrayne and renamed *Brigadier*, and in 1896 was wrecked off Rodel, in Harris.

BRIGHTON

The *Brighton*, reputed at the time of her purchase by the Packet Company to be the 'fastest steamer in England with the exception of the Dieppe boats', was a little larger than the *Aquila* and *Cygnus* and of rather more austere appearance, lacking the elegant clipper bow. The funnels originally had bell tops. In 1860, 'under the superintendence of the engineers and workmen of the Great Western Railway', she was fitted with Partridge's superheaters in the funnel uptakes.[2] The funnels were fitted with doors for access to this apparatus, which was confidently expected to produce marked economies in fuel and boiler maintenance.

The bell tops were removed about 1870 and the extensive renewal of 1877–8 (see page 61) included, in addition to internal remodelling, the fitting of more modern paddle-boxes and a turtle-back hurricane deck. This work was carried out by the Victoria Graving Dock Co, London. At the same time a complete mechanical overhaul was carried out by the Thames Ironworks, including new boilers, new cylinders, 'lagged with felt and mahogany and neat brass bands', new pumps and, a most important improvement, surface condensers. For the last nine years of her existence the *Brighton* showed a marked superiority over the *Aquila* and *Cygnus*.

Colours, etc, of the Packet Company

We have an unusually good record of the colours of the Weymouth & Channel Islands Steam Packet Co's vessels in some contemporary oil paintings in the Jersey Museum. One of the *Cygnus*, executed in 1857 by the well-known Channel Islands artist P. J. Ouless, shows the original colours to have been black hull and black-topped white funnels. The mainmast is also white and the vessel flies a white pennant with her name in red. A later colour scheme, with certain variations, is illustrated by a most attractive set of three pictures (one of each of the three steamers) painted in 1885–6 by A. Meaden. The hull colour is still black, but relieved by white paddle-boxes and upperworks, while shelters and ventilators are brown. The funnels are a deep cream, again with black tops, and the masts buff.

The company's flag was a St Patrick's cross with the initials WCPC in red in the four quarters. The steamers' port of registry (while in Packet Company ownership) was Weymouth.

GREAT WESTERN (1867), *SOUTH OF IRELAND, VULTURE* and *GAEL*

The first two of these vessels, as their names suggest, were built expressly for Ford & Jackson's contract. Though regarded as a pair they were not sister ships, the most noticeable difference being that the *Great Western* had two funnels and the *South of Ireland* only one. A minor peculiarity of the former was the repetition of her name, which appeared twice on each bow and a third time on each paddle-box. With the *Malakhoff*, an older vessel which was never used at Weymouth and therefore does not concern us here, the *Great Western* and *South of Ireland* were transferred to Great Western ownership on 1 February 1872, the combined price for the three being £36,500.

The *Vulture*, the fourth of Jackson's steamers, had no specific connection with the Great Western contract. Jackson bought her as a spare, and though at times employed at Milford she was more often to be found elsewhere. In evidence on the Steam Vessels Bill in 1871, for example, he mentioned that she was 'now employed for the Government to carry troops'. Her suitability for railway cross-channel service was in any case open to question. Another witness at the same hearing, Hugh Nevins, secretary to the Waterford Harbour Commissioners, when asked whether the *Vulture* was 'larger and of a better class' than the others replied that she was 'larger but of the worst class'.

In February 1872, having completed the sale of the three contract steamers, Jackson persuaded the Great Western to have the *Vulture* as well, as a spare. His asking price was £10,000 but he later agreed to take £9,000—and was no doubt pleased with the deal. The *Vulture* became a railway steamer by bill of sale dated 13 April 1872.

At the time of her arrival at Weymouth, in May 1879, she was the largest steamer that had ever entered the harbour. She was, in fact, much too large for the work required of her and became very much of a 'white elephant'—if the mixed zoology of the metaphor may be forgiven. She was heartily disliked by the operating staff; the French objected strongly when she was sent to Cherbourg, and Wimble refused to have her for the Jersey potato traffic.

In his 1883 report Lecky condemned all three vessels as being fitted with 'old-fashioned jet condensing engines and low pressure boilers' in consequence of which their coal consumption was 'exactly double what it ought to be'. Speeds and coal consumption were given as follows:

	Speed	*Coal consumption per trip*
Vulture	9 knots	23 tons
Great Western	10 knots	20 tons
South of Ireland	10 knots	20 tons

The disability of jet condensing, with its concomitants of salt feed and boiler renewal every few years applied, of course, to all the steamers so far mentioned except (after 1878) the *Brighton*. In spite of it Lecky considered the *Great Western* and *South of Ireland* to be 'moderately well suited' to their purpose; the *Vulture*, as might have been expected, was dismissed as 'too old, too large and too slow'.

The fourth Cherbourg steamer, *Gael*, was formerly the property of the Campbeltown & Glasgow Steam Packet Joint Stock Co, from which she was bought for £3,000 (bill of sale dated 8 April 1884). She was a flush-decked vessel with straight stem, two funnels and two masts; the after deck carried a large deck saloon, and cargo holds were provided fore and aft of the machinery space. At the time of her purchase the *Gael* was described by Lecky as rather small and light for her intended service but very carefully built and acceptable as a makeshift.

The work carried out by Lairds to adapt her for the Cherbourg traffic included the gutting of much of her under-deck passenger accommodation to enlarge the holds, and the enlargement of the cargo hatches. Additional bilge keels were fitted to stiffen the hull for lying aground at Cherbourg and a wooden turtle-back was added at the bow to improve seaworthiness and provide covered deck stowage. After being altered she had a cargo capacity of about 20,000cu ft and sleeping accommodation for about 40 passengers (20 first-class and 20 third). Her speed was about 12 knots.[3]

When the Cherbourg service closed, the *Great Western* went back to Milford to become once more a relief vessel on the Waterford service but, as already mentioned, served at Weymouth again after the loss of the *Brighton*. The *Gael* ran in the Bristol Channel during the summers of 1885 and 1886 and the following summer was on charter to the West Cornwall Steamship Co for the fish traffic between the Scilly Isles and Penzance. After re-visiting Weymouth in 1889 both finally returned to Milford and in March 1890 it was decided to dispose of them. *The Great Western* was sold on 30 May to Nathaniel Miller, of Preston, for £2,750. Shorty afterwards, with her name now changed to *Lovedale*, she went to MacBraynes, who kept her until 1904; she was then broken up. The *Gael*, apart from her brief last visit to Weymouth in June 1890, remained at Milford as a relief steamer until 13 May the following year. Then, like the *Great Western*, she was bought by MacBraynes and so returned home to Scotland, where she continued to work until 1923 (broken up and register closed 22 May 1924).

The despised *Vulture* was beyond further employment. Her disposal had already been agreed the previous February, while the service was still running and, as mentioned in chapter 3, at the end of the year she was broken up (register closed 10 February 1886). Oddly enough, of the steamers so far mentioned, she is the only one of which there is any known relic. When she was broken up her bell was kept and at some date after 1889 it appeared at Weymouth marine workshops. For many years it was used to call the times of starting and finishing work and though latterly disused it continued to hang there until 1960. It is now in the Museum of British Transport at Clapham.

While at Weymouth the *Great Western* and *South of Ireland* carried a crew of twenty-two in addition to the captain: first mate, second mate, chief steward, second steward, cook, stewardess, chief engineer, second engineer, six firemen and trimmers, one quartermaster, six seamen and one carpenter.

Of the *Vulture*'s crew there appears to be no record beyond the fact that the captain's name was Haddock.

LYNX, *ANTELOPE* and *GAZELLE*

The Lynx class were not only the first screw steamers in Great Western cross-channel service but the first on any of the English Channel routes to combine twin screws with triple-expansion machinery. Credit for their introduction is due largely to Laird Bros. The Great Western's original intention, in 1887, had been to continue the Channel Islands service with paddle steamers, owing to the shallowness of Weymouth harbour, and Lairds submitted designs accordingly.[4] At the time twin screws and triple-expansion engines were confined, as far as cross-channel practice was concerned, to certain vessels on the Holyhead services. It so happened, however, that the firm most prominently concerned with these was Lairds, and in the light of the 1888 agreement, with its provision for dredging the harbour, they urged the adoption of the same arrangement for the Weymouth steamers.

Within the Great Western's outline specification Lairds were entrusted with the design of both hull and engines. The ships were a marked advance in speed and comfort on any previous member of the Great Western fleet. As befitted their importance, the choice of names was given careful consideration and comprehensive lists, compiled by Lecky, were submitted to Gooch for his personal attention. Altogether well over 100 possible names were suggested. We might, for instance, instead of *Lynx*, *Antelope* and *Gazelle* have had *Diamond*, *Ruby* and *Emerald*, or *Wave Queen*, *May Queen* and *Fairy Queen*! Lecky objected to 'place' names, as carried by the company's Irish steamers, because in messages they tended to be confused with the places themselves.

The hull, with keel, stem and stern framing of iron and plating of Siemens mild steel, had seven watertight compartments, an unusual degree of subdivision for such small ships. The bow was protected by a 40ft turtle-back and other features of interest were the fitting of racks in the holds specially for the stowage of fruit and vegetables and the provision of electric light throughout, installed by the Great Western's own staff. Steam at 150lb was supplied by two single-ended boilers each with three Fox's corrugated furnaces.

The passenger accommodation was described in the *Great Western Railway Magazine* at some length and with a fine freedom of fancy:[5] 'The companion way leading to the main saloon is lofty, cheerful and imposing, handsomely panelled and painted in several most delicate tints, and presents a most chaste and charming appearance'; the main saloon itself was 'a splendid apartment of large size and lofty dimensions', with 'luxurious furniture . . . crimson velvet upholstery . . . Venetian mirrors . . . and a white roof with gold panelling', while the lavatories were 'models of sanitary science' with complete privacy and perfect ventilation. The original certificate was for 413 passengers.

An unusual technical feature was the arrangement of the propellers, the starboard being set a little forward of the port so that they could overlap.[6] It was thus possible to increase both diameter and pitch and to fit correspondingly powerful machinery. To accommodate the overlap the deadwood at the stern was cut away, as in single screw vessels. All three ships improved in normal service on the designed top speed of 16 knots and, for some reason never determined, the *Gazelle* proved to be slightly faster than the other two.

The original specification called for propellers of cast iron but while building was in progress it was decided, at Lecky's instigation, to substitute manganese bronze. This was both lighter and stronger and in comparative trials showed an advantage of half a knot. One set of iron propellers were held as spares. In 1892 two further sets were bought and it then became the practice to use iron in winter, when top speed was not required, and to reserve the more expensive bronze for the summer. The change was always made in St Helier, where the ships could lie aground at low water.[7]

Lean and low and twin-funneled, the *Lynx*, *Antelope* and *Gazelle* were quite unlike their South Western rivals. The *Liverpool Journal of Commerce* described their appearance as 'most beautiful and yacht-like'; *The Comet*, on the other hand, thought them 'wall-sided'. Beauty is indeed in the eye of the beholder! As built, all three were precisely alike, the little differences that often distinguish one member of a class from another being entirely absent. Even in later years, when they had been altered about the deck, it was still unusually hard to tell one from another. They were equipped with sails and when the wind was right the setting of a stay sail was a useful aid to manoeuvring in the island harbours. Apart from that, however, there appears to be no record that sails were ever needed.

Alterations to the passenger accommodation were first made as early as 1890. In the light of experience in service, the sleeping cabins were remodelled and the deck shelters aft of the wheel-house replaced by a ladies' cabin. The latter alteration involved raising the forward lifeboats and at the same time the funnel height was increased.[8] There appears to have been no further major alteration until the stripping of the *Lynx* and *Gazelle* for cargo when, by the removal of the first-class saloon and cabins, a large main hold, on two decks, was created between the forehold and the boiler room. With a characteristic stroke of railway publicity these two were then described as 'the fastest cargo carriers afloat'. As far as it went that was true, but it meant very little as they were never entirely satisfactory in their new role.

Both were broken up in September 1925 but the *Antelope* was still afloat, under the Greek flag, until at least 1933 (Hellenic Coast Lines *Atromitos*).

One last point of interest is that during the final gauge conversion, in May 1892, the steamer used to convey the Cornish mails to and from Plymouth (see MacDermot's *History*, vol 2, p 380) was the *Gazelle*.[9]

IBEX

The *Ibex* was very much an enlarged version of the Lynx class even, it might be said, to the name, which was chosen from Lecky's original list. The hull, with straight stem and elliptical stern, was of steel throughout and divided into ten watertight compartments. Accommodation above the main deck was provided by promenade and poop decks, separated by a well, a feature by which it was always easy to distinguish the *Ibex* from the otherwise generally similar *Roebuck* and *Reindeer*. A departure from earlier practice was the arrangement of the boiler room, the *Ibex* having two double-ended boilers side by side instead of the single-ended 'in line' arrangement of the Lynx class; the working pressure was 160lb. With manganese-bronze propellers her top speed was a little over 19 knots but, as in the case of the Lynx class, cast-iron were substituted in winter.[10] Again as in the Lynx class the holds were fitted with racks and the whole ship was steam heated and electrically lit, the latter installation, as before, being the work of the company's own staff.

The passenger accommodation followed the earlier layout very closely—second-class aft and first-class saloon, smoke room and private cabins amidships, forward of the machinery. The first-class accommodation was 'of a very superior standard', with lavish fittings and decoration: mahogany, walnut and satinwood; morocco leather (for the gentlemen); cushions in canary and gold (for the ladies); and, beneath the coloured glass dome of the dining saloon, paintings of the Channel Islands (specially commissioned), sage green plush and an ornamental open fireplace complete with mantelpiece, mirror and fender. The second class, 'of a far higher standard than usual', included a separate and 'entirely isolated' ladies' sleeping saloon. The original certificate was for 600 passengers, full sleeping accommodation being provided for 210.[11]

The *Ibex*'s renewal in 1901 resulted in some change in appearance. The promenade deck was extended aft by 12ft and the well dividing it from the poop deck bridged over to give continuous access from one end of the ship to the other, and the number of lifeboats was reduced from 5 to 4. About 1910 the number was increased to 6 by mounting a third pair over the poop deck. A minor change dating from about the same time was the removal of the cowl tops originally fitted to the funnels. The *Ibex* was broken up at Sharpness in 1926–7. Despite their long immersion her original boilers served her to the end.

The builder's half-model, showing the hull form, is in the Science Museum at South Kensington.

ROEBUCK (1897) and *REINDEER*

Basically the *Roebuck* and *Reindeer* perpetuated the design and layout of the Great Western's earlier Weymouth steamers, the aim being simply 'bigger and better' to confound the London & South Western. Cargo, though still catered for, was of secondary importance, the whole emphasis being on passenger speed. The cabins and public rooms, on lower, main and promenade decks were arranged very much as in the *Ibex* but the promenade deck was now full length instead of being divided by a well. The standard of furnishing and decoration was again high though rather less lavish than in the *Ibex*; the original passenger certificate was for the same number—600—with 150 first-class berths and 76 second-class.[12]

The machinery layout followed that of the *Ibex* but an unusual feature was that to reduce engine room dimensions, which would otherwise have interfered with the arrangement of the passenger spaces, the engines were inclined inboard. Steam at 175lb was supplied by two double-ended boilers each with six corrugated furnaces, to which air was fed by Howden's system of forced draught. This was unexpectedly successful, the engines developing 900ihp more than the contract figure. Manganese-bronze propellers were fitted as standard—ie irrespective of season. Howdens claimed that with an improved pattern, capable of absorbing the extra horsepower, a speed of 21 knots could be attained, but experiments to that end carried out on the *Roebuck* were not successful. Even at 20 knots they were the fastest steamers on the Channel Islands services. Initially they were prone to excessive vibration—a not uncommon fault in lightly built ships with powerful engines—and at the end of the first season's running were stiffened at the waist. In April 1898 their speed was recognised in a rather unusual way when the Spanish government offered to buy them at valuation plus £30,000 for service in the

Spanish-American war. Though probably flattered the Great Western declined the offer.

When new, both ships had cowl tops to their funnels; these were removed from the *Reindeer* about 1910 and from the *Roebuck* about 1913. Such small details apart, their appearance remained unaltered. A further point of interest concerning the *Reindeer*'s funnels is that she returned from war service with them patched. It was suggested that they should be kept that way, as a memento of her war service, but as they were found to impair steaming they had to be replaced. The *Reindeer* was broken up by T. W. Ward at Briton Ferry in December 1928 (register closed 5 April 1929).

PEMBROKE

The *Pembroke* served in the Great Western cross-channel fleet for longer than any other steamer—forty-five years. For four-fifths of that time she was at Milford and Fishguard, only the last nine years being spent at Weymouth. Originally a two-masted paddle steamer, the company's last and largest and the only one to be built of steel, she was twice reconstructed; first in 1896, when she was given twin screws and triple-expansion engines, and again in 1916, when she became a cargo boat. Although she might have done so temporarily in 1889 had the harbour been dredged in time, she did not operate from Weymouth as a paddle steamer.

Her conversion to screws came about through an accident. On 16 March 1895 she was approaching Waterford when the twin piston rods of the low pressure cylinder broke in the crosshead, damaging that side of the engine beyond repair. The early replacement of the Milford paddle steamers being already in mind the opportunity was taken, on Lecky's recommendation, to convert the *Pembroke*, thus improving both her speed and her accommodation. The work was carried out by Lairds at a cost of about £30,000.

On return to service, early in 1896, she was officially designated reserve steamer for both Waterford and Channel Islands services and the following year made her only appearances at Weymouth as a passenger vessel (see chapter 4). Her regular Weymouth service dated from 1916, after she had been converted to a cargo boat expressly for the Channel Islands trade. Larger than the converted *Lynx* and *Gazelle*, though slightly slower, she was a valuable addition to the Weymouth fleet. She was also, incidentally, the only steamer to be transferred from Fishguard to Weymouth permanently until the *St Patrick*, in 1959.

Her appearance as a cargo steamer was quite distinctive, with one funnel and one mast, and two lifeboats carried very prominently right aft. She was broken up in 1926.

ARMINE

This little-known craft was added to the Weymouth fleet as a result of the final extension of the cargo stage (see page 131), which took in part of the quay hitherto occupied by the coal siding. Although the work was not actually carried out until 1905 it was originally contemplated in 1898 and in anticipation of its early completion a new siding was laid down alongside the Backwater. As this was at some distance from the steamer berths, approval was given in October 1898 to buy 'a small tug or steam launch at a cost not exceeding £250' to tow the coal barges up and down. The outcome was the *Armine*.

The *Armine* was a wooden launch built in 1886 by J. White of Cowes. Nothing appears to be recorded of her history until 1893, when she was fitted with a two-cylinder launch engine of 2·4 nhp (cylinders 6in × 6in), built by Plenty & Son of Newbury, and a vertical launch-type boiler by Abbot & Son of Newark-on-Trent. The working pressure was 100lb and her speed 9 knots. She was first registered in June 1894. Her measurements were: length 37·8ft, breadth 9·0ft, depth 4·3ft, tonnage 7·3 gross.

The *Armine* is understood to have been used for a time as a passenger launch on the River Fal. By 1897 she was at Weymouth, and in 1899 was bought by the Great Western (bill of sale dated 18 January).

The Weymouth steamers were coaled manually through side doors on the lower deck. As soon as one arrived at the landing stage the *Armine*, with barge in tow, would hasten alongside, the object being to get as much as possible into the nearside bunker before the ship moved up harbour and swung. Once swinging had taken place what had been the nearside bunker became the far one and completion of the job meant carrying the coal baskets that much further. Some idea of the amount of labour involved in coaling may be gathered from the average quantities (in tons) burnt by the various ships:

To Jersey and back (direct)		To Jersey and back (via Guernsey)	
Reindeer	45	*Reindeer*	50
Ibex	38	*Ibex*	42
Great Western	34	To Guernsey and back	
Pembroke	24	*Pembroke*	20
Lynx and *Gazelle*	17	*Lynx* and *Gazelle*	14

a total, in summer, of upwards of 350 tons a week.[13]

The *Armine* also performed a variety of other work comprising the normal lot of a harbour launch and to increase her usefulness the twelve-passenger certificate carried when she first became a railway steamer was always carefully renewed. Facetiously she was often referred to as 'Percy Boyle's yacht'. The last coal-burning Great Western steamer at Weymouth, the *Great Western*, finished in 1932, but as long as Boyle remained so did the *Armine*. She was placed on the disposals list in January 1936, immediately after his retirement, and sold in September. Her new owners converted her into a motor boat.

MELMORE

For the first thirteen years of her existence the *Melmore* sailed between Glasgow and ports in Northern Ireland on a service operated by the Earl of Leitrim. She passed to the Great Western by bill of sale dated 4 May 1905.

A single-screw vessel, the only one in the Weymouth fleet, she had two cargo holds and passenger accommodation which included sleeping saloons and a deckhouse aft. At Weymouth, however, this accommodation was largely discounted—the Great Western regarded the *Melmore* as a cargo vessel and her passenger complement was thus restricted in practice to twelve. She carried a small steam crane but, while with the Great Western and sailing between ports which had adequate shore cranes, this was not needed. After a time the jib was removed and the mechanism sheeted over. There is no evidence that the Great Western made any other alterations.

On the slow side and not always reliable, the *Melmore* was not the sort of vessel usually associated with railway cross-channel service. She is recalled by those who knew her as 'a bit of an old tub'. On her disposal by the Great Western (bill of sale dated 10 June 1912) she was bought by a Mr Charles Forbes, who reputedly intended to use her for a treasure-seeking expedition to the Cocos Islands, but further changes of ownership followed and in May 1914 her registry was transferred to Vancouver, BC. Her end is not known.

GREAT WESTERN (1902) and *GREAT SOUTHERN*

These two ships were built for the New Milford–Waterford service as replacements for the old paddle steamers but qualify for inclusion in a Weymouth history through the seasonal transfer recorded in chapter 6.

They were capacious dual-purpose vessels with accommodation for 680 passengers and 500 head of cattle. The passenger accommodation was of a more modest style than on the *Roebuck*, *Reindeer* and *Ibex* but included 65 first-class berths and a saloon attractively panelled in decorative woods and upholstered in velvet.

The hull was divided into seven watertight compartments and forward of the bridge deck included two large holds for general cargo. The engines were four-cylinder triple expansion, supplied with steam at 180lb by two double-ended boilers.

Neither vessel appears to have undergone any substantial alteration during some thirty years service. On 24 August 1933, on the launch of a replacement bearing the same name (which never ran from Weymouth), the *Great Western* became plain *GWR No 20*. The following year both were broken up by Cashmores of Newport (register closed 13 March 1934 in the case of the *Great Western* and 8 September 1934 in the case of the *Great Southern*).

WATERFORD

The *Waterford* was built to replace the *Pembroke* and run with the *Great Western* and *Great Southern* on the Waterford service. The company intended to call her *Great Britain* but the Board of Trade refused to sanction that name as it was already carried by another vessel.

In appearance she was not unlike the *Great Western* and *Great Southern* but, Waterford passenger traffic having much declined since the opening of the Rosslare route, was predominantly a cattle and cargo boat with only limited passenger accommodation. She was the only Great Western steamer fitted with quadruple-expansion engines; steam at 215lb was supplied by four single-ended boilers.

The *Waterford*'s employment at Weymouth was limited to one spell of less than three weeks in 1920 but she turned up in Jersey at various other times to load cattle for Plymouth. In September 1924 she was sold to American owners.

ROEBUCK (1925) and *SAMBUR*

These were the only Great Western steamers built specially for cargo traffic. The hull, with straight stem and cruiser stern, was arranged with three holds, two forward of the machinery space and one aft. The forward and main holds were combined with extensive tween deck stowage on two decks and in addition the main deck provided covered stowage along either side of the machinery space. This subdivision was designed for the fruit and vegetable traffic, to ensure that the lower packages were not crushed by those on top but it was also invaluable for the very mixed general cargoes *to* the islands. The sides of these vessels maintained an unbroken line from focsle to poop, thus providing shelter for commodious well decks in way of the main and after hatches. The total cargo capacity was about 67,000cu ft.

The designed length was 230ft overall but because of berthing limitations at the time this was reduced by the stern by 20ft, involving the elimination of a proposed fourth cargo hatch.[14] As a result these two ships always had a slightly 'chopped off' look about them and a characteristic bow-up trim. When new they were equipped with derricks on each mast but for service between ports with adequate shore cranes these were merely in the way and were soon removed. The engines were the usual inverted triple-expansion, supplied by two single-ended oil-fired boilers working at a pressure of 185lb.

Accommodation for 12 passengers was provided in a small saloon on the shelter deck. The arrangement was not very satisfactory for night crossings, however, so in 1928 bunks were fitted (for 10) and a new day saloon constructed on the main deck, abaft the machinery space. These facilities were popular with 'commercials' travelling with bulky skips.[15] In 1947 the space occupied by bunks was taken to provide improved accommodation for the captain and other officers and two years later similar consideration was extended to the crew by adapting the main deck stowage at either side, amidships.

In their last years their comparative unsuitability for container traffic, owing to the arrangement of their decks, rather restricted the usefulness of these two vessels, but they soldiered on, alongside much more modern tonnage, until 1964. The *Sambur* finished service on 29 March and then, on expiry of her current certificate, was withdrawn and laid up at Southampton to await disposal. In June she was towed to Holland for breaking up.

The *Roebuck* continued for eleven months longer and in November 1964 she and her crew enjoyed the temporary diversion of being hired to a film company. With her funnel and masts painted white and her forward derrick restored, the old ship masqueraded for about three weeks as the wartime Norwegian coaster *Galtesund*. Her service came to an end on 27 February 1965, not quite forty years from the day of her first arrival. She remained at Weymouth until the end of July and then, under her own steam, sailed for Sheerness to be broken up. Her purchasers, Lacmots, of Queenborough, later resold to Scrappinco SA, of Brussels, and she was eventually broken up in 1966.

ST JULIEN and *ST HELIER*

These two solidly handsome passenger and cargo vessels were the first turbine steamers at Weymouth and also, at the time of their introduction, the largest in the Channel Islands trade. With their high focsles and cruiser sterns they were very different in appearance from the nineteenth-century 'sea shovels' which they replaced.

They were built to Lloyd's highest class, with the hull divided by eleven watertight bulkheads. The first-class accommodation, amidships, included a smoke room panelled in French walnut, a large dining saloon in mahogany, and a ladies' room, all on the promenade deck; six special two-berth cabins on the boat deck; and sleeping berths for a further 128 in cabins and open saloons on the promenade, main and lower decks.[16] The second-class accommodation was aft. It included an oak-panelled saloon and smoke room on the promenade deck, and open berths for 120 on the main and lower decks. The original passenger certificate was for a total of 1,004. Cargo holds, forward and aft of the main superstructure, had a combined capacity of 23,500cu ft.

The propelling machinery consisted of two sets of Parsons compound turbines, of a combined horsepower of 4,350, supplied with steam at a pressure of 230lb by four single-ended oil-fired boilers and driving through single-reduction gearing. On trial over the measured mile both ships averaged 19½ knots, but the high service speeds provided in the 1890s to meet South Western competition now gave way to a more sedate 18 knots, which was sufficient to meet the needs of the joint timetable.

As built, each ship had a pair of rather massive funnels but early in 1928 the after one, a dummy, was removed, because it was thought to hinder manoeuvring in a high wind. Its removal spoilt the symmetry of the design, the suggestion of 'something missing' being particularly apparent when the ships were viewed from the quarter. An amusing story is told of Charles Langdon, first master of the *St Julien*. Soon after the ships entered service the company published a jig-saw puzzle of the *St Julien* and he used to do the puzzle without the after funnel, to show how she would look.[17] He did not live to see the alteration put into practice. The ships' appearance was further altered at the same time by the removal of the after docking bridge, and internally there was a rearrangement of the second-class accommodation, the smoke room being merged into an enlarged dining saloon.

Further interior remodelling was undertaken in 1937. The shelter windows forward of the first-class entrance on the promenade deck, which had always been prone to weather damage, were eliminated by reconstructing the first-class smoke room to take in the full breadth of the ship and rearranging the adjacent cabins. There were also additional bars and improved seating and sleeping accommodation in both first and second class (the latter now designated third). External appearance was again altered at this time by cutting about 5ft from the funnel height, leaving only a narrow black top, and fitting a cowl. The cowl was removed from the *St Julien* during the early part of the war but retained by the *St Helier* until about 1945. A full-depth black top was later restored to both ships (about 1946 or 1947).

A post-war feature by which the *St Helier* could always be distinguished was a set of oversize davits. The original ones were removed in 1942 to enable the ship to carry landing craft and apparently got lost! A final change in appearance took place in 1959, when the hull plating between the promenade deck and the rail, painted white since transfer to the Southern Region, reverted to black, as in Great Western days. White was retained for the focsle.

After being laid up on withdrawal from service both ships were sold for breaking up to Et. Van Heyghen Freres SA, of Ghent. The *St Helier* left Weymouth for the last time on 17 December 1960, under tow, and the *St Julien*, similarly, on 10 April 1961. Both were broken up at Antwerp.[18]

The regular 'migration' of Fishguard steamers to Weymouth had no counterpart in the reverse direction and Weymouth steamers operated from Fishguard only rarely. One or two such instances have been mentioned in chapter 6 and the *St Helier* and *St Julien* were involved in another during the latter part of 1926, when they maintained the Rosslare service for some weeks during and following the coal strike.

For many years they were identified with two well known Jerseymen—Captain Reginald Pitman (*St Helier*) and Captain Leyghton Richardson (*St Julien*).

ST PATRICK (1930)

The 1930 *St Patrick* was generally similar in appearance to the *St Helier* and *St Julien* but slightly larger and slightly faster. The most noticeable differences were that her funnel was better proportioned and more symmetrically placed than in the older ships in their one-funnel days, and that the focsle was extended to meet the superstructure instead of being divided from it by a well. She had one additional watertight bulkhead and a cargo capacity of about 23,000cu ft.

The general similarity extended to the internal layout but the accommodation was of a rather better standard. The first-class dining saloon was finished in quartered mahogany and seated 68, the majority at small tables; the third-class seated 62. Both were on the promenade deck, as in the *St Helier* and *St Julien*, and much play was made of their large windows, through which diners might admire the coastal scenery. The first-class smoke room was panelled in laurel wood, with walnut furniture, and the ladies' lounge in grey sycamore. The *St Patrick* was certified to carry 913 passengers, sleeping berths being provided for a maximum of 216 first-class, in cabins, open saloons and a small number of specially furnished staterooms, and 116 third, in ladies' and gentlemen's saloons on the main and lower decks. The staterooms adjoined the first-class dining saloon and during the summer, while the ship was at Weymouth and sailing by day, could be adapted to serve as port and starboard tea lounges. The third-class accommodation on the main deck could be similarly adapted to serve as ladies' and gentlemen's lounges.

The propelling machinery was similar to that installed in the *St Helier* and *St Julien* but was of slightly greater horsepower (4,720) and an innovation was diesel auxiliary power.

ST DAVID and *ST PATRICK* (1947)

Only one of this pair, the *St Patrick*, could properly be regarded as a member of the Weymouth fleet, the *St David* having always been at Fishguard except for a few weeks on first entering service, as already mentioned. They are well proportioned vessels, with raked stem, cruiser stern and compact superstructure, and although somewhat dated now, after more than twenty years service, were for some time the only modern ships on their respective routes. An important advance on the earlier ships was the concentration of all passenger accommodation, third-class as well as first, amidships, between the forward and after cargo hatches. Prior to alteration it was distributed on four decks, promenade, shelter, main and lower, the first-class public rooms being on the promenade deck and the third-class on the shelter deck. Furnishing was to a high standard, in a variety of decorative hardwoods—burr oak, eucalyptus, Australian walnut and bird's-eye maple. The main machinery consists of two sets of Parsons single-reduction turbines of a combined shaft-horsepower of 8,500, supplied with steam at 250lb by three Babcock & Wilcox watertube boilers. Diesel generators are provided for use in port, and a bow rudder to assist in manoeuvring astern.

Although both ships were built to basically the same design, the *St Patrick*, being intended as much for the daylight Channel Islands service as for the Fishguard night crossings, differed from the *St David* internally. Between the first-class dining saloon and smoke room the promenade deck was arranged as port and starboard lounges instead of first-class cabins, and additional day accommodation was also provided for third-class passengers, at the expense of ladies' and gentlemen's open berths on the shelter deck, and by reducing by approximately half the *St David*'s extensive main-deck car stowage. These differences reduced the number of berths to 295, as against 353 in the *St David*. They are reflected in the external appearance of the two ships, the *St Patrick* having a continuous line of observation windows on the promenade deck whereas the *St David* has only cabin windows, at intervals.

From 1948 until 1960 the *St Patrick* was the pride of the Weymouth summer service and until 1959 kept alive the old Great Western colours. Intending passengers often named her when booking passages. With the advent of the *Caesarea* and *Sarnia*, however, she became rather the 'poor relation', the internal alterations made in 1961 to adapt her for one-class service merely succeeding in destroying her original character without making her fully the equal of the new ships. The alterations in question included the provision of additional catering facilities and an extensive redistribution of accommodation. Cabins at the forward end of the shelter deck were replaced by an open saloon with reclining seats and others, on the main deck, were re-allocated to the crew.

The *St Patrick*'s regular Weymouth service ended on 10 October 1963. In December 1964, after terminating the St Malo service, she was transferred to Dover and since then has undergone certain further alterations, notably the fitting of entrance doors amidships in place of the old single gangway position aft. Latterly she has been based at Folkestone, but reappeared briefly at Weymouth in August 1968 while the *Caesarea* was temporarily out of service for damage repairs.

Colours, etc, of the Great Western

The hull colour of Great Western steamers appears always to have been black but the painting of other features underwent change from time to time. In the paddle steamers, upperworks were white; in the Lynx class, a change was made to a deep buff for the turtle-back and the hull plating from the bridge deck down to the level of the main deck rail, but in all subsequent passenger vessels the superstructure was again painted white. There was also a change of funnel colour at about the time the Lynx class were introduced, from cream with black top to a deep red with black top. It is probable, though not certain, that the change coincided with the building of these ships and that they were the first to carry the new colour. Even the little *Armine* had her funnel done in red and black, 'just like big sisters' '.

The sterns of the older ships, up to the *Great Western* and *Great Southern* (1902), were embellished with the company's coat of arms flanked by the ship's name and port of registry and ornate gilt scrollwork. The appearance of the *Ibex*, *Roebuck* and *Reindeer* was further enhanced by a raised white beading round the hull at the main and promenade decks. After 1925 the *Reindeer*, then sole survivor of the nineteenth-century ships, was deprived of ornamentation; her stern then merely showed her name and port of registry, though the white beading was retained. Twenty-two years later the coat of arms reappeared, on the bow of the *St David* and *St Patrick*. It was, alas, removed from the *St Patrick* at about the time of her transfer to Dover but on the *St David* it still survives, a pleasant reminder of company days.

The Great Western house flag was white with a narrow red band at top and bottom and in the centre the garter coat of arms. The garter was outlined in yellow edged with black and bore the company's name in black letters. The London and Bristol mottoes were omitted. Name pennants were red with white letters.

When the company's Marine Department was set up, in 1872, its headquarters were established at New Milford (Neyland) and, until 1897, the port of registry of Great Western ships was Milford Haven. For some years it was customary for the *Roebuck* (1897) and *Reindeer* to be laid up at Milford for the winter, but the other Weymouth steamers did not normally see their 'home' port except on passage to and from annual survey. The *Great Western* and *Great Southern* and all later ships were registered in London but in September 1929 the *St Julien*, *St Helier*, *Roebuck* (1925) and *Sambur* were re-registered at Weymouth, reviving local 'allegiance' after a lapse of forty years.

Notes to this chapter are on page 226

CHAPTER NINE

THE HARBOUR TRAMWAY

EARLY PROPOSALS

THE earliest proposal to connect Weymouth harbour with the country's then rudimentary railway system was put forward in 1836. Among the bills deposited that year was one for a Bath & Great Western Union Railway, forming a junction with the Great Western near Bath and running to Weymouth via Wincanton, Cerne Abbas and Dorchester. This, of course, was the line referred to by Captain Stevens (see page 30). However, the bill was withdrawn and three other early proposals for a harbour line, in 1845–6, also failed, as already mentioned in chapter 2.

The question was not raised again until March 1861, by which time the steamers had been operating for nearly four years against the handicap of having no direct rail connection. James Aldridge Devenish, a director of the Packet Company, wrote then to the Great Western to the effect that he was prepared to lay before them what he called a 'well digested scheme for a tramway'.

He proposed to form a company, with a capital of £10,000 in £10 shares, for the specific purpose of linking the harbour with the station. The preamble to a draft prospectus reads:

> On the completion of the Railways, or concurrently, it was always intended to form a Tramway from the Stations [*sic*] to the Harbour as in other Seaport Towns, although greatly needed this has not been done, it is submitted in consequence hitherto neither the Town or Railways have derived the full advantage of the two lines being opened to Weymouth.

Estimated costs of construction were as follows:

	£ s d
Rails	420 0 0
Bolts and fastenings	120 0 0

	£	s	d
Laying in Point and Crossing Quay Works	400	0	0
Timber for Road	840	0	0
Tunnel under Bridge	700	0	0
Laying Road and Repairs to Wall along Commercial Road	500	0	0
Timber Viaduct from the Foundry to Ferry's Yard	800	0	0
Engineering and Superintendence	250	0	0
Parliamentary and Law Expenses	500	0	0
Contingencies	300	0	0
Total by viaduct	4830	0	0
Stone wall instead of viaduct add	750	0	0
	£5580	0	0

It was expected that goods passing over the tramway would pay a toll of 4d (1½p) a ton, to which the cost of locomotive power was estimated to add 6d (2½p), making a total of 10d (4p). The rate for road cartage was 1s 6d a ton (7½p).

THE WEYMOUTH & PORTLAND RAILWAY

Nothing came of the proposal in this form. Instead, the promoters aligned themselves with a proposed Weymouth & Portland Railway. A meeting to consider the combined scheme was held at the Royal Hotel, Weymouth, in October 1861 and the necessary plans and bill were deposited for the ensuing session. The link with the Packet Company remained, the Portland chairman being the same J. A. Devenish, while from 1 January 1862 Joseph Maunders, secretary to the Packet Company, discharged that office in the Portland company as well.

The Weymouth & Portland Railway Co was incorporated on 30 June 1862 and section 16 of the act authorised the construction of 'a railway or tramway' commencing 'by a junction with the Portland line at or near the junction of that line with the Great Western Railway'—ie, about 170yd north of Weymouth goods station—and terminating 'at or near the Toll House on the Pile Pier in the Parish of Melcombe Regis'.[1] Construction of the line, including the tramway, started in December 1862. The contractors were John Aird & Son, of Lambeth.

For the first 12 chains or thereabouts the W&P was on Great Western property. The course of the tramway then diverged from the Portland line proper, taking the water's edge down the Backwater to the harbour, as far as possible utilising public roads. For practical purposes this course is level throughout, but construction of the tramway was not entirely straightforward as there were two obstacles.

The first was the right-angled bend, known as Ferry's Corner, some 54 chains from the junction. Commercial Road, along which the line was to run, was interrupted at that point, for about 200yd, by various warehouses and other premises with frontage directly onto the water. This was the reason for the timber viaduct mentioned in Devenish's original proposal, and to negotiate the corner easily it was proposed to take a wide sweep over the water by such a viaduct, having thirty-seven arches each of 20ft span.[2] In January 1863, however, the company had second thoughts and dropped the idea of a viaduct in favour of an embankment along the water's edge, 'to deepen the waterway and benefit waterside occupiers'. The corporation agreed to the change and granted the company the right to excavate the necessary material from the Backwater free of charge. As much of the made land as was actually necessary for the track was to be conveyed to the company free of all liability whenever they might choose, and the corporation also paid agreed compensation to the occupiers deprived by the embankment of their direct access to the harbour.

The company probably hoped that the 'benefit to waterside occupiers' might be reciprocal, in the way of extra business for the railway, but whatever the reason the decision was shortsighted. The radius of the curve was reduced from the 8 chains of the viaduct to only 223ft, with the result that in 1889, when bogie stock was introduced to the tramway, it was able to negotiate the corner only by the use of special couplings.

The second obstacle was just beyond the corner, where the

quayside was intersected by the raised approach to the town bridge. Passing this involved the construction of an archway (the 'tunnel' referred to by Devenish) and raising the level of the road to give the necessary clearance. Nearby residents objected. Of various alternatives suggested the most interesting was to raise the railway and lower the road, so that they would cross on the level, and replace the existing swing span by a telescopic bridge, but in the end the company merely compromised by limiting the extent to which the road was raised. This improved the level of the road, so placating the objectors, but upset the level of the tramway, as proper clearance could be obtained only by making the line dip sharply under the bridge. This made it liable to flooding.

Construction went ahead apace and by May 1864 both 'main line' and tramway were complete. In accordance with the act of incorporation, and at the behest of the Board of Trade, standard-gauge track was laid as well as broad so that the line, including the tramway, would be available to the traffic of both the Great Western and the South Western. By an agreement made in March 1862, and confirmed by the act, the line was to be managed, maintained and worked by a joint committee of the two companies on a perpetual lease. Board of Trade inspection, on 19 May 1864, was confidently expected to be followed by the public opening but defects in two viaducts between Weymouth and Portland and, later, a protracted dispute with the leasing companies over station accommodation at Weymouth delayed the opening until 16 October 1865. The tramway, of course, was not directly concerned in these arguments but as an integral part of the W&P it perforce lay idle until they were resolved.

The tramway was single throughout except at the terminus, where it divided to provide a short siding. With a length of 79 chains it was a little longer than originally proposed (67 chains, terminating at the custom house) but 4½ chains shorter than authorised. It was originally laid with special rails but exactly what these were like is something of a mystery. It is on record that for the company's first general meeting, in September 1862, a small model of the 'tramroad to the quay' and of the 'inverted iron rail' intended to be used was ordered to be prepared and to lay [*sic*] at the secretary's office for inspection.[3] It was presumably some kind of flanged rail but whatever it was it appears to have fallen short of expectations. In April 1869 the *County Chronicle* reported that 'experience has proved that the hollow rails . . . on the tramway . . . have not been satisfactory because of the "biting" of the wheels of the trucks. Railway metals have therefore been substituted, which will save both time and labour'. The 'railway metals' in question were the normal broad gauge bridge rails, laid on sleepers.

Although, like the rest of the W&P, the tramway was the responsibility of the joint committee, to the end of company days it was always worked by the Great Western. In the early days, tramway and Portland goods traffic was worked together, the wagons being marshalled, from north to south, in the following order: brake van, Portland wagons, tram wagons. The engine propelled them towards the goods yard gate, at which point those for the tramway were uncoupled and left to be taken forward to the quay by horses as convenient, while the engine ran round to head the rest of the train to Portland in the normal way. While propelling wagons onto the tramway the engine was required to whistle continuously as a warning to people on the road but frequently, it seems, the tram wagons were cut off and loose-shunted 'at a fast rate', a rather alarming practice that saved a few yards horse haulage but much displeased the neighbours.[4] In fact, in an age happily remote from motor traffic, wagons running along the public road caused local residents a good deal of annoyance, real or imagined. In June 1873 a length of quay wall just below the town bridge subsided into the harbour, carrying about two chains of the line with it, and supposed heavy loads on the tramway were inevitably blamed for that. The Great Western denied liability but the corporation argued for a month before accepting responsibility. Repairs and strengthening took until the following February to complete, putting the tramway out of use for a time.

A SMALL LOCOMOTIVE

The increase in traffic following the gauge conversion underlined the limitations of horse haulage. Wagons left lying about at the quay caused constant obstruction and what the *County Chronicle* described as 'very considerable complaints by the inhabitants . . . about the wretched state in which the quay is left and the noise made by the horses from morn to night'. It was felt that if an engine were attached to the trucks they could be 'got away . . . and the inconvenience and noise got rid of'. When the Great Western wished to introduce locomotives, for the Cherbourg traffic, these complaints offered a convenient hedge against possible opposition to the idea and in February 1878 the company wrote to the corporation about what they understood to be 'the desire of the Council and the inhabitants generally' that the tramway should be worked by a small locomotive.

Sure enough, when this letter was considered by the council there were objections from several councillors and the town clerk argued that the company had no power under its act to put a locomotive on Commercial Road, a public highway. The objectors were probably afraid that the quay wall might fall down again. But the mayor thought differently. In his opinion it was 'most desirable' to do away with the nuisance complained of by means of a small engine 'consuming its own smoke' and he further observed, helpfully if rather quaintly, that the 'smooth drawing away of the trucks by an engine would be more beneficial to the quay than otherwise'. In reply to a question, the borough surveyor said that the engine would weigh 'one ton less than a loaded truck'.

When Sir Alexander Wood visited Weymouth to make arrangements for the Cherbourg steamers (see page 62) the company sent an engine along so that the town councillors might have a trial trip. Once again we are indebted to the *County Chronicle* for a first-hand account of the event:

> On Tuesday afternoon [19 March 1878] the Directors of the Great Western company afforded the Corporation an oppor-

> tunity of inspecting one of the small locomotives which it is proposed to use on the tramway. To this was attached a composite carriage, consisting of first, second and third compartments, in which sat the Mayor and several members of the Council. The engine, which weighs 12 tons 5 cwt, drew the carriage along in the smoothest possible manner and everyone seemed to be of the opinion the quay walls would not be so much injured by it as by the constant jolting of trucks when drawn by horses . . . It is said the Great Western Railway company will undertake the sole responsibility in case accident should occur to the public from the use of the engine. Whilst the engine was travelling about four miles an hour one of the members of the Council suddenly got in front of it to ascertain how quickly it could be stopped, and it was brought up almost within its own length.

Apparently reassured by this demonstration, the council at its next meeting approved the use of an engine. More than two years elapsed before one was used regularly, however. In the meantime the tramway was improved by the addition of various sidings, the most important of which was the extension of the two dead ends at the terminus to increase accommodation alongside the cargo stage and form a run-round loop for engine release. These modifications were completed at about the same time as the first extension of the stage, and a tramway locomotive was first used in regular service on Monday 7 June 1880.[5] From that date it became more convenient to work the tramway independently and the old method of working it, as an integral part of the Portland line, came to an end.

The engine was used mainly to haul wagons from and to the station, minor shunting on the quay continuing to be done by horses. These were supplied by the Great Western's outside cartage contractors and their use persisted until early in the present century. In fact, 'shunting with horses' was still mentioned in the tramway working instructions as late as 1931.

With the introduction of locomotive haulage it became necessary to lay down regulations for the tramway's operation, the original version of which is reproduced opposite. A reissue of the regulations dated July 1880 suggests a certain touchiness on

GREAT WESTERN RAILWAY.

REGULATIONS

FOR

Working the Weymouth Tramway with Locomotive Engine.

THE hours the Engine is to be at work will be regulated by Mr. Collett, the Station Master (who has the General Superintendence of the Tramway), according to the requirements of the traffic, but will be under the immediate orders of Inspector Pollard, who (under Mr. Collett) has charge of the work on the Tramway, and who will be responsible for all regulations with regard to the working of the Engine being strictly carried out.

The Engine must always be accompanied by a Policeman in uniform, who will be responsible for seeing that the road is clear in front of the Engine, and who must warn every one on or about the Tramway of the Engine's approach, and must also see that the Engine does not travel faster than the specified speed. He must either walk in front of the Engine, or ride on the front buffer plank.

In going round sharp curves, and at those places where there are many people or Children on or about the Tramway, the Policeman must always walk a short distance ahead of the Engine, so as to be able to warn people of its approach and to keep the road clear. Where the road is straight, and there are no people about, he may ride upon the Engine.

He must be provided with a Guard's Whistle, and a red flag by day and a Guard's Hand Lamp by night.

The speed of the Engine must not exceed Four miles an hour, and it must travel slower where it is necessary to ensure safety.

The greatest care and vigilance must be exercised, by each person accompanying the Engine and Train, to guard against accident, and ensure the safety of the public; and the Engine Driver must implicitly obey any signal or instruction given by the Policeman.

The Policeman must keep a record of the time of starting and arrival of each trip the Engine makes between the Quay and the Great Western Station, the number of Wagons conveyed each trip, and must make a note of any special circumstance that may occur; these he will enter on a proper Guard's Report at the end of the day, and send in to Mr. Collett.

G. N. TYRRELL,

Superintendent of the Line.

June 7th, 1880.

Regulations for working Weymouth harbour tramway, 1880 (*British Transport Historical Records*) the part of the London & South Western at Great Western control of the tramway. This revised version is headed 'Joint Weymouth Tramway' instead of 'Great Western Railway' and concludes with the unoffending 'By Order' (without specifying whose). The main wording remains unchanged but the working of the engine was now to be 'regulated according to the requirements of the traffic of the Great Western and South Western Companies . . . without undue preference'. The need to study the convenience of traders loading and unloading trucks at 'Stores on the Tramway' was also mentioned, recalling that the line was also used as a private siding. The bulk of the traffic passing over it was, of course, associated with the steamers but, in addition, wagons were dropped off intermediately at various waterside premises. This practice (later facilitated by sidings) lasted until the early 1950s.

The careful concern for public safety was not always apparent in practice. One day the tramway engine 'came round the corner straight onto the plank being used for unloading a coal ship' and a year or so later a boy was run over by a wagon and killed. As he had climbed onto the moving train after the flagman had passed, and slipped off, the inquest jury returned a verdict of accidental death and attached no blame to the railway. Evidence was given, indeed, that the tramway was 'infested with children' and that boys frequently jumped on the trams [*sic*] as they were passing and gave a great deal of trouble, but the incident attracted more than usual notice as this particular boy happened to be the son of the then town clerk of Weymouth. The jury added a rider as to the need for caution in shunting.

PASSENGER TRAFFIC

During the early eighties further sidings and loops were laid in so that wagons for waterside premises would no longer have to be left lying about; before passenger stock was permitted it was also necessary to improve alignment and clearances. The tramway was tested for passenger traffic on 20 June 1889. 'For this purpose,' the *County Chronicle* tells us, 'one of the largest coaches —an eight-wheeler—was attached to the tramway engine and conveyed from the station to the staging. The coach cleared everything, but a few alterations will have to be made in the removal of telegraph poles &c.'

As already mentioned in chapter 4 these further alterations were still incomplete when the new service opened. In addition, before passenger traffic could start, improved signalling and interlocking had to be completed at Weymouth Junction. Board of Trade sanction for passenger trains to use the tramway was conveyed to the company on 8 August 1889[6] and relevant general manager's circulars confirm that they ran for the first time on or near that date.[7] The additional length of tramway, alongside the new landing stage, was a Great Western responsibility, not joint with the South Western. The same was true of the further extension allied to the reconstruction of the pier in 1931–3.

After 1889 the tramway itself was not further altered or improved until 1938, when the quay was widened at Ferry's Corner to eliminate the need for the special couplings which had been endured ever since 1889. Bogie stock, as already mentioned, could negotiate the old alignment at that point only with the ordinary screw couplings disconnected and hung up and replaced by three-link loose ones. To give complete flexibility these were of abnormal length, each link being about 16in long instead of the usual 12in. The only exception to this requirement was the articulated stock introduced in 1925 and used on the summer boat trains until about 1933 or 1934. With these vehicles the tedious uncoupling was minimised, which made a small but useful contribution to that summer's accelerations. An added complication with corridor carriages was the necessity to disconnect gangways and lock vestibule doors. A shunter once lost his life through a disconnected gangway. Passing through the train as the empty stock was being worked back to the junction one night he slipped between two carriages and was run over.

Widening proposals were actually in hand at about the time of this accident (April 1930) and reached the stage of a draft agreement between the corporation and the three companies (W&P, GW and Southern). For some reason, however, the proceedings were then broken off, and the question was not reopened until 1937. On 19 March 1938, after some months of further negotiation, an agreement was signed by the companies and the corporation for the building of a new quay wall and filling to carry a curve of more reasonable radius, extending over a length of about 1,100ft.[8] The work was started during the summer of 1938 and completed towards the end of the year, enabling carriage stock, with certain specific exceptions, such as the 70ft vehicles, to use the tramway unhindered.[9] Not the least interesting aspect of the improvement is the similarity between the new alignment and that of the proposed viaduct of 1862! (see page 158).

A use was still found for one of the three-link couplings as late as 1959. During the flower season, in the early part of the year, it was customary to marshal the flower vans at the pier behind the passenger carriages. On leaving, the passenger train drew the vans forward to a more convenient position for loading, and a long coupling, being easily slipped off by the shunter's pole, was a handy way of doing this. The practice fell into disuse after the re-routing of the boat trains to Waterloo, as with Buckeye-fitted Southern stock it was no longer practicable.

TOW-ROPING

Another tramway practice that obtained for many years was tow-roping, which enabled an engine on one track to move wagons on the adjacent one. As congestion increased, and movement became more restricted, this method of shunting was increasingly resorted to. It was, of course, not peculiar to Weymouth Quay but elsewhere was confined to stations of comparative unimportance. The tow-rope was a steel cable about 24ft long, fitted at one end with a link for attachment to the engine drawhook and at the other with a hook for insertion in the wagon solebar. Up to forty-five wagons were sometimes moved in this way.

There appears to be no record of when tow-roping was first used at Weymouth but the rope may be seen draped along the running plate in any photograph of a tramway engine taken after about 1900. The 1933 improvements reduced the need for the rope but it was not finally discarded until 1952, after the rebuilding of Custom House Quay. Prior to that the loop line along the quay wall, known as Templeman's siding (originally laid to serve a nearby flour mill of that name), was prohibited to locomotives and movement of wagons over it usually required the rope.

Since the war some sidings, no longer used, have been lifted, the last in 1957. But early in 1962, as part of the general improvements outlined in chapter 7, two additional ones were laid between the old and new alignments at Ferry's Corner. At the same time the track under the town bridge was raised to reduce flooding at spring tides. There was, of course, a limit to how far this was feasible but relaxation of the standard overhead clearance and the acceptance of some restriction on vehicle height achieved a saving of just over six inches. Some flooding still occurs, giving rise to a curious situation—while the ships come and go when they please the connecting trains have sometimes to wait for the tide! Fortunately the local tidal constants are such that the boat trains are rarely interfered with, and other traffic can usually be retimed.

ENGINES OF A SPECIAL CLASS

Much of the tramway's interest, it need hardly be said, derives from the engines, particularly the early ones, which the working instructions used to describe rather grandly as 'engines of a special class'. In fact, the only respects in which they might have been considered as one particular class were non-Great Western origin —all were acquired through absorption of other companies—and size; the sharp curvature and the state of the quay wall precluded all but the smallest and lightest available. In every other respect they displayed an entertaining diversity:

No	Type	Weight Total		Weight Max. Axle		Origin	Blt	Tramway Service
		T	*C*	*T*	*C*			
2	2–4–0T	13	17	4	16	SDR	1871	1878, ?1880–
1376	0–6–0T	22	6	7	12	B&E	1881	by 1886–1928, 1931
1377								by 1886–c Dec 1926
1391 *Fox*	0–4–0T	18	0	11	8	WCR	1872	Apr 1903–May 1906, Mar–Oct 1908
1337 *Hook Norton*	0–6–0ST	23	12	8	7	HNIP	1889	Nov 1904–1907, Jan 1914–Jan 1926
1386	0–6–0ST	24	13	9	0	W&C	1875	May 1909–Mar 1911
2194 *Kidwelly*	0–6–0ST	32	1	11	1	BP&	1903	c Apr 1926–1940
2195 *Cwm Mawr*						GV	1905	1926–Mar 1939, Nov 1945–Jun 1946
1331	0–6–0ST	31	12	10	16	W&C	1877	1928–Oct 1935
679	0–6–0ST	26	17	10	8	ADR	1890	c Jan–Jun 1929
1397	0–6–0ST	30	16	10	17	CMR	1873	June–Jul 1931 (on loan)

SDR South Devon Railway
B&E Bristol & Exeter Railway
WCR West Cornwall Railway
HNIP Hook Norton Ironstone Partnership
W&C Whitland & Cardigan Railway
BP&GV Burry Port & Gwendraeth Valley Railway
ADR Alexandra Docks & Railway
CMR Cornwall Minerals Railway

The identity of the first engine cannot be established beyond all doubt but circumstantial evidence and credible local hearsay support the contention that it was No 2. There was in any case no other engine in Great Western stock weighing as little as the $12\frac{1}{4}$ tons quoted by the *County Chronicle* (assuming that figure to have been correct) or 'one ton less than a loaded truck'. No record of this engine's exact weight in 1878 appears to have survived, but, if proper allowance for a later increase in tank capacity is made in the figure quoted in the table, $12\frac{1}{4}$ tons is about right.

In 1904 the Bristol divisional superintendent raised the question of more powerful engines but the divisional engineer demurred:

> The engine at present working on the Tramway has a total weight of 22t.6c. spread over three pairs of wheels coupled and this I consider is the maximum weight that should go over the Tramway. The Quay walls were never constructed to carry heavy weights . . . Why cannot the trains when very heavy be taken with two small engines?

His suggestion was put to the divisional locomotive superintendent who looked carefully into the matter and gave instructions that whenever there was a heavy train it was to be worked 'by one of the usual tram engines assisted by the Fox' which would, he thought, 'get over the difficulty'.[10]

Whether *Fox* ever did assist No 1376 or No 1377 history does not record, alas; it would have been a fascinating sight! Double heading has always been rare, though not unknown.

The first standard Great Western engine to be allocated permanently to the tramway was No 1367, which arrived in 1935 and, with only brief interruption, stayed until 1962, a period exceeded only by the exceptional stint of Nos 1376 and 1377. A maximum axle loading was first specified in the instructions in 1947. The limit, 15 tons 7cwt, permitted engines up to the 7400 class although engines of that class were not at that time used on the tramway regularly. In 1951 the limit was raised to $16\frac{3}{4}$ tons, to accommodate the 5700 class.

The post-war reconstruction of Custom House Quay had a

rather peculiar outcome. The new quay wall was designed to meet loading criteria laid down by the Railway Executive, and these were based on the 5700 class—ie, a total weight not exceeding 47½ tons spread over three axles and a wheelbase of at least 15ft 6in.[11] After a time, somebody seems to have realised that the resultant loading of approximately 3·1 tons per foot precluded the 1366 class, which hitherto had been accepted quite happily. Although smaller and lighter than the 5700 class they had a wheelbase of only 11ft, which gave a corresponding figure of 3¼ tons.

In March 1953 Weymouth's 1366s were therefore replaced by 7400s. The latter had been used on the tramway before, occasionally, but were not popular with the drivers as they were 'too high in the wheel'. Six months later, in response to representations, the 1366s were granted dispensation to return. From about 1956 their tramway duties were shared by engines of the 5700 class but the slightly heavier 8750 class were not accepted until May 1960 when, to meet a temporary shortage of permitted classes, the corporation authorised the necessary relaxation. Thereafter the two versions of 'large pannier' were regarded as one for tramway working. A marked contrast in the meantime was the brief transfer of No 1361, the first of that class on the tramway otherwise than on loan.

Standard Great Western classes used on the tramway were as shown in the table opposite.

DIESELS

In April 1961 a stranger appeared in the form of 204hp diesel-mechanical shunter No D2292, on trial, but the regular use of diesels on the tramway was delayed until the following year by a manning disagreement. The union demand for double manning, not unreasonable in view of the peculiar difficulties of working on the public roads in modern traffic conditions, was eventually conceded. No D2292 was first used in normal working in January 1962, when the pier was temporarily isolated by relaying under the town bridge, and thereafter, as others arrived, steam was

Class	Type	Weight Total		Max. Axle		Per Foot	Weymouth Tramway Engines
		T	C	T	C	Tons	
1366	0-6-0PT	35	15	13	0	3·25	1366: Jun–Oct 1948, Nov–Dec 1954 1367: Apr 1935–Mar 1953, Sep 1953–June 1962 1368: Mar 1947–Mar 1953, Dec 1954–Apr 1962 1369: Mar 1960–Jun 1962 1370: Jun 1946–Mar 1953, Sep 1953–Dec 1959 1371: Apr 1939–Mar 1947
7400*	0-6-0PT	45	9	15	7	3·10	7408: Mar 1953–Jan 1955 7415: Mar–Sep 1953 7418: Mar–Sep 1953 7421: Mar 1953–June 1954
5700	0-6-0PT	47	10	16	15	3·07	various, 1956–1963 (not allocated specifically for tramway)
8750	0-6-0PT	49	0	17	0	3·16	various, 1960–1963 (not allocated specifically for tramway)
1361	0-6-0ST	35	4	12	0	3·21	1361: Jan–Apr 1960, others at various dates, on loan

* Occasional use from at least 1951.

gradually displaced. The 1366s were gone by the end of June though the 8750s continued to appear at intervals for another eighteen months. The last Great Western engine to run on the tramway was No 4610, which hauled the up boat train on Christmas Eve 1963.

By early the following year the panniers had left Weymouth altogether, their other duties being relinquished to Ivatt 2P 2-6-2Ts, and, although the latter were given clearance to run over the tramway in case of emergency, the chance of steam reappearing seemed slender. However, a diesel failed and early in July No 41261 became the largest engine ever seen on Weymouth Quay. This engine and others of the class made several more trips during that summer. One reason was to save manpower; a diesel on the tramway needed two men but on yard shunting only one, a steam locomotive needed two anyway. So it saved a man to put steam on the tramway and keep the diesels in the yard. Although much heavier than the panniers the 2Ps were well within tramway limits by virtue of their five axles. They were, of course, not at all suitable for the job, but those who saw them will long cherish the memory of these 63 ton locomotives trundling along the public highway.

Of the Great Western engines the ones the men liked best were probably the 1366s. The big panniers would 'pull anything' but suffered from restricted visibility from the cab (less marked in the 8750s than in the earlier engines) while the 1361s were simply 'not strong enough'. All the regular engines are included in the tables but it is impossible to list the many that worked on loan at various times. These were often of the 1361 class or 1392 class (ex Cornwall Minerals Railway) but perhaps the most interesting was LNWR 0–4–0ST No 3033, reported on the tramway in June 1917.[12]

Today the diesels have the quay to themselves, and on the whole they perform admirably. Because they were then fitted with only the vacuum brake, the 204hp engines were replaced for a time in 1967, when air-braked stock was introduced on the boat trains, by 350hp diesel-electrics. They are now dual-fitted —with an array of hoses to meet any eventuality!

BITS AND PIECES

Perhaps the most familiar feature of the tram engines is the brass warning bell which each of them carries and which is required to be rung all the time the engine is moving. Over the years a minor source of interest has been the variety of bell mountings employed, from an elegant arrangement of trunnions and quadrant wheel, which survived until about 1930, to a broken ring spanner pressed into service by a latter-day fitter in a hurry. Like the tow-rope, the bell is of uncertain date. The earliest definite reference discovered is dated September 1899 but there is reason to think that it was in use by about 1890.

In steam days each of the regular engines was also fitted with a special footstep for the shunters, at the front on the right-hand side. Like the bell mountings these added to the prevailing diversity by being of various styles, from a simple bent iron to a heavy flared plate terminating in a step 2ft across. When cleanliness was a virtue the tram engines always received special attention, as they were much on public view, and for the connoisseur their interest was further enhanced by the assortment of 'bits and pieces' often strewn about them—shunter's pole, spare lamps, a tramway coupling or two, loose point levers, the tow-rope and, of course, fire irons and bucket. The 'steam' headlamp code was officially 'ordinary passenger', which covered all traffic; but in practice any of the lower—and more easily accessible!—positions might be used instead. Diesel practice is to display two 'side lights', motor car fashion, as a minimum. In 1967 consideration was given to the fitting of an amber flashing lantern, as used on certain kinds of road vehicle, but the idea was not adopted.

A corollary of the disappearance of steam which may be mentioned in passing was the introduction of boiler vans for use on the winter boat trains. Two were built at Ashford in 1963. By the time they were available, however, the winter boat train had become irregular and infrequent and their work on the tramway was limited to perhaps half a dozen appearances during the winter of 1963–4.

The tramway today is really an anachronism—indispensable, as long as the ships remain, but anachronism none the less. Its abandonment was envisaged as long ago as 1884, in Brereton's plan for Backwater docks, and in 1923, when new steamers and a new town bridge were both in contemplation, it was suggested that the latter might have an opening span giving access to berths alongside the station, so obviating the 'vexatious and uncomfortable' crawl through the streets.[13] Today the vexatious and uncomfortable crawl is aggravated in summer by street congestion and obstruction by parked vehicles. The latter problem has become worse in recent years and even the widespread use of yellow lines cannot entirely cure it. There have been occasional brushes between trains and road vehicles, and, because of the danger of drivers following too close behind a loose-coupled train to allow for buffer rebound if it stops, last vehicles have been adorned since 1961 with boards warning 'Keep 50ft clear'.

Movement to and from the tramway at Weymouth Junction is controlled by Weymouth signal box, the boat trains being advised between the box and the quay by telephone. The working of the tramway itself is controlled by the yard inspector, under detailed and comprehensive instructions; these at one time ran to a six-page pamphlet. Several of the more interesting provisions, such as the disconnection of couplings and gangways, are now only memories, but two items at least survive unchanged from 1880—the flagman (now 'shunter-in-charge') walking ahead of each train and a speed limit of 4mph. Even the policeman may still be seen on occasion, though since 1880 his role has changed. Then it was to protect the public from the approaching train; nowadays he cycles ahead to try to protect the train from obstruction by the great motoring public!

Notes to this chapter are on page 227

CHAPTER TEN

THE CHANNEL ISLANDS SERVICE TODAY

TODAY the steamers are carrying more passengers than they have ever carried and to that extent the uncertainty of recent years seems to have receded. For a time, in the light of earlier retrenchment, failure to complete the pier rebuilding programme gave rise to a suspicion that the BRB was reluctant to face further outlay at Weymouth, despite its commitment to the corporation under the 1960 agreement. Comparatively modern buildings at the east end made way in 1963 for a prefabricated wooden store and office block but the 1889 baggage shed survived, shabby and inconvenient, to mock the smart new ships. Not until November 1965, after various changes of plan and two postponements because of 'financial stringency', was replacement put in hand. A new two-storey steel-framed passenger terminal, incorporating a customs examination hall and booking hall on the ground floor and offices on the first, was completed and brought into use in June 1967. Official opening, by the mayor of Weymouth, followed on 31 July.

Completion of this work coincided with the introduction of electric traction between Waterloo and Bournemouth and a general acceleration right through to Weymouth, and 1968 and 1969 were marked by a spectacular increase in passengers—over 48 per cent in two years compared with a previous average of about 2 per cent a year. Various factors have no doubt combined to achieve this result—faster trains and the new terminal among them—but probably the most important is the substantial difference between the sea and air fares, particularly for mid-week and family travelling. Strictly comparable figures for air passengers are not available but it is clear that during the same period there was some decline, reversing the established trend.

The day excursion programme, of course, finally collapsed after the *St Patrick* left and attempts to revive it have been unsuccessful. The first, in 1965, was when the SNCF Newhaven–Dieppe steamer *Lisieux*, chartered by the French Line (CGT) to run between St Malo and Jersey, extended her itinerary to include a weekly call at Weymouth. She called for seven weeks, following the same routine as the *St Patrick* the previous year. BR acted as agents. A second attempt was made in 1967, when a firm called Jersey Lines announced an ambitious programme of cross-channel sailings by *La Duchesse de Bretagne*—alias *Brighton*, likewise ex-Newhaven–Dieppe and, despite her change of name, distantly recalling the Packet Company. BR again acted as agents. The fact that *La Duchesse* carried cars as well as passengers led to a dispute, however, since direct competition with BR vessels contravened a condition of the *Brighton*'s sale. Jersey Lines therefore confined their interest in Weymouth to a weekly excursion—passengers only—and after one season did not return. (They later went bankrupt). As regards the conveyance of cars the truth was that an unsatisfied demand existed—it was a case of the 'bye-boat' again, one might say—and in July extra cargo-boat sailings were started specifically for vehicles. The number of accompanied cars carried rose from under 6,000 in 1966 to over 16,000 in 1969, to the undoubted benefit of BR's passenger figures.

It is much to be deplored that success does not extend beyond the passenger service. Weymouth's cargo traffic, like so much of BR's freight business since the war, has suffered mixed fortunes and, in certain important sectors, virtual extinction.

An early casualty was the French broccoli, but much more serious has been the drop in Channel Islands perishables. Imports of Jersey tomatoes, for instance, declined steadily from over 15,000 tons in 1947 to a mere 139 tons in 1969. The potato trade, which in the 1870s did so much to set the port on its feet, and which up to 1939 averaged 11,000–12,000 tons a season, reached 5,000 tons in only one subsequent year and by 1966 had dwindled to nothing. (For such Jersey traffic as is still carried by BR ships, exporters favour Southampton).

The most recent and most serious loss has been a large part of Guernsey's tomato trade. From 1960 concentration of these shipments on Weymouth raised the port's average tomato tonnage to an unprecedented 41,000. Palletisation, mechanical handling, extra sailings and other reorganisation were all geared to their rapid clearance. In vain: in 1964, when the freight contract came up for renewal, BR found it necessary to increase rates by up to 40 per cent, and half the tonnage was lost to the Guernsey-based Commodore Shipping Company, running into Shoreham. Prior to 1964 only shipments to Ireland were outside BR's province: in 1969 Weymouth's—ie BR's—share of a record 9½ million boxes was only 4 million (25,000 tons).

Competition from Channel Islands shipping companies; the effect on costs of the invidious distinction between Weymouth—a National Dock Labour Board port—and 'independent' ports, such as Shoreham and Portsmouth; air freight; and the switch from rail to road, for reasons only too well known, have all contributed to the disintegration. More than half Jersey's flowers now leave the island by air, for example, and even at Weymouth there has been a steady extension of road haulage owing to bad rail transits to certain markets. 'Perpots' (perishables and potatoes)—the elaborate programme of special trains mounted for many years during the season—have become just another part of Weymouth's history.

A recent decision threatens much of what is left. BR proposes to rationalise Channel Islands cargo services in collaboration with Commodore, extending the use of containers—or 'unitisation'—to a wide range of cargoes; and in that context Weymouth's old handicap of lack of space becomes insuperable.

Always problematical, this service was seldom more so than today. Its recent past has seen both achievement and disappointment; its future is yet unresolved. We can but wish it well.

NOTES AND REFERENCES

This book is based substantially on official records, of which the most important are as follows:

British Transport Historical Records (BTHR):

GW 1 Minute books of the GWR board and, more particularly, those of the Traffic Committee (1890–1908) and Steamboat Committee (later Docks & Steamboat Committee) 1909–38; also Steamboat Committee reports, 1871–97

MPR 471–4 Channel Islands correspondence

GW 8/3 Letters to Gooch re Irish traffic

GW 8/4 Letters to Gooch re Cherbourg traffic

GW 9/330 Cherbourg correspondence

GW 9/445 Weymouth harbour tramway correspondence

GW 18/11 Grierson's report on the Channel Islands service, 19 June 1873

GW 18/50 ditto, 3 February 1879

TT GWR public timetables, 1857–1947
LSWR public timetables, 1860–99

Weymouth Central Library:

Boyle papers (L382 WE 2)—an important collection of reports, memoranda, etc, formerly in the keeping of the late Percy Boyle

Manuscript records formerly kept by the GWR at Weymouth:

Steamer books (a daily record of steamer working from 1894 to 1947)

Particulars of passenger and cargo traffic from 1890

Public Record Office (PRO):

Adm 1/4066–7 Packet agent's letters to the Admiralty

Adm 1/4075–6 Admiralty letters from the Post Office

Post Office archives:

Postmaster General's reports, 1793–1806

Freeling's minutes, 1794–1811

Packet minutes, 1812–36

Packet report books, 1807–30

Parliamentary papers:

Fifth Report of Select Committee on the Roads from London to Holyhead, 12 June 1822

Twenty-second Report of the Commissioners of Revenue Inquiry, Part 5, 25 June 1830

Report of Select Committee into Post Communication between Great Britain and Ireland, 9 August 1832

Sixth Report of the Commissioners of Post Office Management, 20 April 1836

(These papers, barely touched on in the present work, contain a vast amount of information on early steamships in general and the packet service in particular).

Report of Admiralty Committee on Channel Islands Mails (Blue Books) 25 April 1841

HM Customs and Excise:

Registers of shipping, notably for the ports of London, Weymouth and Milford.

Other sources include the following:

Newspapers:

Dorset County Chronicle, 1825–1913 (*DCC*)
The Star (Guernsey)
The Comet (Guernsey)
The Times
Dorset Daily Echo

Periodicals:

Great Western Railway Magazine
The Railway Gazette
Shipbuilding & Shipping Record
Engineering
The Engineer

Other published works:

Alexandre, J. P., *Early Postal Service to the Channel Islands* (Soc Jersiaise, 1933)

Boyle, Percy, *The Channel Islands Service* (GWR (London) Lecture & Debating Society No 190, 1926). (This paper was largely the work of the late Arthur Moule Gill, Boyle's chief clerk at the time and a well-known local historian).

Brown, Ashley, *Dunkirk and the Great Western* (GWR, 1945)

David, J. M., *Early Channel Island Steamers, 1823–1840* (Soc Guernesiaise, 1954)

Sharp, Eric W., *The Harbours and Shipping of Guernsey at the Turn of the 19th Century* (Soc Guernesiaise, 1959)

Trotter, J. M. Y., *Early Guernsey Postal History* (Soc Guernesiaise, 1950)

NB References to certain of the foregoing official sources—eg GWR minute books and correspondence and records of the Post Office and Admiralty—and the *County Chronicle* are too numerous for individual inclusion in the notes and in general are omitted.

CHAPTER ONE

(The Channel Islands Packets, 1794–1845. Page 11*)*

1. On various dates in February 1794.
2. For a comprehensive account of the origins and early conduct of the service see J. P. Alexandre, *Early Postal Service to the C.I.*
3. 34 Geo III, c 18.
4. A uniform fare to the two islands has applied ever since.
5. J. M. Y. Trotter, *Early Guernsey Postal History.*
6. J. M. Y. Trotter, *Guernsey, the Franking System and Mr Robilliard* (Bulletin of the Postal History Society No 222, 1962).
7. *A Summer Stroll through the Islands of Jersey and Guernsey,* Jersey, 1809 (Priaulx Library, Guernsey).
8. Alexandre.
9. Post Office, Treasury letter books 12–185, 14–226 and 15–168/9.
10. The *Medina* was built in 1822 to run between Southampton and Cowes.
11. 19 July 1827.
12. A method of diagonal trussing devised in 1820 by Sir Robert Seppings, Surveyor of the Navy.
13. J. M. David, *Early Channel Island Steamers.*
14. Commissioners of Revenue Inquiry, 25 June 1830.
15. Select Committee on Post Communication, 9 August 1832.
16. Carriage of mails in private vessels was covered by the Post Office Act, 1815 (55 Geo III, c 153).

17. Commissioners of Post Office Management, 20 April 1836.
18. The agents were usually civilians.
19. Holyhead was convenient for the west coast stations and the Dover packets went round to the Thames. In 1832, exceptionally, the *Watersprite* was repaired and coppered in Jersey (*DCC* 22 February 1832).
20. PRO Adm 1/4075.
21. *The Star*, 19 and 26 April 1838.
22. *DCC*, 25 April 1839.
23. Admiralty Committee on Channel Islands Mails, 25 March 1841.
24. Admiralty Library, 'List of the Navy'.

(The main sources for this chapter are the Post Office and Admiralty packet records and the *County Chronicle*).

CHAPTER TWO

(1845–59: Arrival of the Railway and Rival Steamers. Page 33*)*

1. For an extended account of the development of lines to Weymouth see *Railways of Dorset* (Railway Correspondence & Travel Society, 1968).
2. Evidence in committee (House of Lords record office).
3. 11 and 12 Vic, c 125, s 47.
4. *The Star*, 6 August and 19 December 1850.
5. 16 April 1857.
6. 28 May and 11 June 1857.
7. The steamer did not normally enter Guernsey harbour but merely anchored outside. In Jersey she berthed alongside except when the tide was too low, passengers then being rowed ashore by local boatmen at a charge of 3d.
8. 18 August 1857.
9. *The Star*, 28 May 1857.
10. *The Times*, 22 September and 13 October 1859.

(The main sources for this chapter are BTHR MPR 471 and the *County Chronicle*).

CHAPTER THREE

(*1860–89: Precarious Progress, and Steamers to France*. Page 51)

1. This was the dividend guaranteed by the LSWR under the working agreement (BTHR LSW 3/96).
2. House of Lords record office.
3. 34 and 35 Vic, c 112.
4. BTHR GW 18/11.
5. *Great Western Railway Magazine*, 1896, p 86.
6. *The Southern Times*, 7 September 1878.
7. This fitted in with the 5.15 pm Milford boat train, the Weymouth portion of which already conveyed Channel Islands passengers.
8. Boyle, *The Channel Islands Service*, records that outward cargo included 'the whole of the pipes for the drainage of the city of Paris', amounting to thousands of tons.
9. BTHR GW 18/50.
10. It was in Weymouth as well, for that matter.
11. Weymouth's tidal range is one of the smallest in the country; Jersey's, oddly enough, is exceptionally large.
12. Boyle papers, report on Weymouth–Cherbourg service, 27 May 1883.
13. BTHR MPS 2/75.
14. Available references to this vessel are inadequate for her identification; Boyle records that she was 'most unsuitable', rolling heavily and 'frequently throwing her deck cargo of fish overboard', but does not say whether the fish in question was inward cargo or outward.
15. Board of Trade Library.
16. *The Star*, 29 June 1889.
17. Ibid, 17 August 1889.
18. This was a sort of subsidiary of the Great Western, put up for the express purpose of guaranteeing a large regular coal traffic over the company's lines (see E. T. MacDermot, *History of the Great Western Railway*, vol 1, pp 406–7).
19. The precise time of departure varied a little from time to time.

20. The South Western's steamer powers were made perpetual in 1860 and two years later it absorbed the Navigation Co completely.

(The main sources for this chapter are the company's minute books, BTHR MPR 471–3, GW 8/4 and 9/330 and the *County Chronicle*).

CHAPTER FOUR

(1889–99: The Race to Jersey. Page 79*)*

1. 50 and 51 Vic, c 153.
2. Boyle papers, memorandum of meeting, 12 July 1887.
3. 17 Vic, c 35, s 42.
4. This charge remained unchanged until 1960, when it was raised to 1½d.
5. Boyle papers, report of meeting to consider arrangements for the new Channel Islands service, 18 May 1889.
6. The Cherbourg steamers and, until 1868, the Packet Co also, relied for boiler maintenance and small mechanical repairs on the Locomotive Department. An interesting reminder of this came to light only recently; some drawings of the boilers of the *Brighton* and *Cygnus*, prepared by the then shed foreman in 1867, were still rolled up in a drawer in the shed office in 1967, eighty years after the *Brighton* sank!
7. BTHR GW 4/515, general manager's circular No 753, 12 August 1889.
8. BTHR, LSWR Steam Packet Committee minutes.
9. December 1890.
10. BTHR GW 18/183.
11. *Railway Times*, 9 August 1890.
12. BTHR LSW 4/15.
13. Boyle papers, report of meeting to consider Channel Islands working during 1891 season, 30 January 1891.
14. *The Times*, 8 September 1891.
15. As is well known the train eventually went into service between Paddington and Birkenhead but this account appears to have been the first published reference to it; as such it is of much interest.

16. Even from The Needles the crossing is 10 miles longer than from Weymouth.
17. Report of court of inquiry into accident to the *Ibex*, 10 June 1897 (Weymouth library L 387.2 WE 2).
18. 61 and 62 Vic, c 254.
19. BTHR, LSWR Steam Packet Committee minutes.
20. Boyle papers, agreement No 549.
21. BTHR LSW 4/1, report of court of inquiry into loss of the *Stella*, 27 April 1899.
22. E. W. Sharp, *The Harbours & Shipping of Guernsey*.

(The main sources for this chapter are the company's minute books, BTHR MPR 472–4 and the *County Chronicle*).

CHAPTER FIVE

(*1900–14: Consolidation, and Steamers to France again.* Page 113)

1. *Railway Times*, 10 and 17 February 1900.
2. The loudest grumbling came, predictably, from the island growers.
3. *The Times*, 3, 5 and 6 February 1900.
4. *The Star*, July and August 1900 (various dates).
5. House of Lords record office.
6. 9 Ed VII, c 44.
7. Information kindly supplied by Mr W. J. Bellamy.
8. MacDermot, vol 2, p 446.
9. Boyle papers, agreements Nos 700, 700A & 700B.
10. Information kindly supplied by Mr W. J. Bellamy.
11. Ibid.
12. French strawberries, carried in chartered vessels, remained an important seasonal trade for the company at Plymouth up to 1939.
13. 3 Ed VII, c 196, s 61 and 62.
14. Boyle papers, general manager's notes on meeting with Admiralty Director of Works, 22 October 1912.
15. 3 and 4 Geo V, c 56, s 64, 67 and 68.
16. Boyle papers, report on 'run' in Weymouth harbour (undated).

17. Ibid, memorandum of meeting, 24 October 1912.

(The main sources for this chapter are the company's minute books and the Weymouth steamer books).

CHAPTER SIX

(1914–40: Problems Surmounted and Progress Redoubled. Page 133*)*

1. In May 1915 the *Mersey* was damaged in collision with the ss *Poona* and was off service until the end of July.
2. *The Railway Magazine*, April 1922.
3. MacDermot, vol 2, p 462.
4. Boyle papers, memorandum on wage rates.
5. She was, of course, too big to enter Weymouth harbour, or Guernsey or Jersey.
6. Boyle papers, memorandum on working costs.
7. *The Star*, 25 June 1925.
8. Boyle papers, report of court of inquiry into accident to the *St Patrick*, 14–24 November 1932.
9. *The Star*, 1 July 1933.
10. Harbour improvements were also carried out in Jersey and, more particularly, Guernsey.
11. July 1934.
12. August 1934.

(The main sources for this chapter are the company's minute books and the Weymouth steamer books and cargo books).

CHAPTER SEVEN

(1945–65: Under New Management. Page 156*)*

1. Admiralty Library, *Red List* (relevant dates).
2. Ibid, also *Pink List* (relevant dates).
3. Information kindly supplied by Captain R. R. Pitman.
4. *Great Western Railway Magazine*, November 1945.
5. Coastal cruises were also resumed after the war but lasted for only two seasons; the last was run on 8 September 1949, by the *St Helier*.

6. A detailed account of the new works may be found in *Railway World*, July 1961.
7. Invariably the *St Patrick*.

CHAPTER EIGHT

(*The Great Western's Weymouth Fleet*. Page 172)

1. *The Illustrated London News*, 11 November 1854.
2. A sort of tubed drum, rather like a miniature locomotive boiler, placed vertically in the uptake; it was patented by a Mr Partridge, of Woolwich Dockyard (*DCC* 17 May 1860).
3. BTHR GW 8/3.
4. *Liverpool Journal of Commerce*, 15 August 1889.
5. September 1889.
6. For general arrangement drawings see *Engineering*, 30 March 1890.
7. Information kindly supplied by Mr W. J. Bellamy.
8. *Antelope* and *Gazelle*; the *Lynx* apparently remained unaltered until 1896 but the evidence is inconclusive.
9. *The Comet*, 28 May 1892.
10. She was running with her 'winter' propellers when she struck the Noirmontaise; the marginally higher speed attainable with bronze might just have saved the tide—and the day.
11. *Liverpool Journal of Commerce*, 25 August 1891.
12. For general arrangement drawings see *Engineering*, 24 September 1897.
13. Boyle papers, memorandum on coal consumption. The coal used was specially selected large steam coal from Dowlais.
14. Information kindly supplied by Captain R. R. Pitman and Mr W. G. Salmon.
15. Information kindly supplied by Mr Hector Lowman.
16. The original drawings showed sleeping berths in the dining saloon as well—an objectionable feature of the old ships that was wisely abandoned (Boyle papers, memorandum on new Channel Islands steamers, 4 December 1923).
17. Information kindly supplied by Captain R. R. Pitman.
18. In March 1961 the *St Helier* was officially 'partially dis-

mantled and no longer capable of being used in navigation'; she was possibly in use as a hulk for some purpose.

(Sources for this chapter other than those noted include the company's minute books and the periodicals listed on page 219).

CHAPTER NINE

(*The Harbour Tramway*. Page 196)

1. 25 and 26 Vic, c 71.
2. Deposited plan, Dorset Record Office.
3. *DCC*, 2 October 1862.
4. *DCC*, 10 May 1877, report of accident on the tramway.
5. *DCC*, 10 June 1880.
6. Board's minute, 9 October 1889.
7. BTHR GW 4/515, circulars Nos 752 (30 July 1889) and 753 (12 August 1889).
8. BTHR WAP 4/1; see also *The Railway Magazine*, November 1938, p 382.
9. Permitted vehicles were identified by cast-iron plates bearing the letters WxQ, affixed to their ends.
10. BTHR GW 5/9, 93/4.
11. Information kindly supplied by Mr A. J. Wallis.
12. *Railway and Travel Monthly*, June 1917.
13. Boyle papers, memorandum on new Channel Islands steamers.

(The main sources for this chapter are the *County Chronicle*, BTHR MPR 472 and GW 9/445 and the several agreements between the companies and Weymouth Corporation).

APPENDICES

Appendix One

REGISTER OF SHIPS

Except in the case of the government packets, measurements are taken from the official registers of shipping and are as defined for registry purposes at the relevant dates. The measurements of the packets are taken from various sources as shown in the footnotes to the first part of Table 2. Tonnages are those recorded for the ships when built. Subsequent variations are omitted, as these nearly always arose from internal rearrangement or revision of tonnage rules without affecting the outward appearance of the ships concerned.

Table 1 THE SAILING PACKETS (1794–1827)

Name	Built	L ft in	B ft in	D ft in	Tonnage	Channel Is. service Com'd	Channel Is. service Ended
Royal Charlotte§	—	—	—	—	63	Feb 1794	c Jun 1795
*Rover**	West Cowes, 1789	53 0	18 2	8 9	67	Feb 1794	c Jul 1811
*Earl of Chesterfield**	Bridport, 1795	56 0	19 0	9 0	78	Jun 1795	Nov 1806
*Chesterfield (I)**	Portland, 1806	58 4	18 11	9 5	85	Nov 1806	Oct 1811
*General Doyle**	Looe, 1803	57 8	19 3	9 0	83	Oct 1806	Nov 1809
*Francis Freeling**	Portland, 1809	57 7	19 4	9 2	86	Dec 1809	Sep 1826
Rapid§	—	—	—	—	—	c Jan 1812	c Nov 1812
*Chesterfield (II)**	Portland, 1812	63 4	20 0	10 1	107	Nov 1812	c Jan 1813
*Hinchinbrook**	Bridport, 1811	60 0	19 8	10 0	90	Jul 1811	Feb 1826
Sir William Curtis‡	Hastings, 1815	58 5	17 7	9 0	75	Jun 1816	1817
*Countess of Liverpool**	Portland, 1814	62 2	20 1	10 3	104	Feb 1814	Jul 1827
Queen Charlotte§	—	—	—	—	—	c Feb 1826	Jul 1826
Iris§	—	—	—	—	69	Oct 1826	Jun 1827
Dove§	—	—	—	—	—	Nov 1826	Jul 1827

* Port of registry Weymouth.
‡ Port of registry Sandwich.
§ Port of registry not known and no further details available.

Of the half dozen 'home' packet stations Weymouth is the only one for which the eighteenth-century register is extant, and as a record of such a station this list is probably unique. The regulation minimum tonnage for a Channel Islands packet was 50.

Table 2 WOODEN PADDLE STEAMERS (1827–45)
(i) Post Office and Admiralty packets

Name	*Date* *(a) blt* *(b) to Wmth*	*Builder* *(a) ship* *(b) engines*	*L* *ft in*	*B* *ft in*	*D* *ft in*	*Tonnage*	*Engines* *(a) dia* *(b) str*	*NHP*
Ivanhoe[1]	(a) 1820 (b) 1827	(a) J. Scott & Sons, Greenock (b) Maudslay Sons & Field (1826)	103 9	16 9	11 3	158	(a) 31 7/8" (b) 36"	2 × 30
Watersprite/[2] *Wildfire*	(a) 1826 (b) 1827	(a) Geo. Graham, Harwich (b) Boulton, Watt & Co	107 0	17 2	11 8	162	(a) 31 1/4" (b) 36"	2 × 30
Meteor[3]	(a) 1821 (b) 1828	(a) Wm. Evans, Rotherhithe (b) Boulton, Watt & Co	n/a	n/a	n/a	190	n/a	2 × 30
Flamer/ Fearless[4]	(a) 1831 (b) 1831	(a) Hy. Fletcher Son & Fearnall, Limehouse (b) Boulton, Watt & Co	111 0	17 0	11 4	165	(a) 31 1/2" (b) 36"	2 × 30
Pluto[5]	(a) 1831 (b) 1837	(a) Woolwich Dockyard (b) Boulton, Watt & Co	135 0	24 0	11 10	365	n/a	2 × 50
Dasher[5]	(a) 1838 (b) 1838	(a) Chatham Dockyard (b) Seaward & Capel, Limehouse	120 0	21 8	13 0	260	n/a	2 × 50
Cuckoo (ex *Cinderella*)[6]	(a) 1824 (b) 1839	(a) Wigram & Green, Blackwall (b) Boulton, Watt & Co	119 6	19 8	12 6	234	(a) 39 1/2" (b) 42"	2 × 40

[1] Dimensions from *6th Report of the Commissioners of Post Office Management*, 1836; original engines by D. Napier; Greenock register (1820) gives dimensions as 102′ 3″ × 18′ 4″ × 11′ 2″. Stevens's tonnage (page 26) is probably in error.

[2] Dimensions from *6th Report*; lengthened 1836 to 114′ 0″ BP, 185 tons (contemporary plan); re-engined at Blackwall 1836 to 2 × 40hp rather than 75hp as Stevens expected (page 25).

[3] There appears to be no surviving record of the *Meteor*'s dimensions.

[4] Dimensions from *6th Report*.

[5] Dimensions from contemporary plan.

[6] Dimensions from *6th Report*; power later increased to 2 × 50hp.

n/a—not available.

(ii) Commercial Steam Packet Co

Name	*Date* (a) *blt* (b) *to Wmth*	*Builder* (a) *ship* (b) *engines*	*L* *ft*	*B* *ft*	*D* *ft*	*Tonnage*	*Engines* (a) *dia* (b) *str*	*NHP*
Calpe	(a) 1835 (b) 1839	(a) McGhie & Hawks, Rotherhithe (b) n/a	125·4	19·5	12·8	259	n/a	2 × 40
Kent	(a) 1829 (b) 1839	(a) J. & G. Bauckham, Gravesend (b) n/a	125·0	17·4	10·5	182	n/a	n/a
City of Glasgow	(a) 1822 (b) 1839	(a) J. Scott & Sons, Greenock (b) D. Napier, Glasgow	119·4	20·5	11·2	217	n/a	2 × 50
Grand Turk	(a) 1837 (b) 1839	(a) Robt. Duncan & Co, Greenock (b) Murdock Aitken & Co	135·9	20·2	13·0	369	n/a	2 × 80

n/a—not available.

Table 3 IRON PADDLE STEAMERS (1857–89)

Name	*Date* (a) *blt* (b) *to Wmth*	*Builder* (a) *ship* (b) *engines*	*L* *ft*	*B* *ft*	*D* *ft*	*Tons gross*	*Engines* *dia × str*	*NHP*
LSWR (New South Western Steam Navigation Co)								
South Western	(a) 1843 (b) *	(a) Ditchburn & Mare, Blackwall (b) John Seaward & Co, Limehouse	143·0	18·0	10·8	203	$36\frac{1}{2}$" × 36" (2) (sl)	80
Wonder	(a) 1844 (b) *	(a) Ditchburn & Mare, Blackwall (b) Seaward & Capel, Limehouse	158·0	20·6	10·0	250	53" × 42" (3) (atmos)	130
Express	(a) 1847 (b) *	(a) Ditchburn & Mare, Blackwall (b) Maudslay Sons & Field	159·0	21·4	10·4	255	55" × 42" (2) (atmos)	160
Weymouth & Channel Islands Steam Packet Co								
Aquila	(a) 1854 (b) 1857	(a) Jas. Henderson & Son, Renfrew (b) McNabb & Clark, Greenock	180·4	21·0	10·9	264	42" × 42" (2) (osc)	110
Cygnus	(a) 1854 (b) 1857	(a) Jas. Henderson & Son, Renfrew (b) McNabb & Clark, Greenock	182·0	21·4	9·7	245	$42\frac{3}{8}$" × 42" (2) (osc)	120

Brighton	(a) 1857 (b) 1858	(a) } Palmer & Co, (b) } Jarrow	193·5	20·9	10·0	286	$43\frac{3}{4}$" × 48" (2) (osc)	140
Great Western Railway								
Great Western	(a) 1867 (b) 1878	(a) } W. Simons & Co, (b) } Renfrew	220·4	25·2	12·4	447	48" × 45" (2) (osc)	190
South of Ireland	(a) 1867 (b) 1878	(a) } W. Simons & Co, (b) } Renfrew	220·2	25·8	12·4	474	50" × 48" (2) (osc)	200
Vulture	(a) 1864 (b) 1879	(a) } Jas. Aitken, (b) } Whiteinch	243·2	25·7	17·3	793	54" × 60" (2) (osc)	200
Gael	(a) 1867 (b) 1884	(a) Robertson & Co, Greenock (b) Rankin & Blackmore, Greenock	211·0	23·2	10·6	403	45" × 63" (2) (osc)	150

* Intermittent service only, 1857-9; *South Western* Aug-Dec 1850 also. sl = side lever atmos = atmospheric osc = oscillating

Table 4 STEEL SCREW STEAMERS, RECIPROCATING ENGINES (1889–1925)[1]

Name	*Date* *blt*	*Builder (ship and engines)*	*L* *ft*	*B* *ft*	*D* *ft*	*Tons gross*	*Engines* (Melmore *single screw all others twin screw)*	*HP* *(a) ind (b) nom*	*Speed*[2] *knots*
Lynx[3]	1889	Laird Bros, Birkenhead	235·5	27·6	13·1	596	16½", 26", 41" × 30" str	(a) 1700 (b) 168	16½
Antelope	1889	Laird Bros, Birkenhead	235·5	27·6	13·1	596	16½", 26", 41" × 30" str	(a) 1650 (b) 168	16½
Gazelle	1889	Laird Bros, Birkenhead	235·5	27·6	13·1	596	16½", 26", 41" × 30" str	(a) 1650 (b) 168	16½
Ibex	1891	Laird Bros, Birkenhead	265·0	32·6	14·2	1160	22", 34", 51" × 33" str	(a) 4000 (b) 282	19
Roebuck[4]	1897	Naval Constn & Armaments Co, Barrow	280·0	34·5	16·8	1281	23", 36", 56" × 33" str	(a) 5300 (b) 330	20¼
Reindeer	1897	Naval Constn & Armaments Co, Barrow	280·0	34·5	16·8	1281	23", 36", 56" × 33" str	(a) 5300 (b) 330	20¼
Pembroke rebt	1880 1896	Laird Bros, Birkenhead	254·0	30·9	15·0	976[5]	19", 30", 46" × 30" str	(a) 3300 (b) 650	16
Melmore acqd	1892 1905	D. J. Dunlop, Port Glasgow	156·2	25·8	11·3	412	15", 23", 38" × 27" str	n/a	10
Great Western	1902	Laird Bros, Birkenhead	275·8	36·3	15·2	1339	19", 29½", 2 × 33" × 30" str	(a) 3250 (b) 228	16

Great Southern	1902	Laird Bros, Birkenhead	275·8	36·3	12·2	1339	19", 29½", 2 × 33" × 30" str	(a) 3250 (b) 228	16
Waterford	1912	Swan Hunter & Wigham Richardson, Newcastle	275·2	38·2	16·5	1209	16", 23", 33", 48" × 33" str	(a) 2400 (b) 438	15
Roebuck	1925	Swan Hunter & Wigham Richardson, Newcastle	201·2	33·7	15·3	776	14½", 23", 38" × 27" str	(a) 1350 (b) 226	12¼
Sambur	1925	Swan Hunter & Wigham Richardson, Newcastle	201·2	33·7	15·3	776	14½", 23", 38" × 27" str	(a) 1350 (b) 226	12¼

[1] Including the cargo steamers *Roebuck* and *Sambur*, built 1925.
[2] Speeds are included in the official registry from this date onward.
[3] Renamed *Lynn* 19 January 1915; *Lynx* 1 April 1920.
[4] Renamed *Roedean* 19 January 1915 (official date of change; vessel sunk four days previously).
[5] On conversion to screws; original tonnage (as paddle steamer) 927.

Table 5 TURBINE STEAMERS (introduced 1925)

Name	*Date blt*	*Builder (ship and engines)*	*L ft*	*B ft*	*D ft*	*Tons gross*	*Speed knots*
St Julien	1925	John Brown & Co, Clydebank	282·2	40·0	16·3	1885	18
St Helier	1925	John Brown & Co, Clydebank	282·2	40·0	16·3	1885	18
St Patrick	1930	Alex. Stephen & Sons, Linthouse, Glasgow	281·3	41·1	16·3	1922	19
St David	1947	Cammell Laird & Co, Birkenhead	306·5	48·2	17·2	3352	20¾
St Patrick	1947	Cammell Laird & Co, Birkenhead	306·5	48·2	17·2	3482	20

Table 6 JAMES FISHER & SONS, BARROW-IN-FURNESS

Although only chartered, the 'Fisher Boats' were almost entitled, by their close association with the company over a long period, to be regarded as Great Western vessels. From about 1887 until 1904 Weymouth's Jersey potato traffic was almost entirely dependent on them and the regular connection survived, albeit on a reduced scale, until 1915:

Name	*Date blt*	*Tons gross*	*Name*	*Date blt*	*Tons gross*
Sea Fisher	1883	297	*Race Fisher*	1892	494
Bay Fisher (I)	1884	369	*Sound Fisher*	1894	463
Lough Fisher	1887	418	*Firth Fisher*	1898	456
Strait Fisher	1890	465	*River Fisher*	1899	457
Stream Fisher	1891	479	*Bay Fisher (II)*	1904	478

The connection was revived to a limited extent in the thirties.

Table 7 OTHER RAILWAY VESSELS AT WEYMOUTH (1948–69)

Name	*Home Port*	*at Weymouth*
Felixstowe[1]	Harwich	1948
Isle of Sark[2]	Southampton	1950, 1956
Hythe[1]	Southampton	1951–5
Isle of Jersey[2]	Southampton	1956
Whitstable[1]	Southampton	1957–9
Ringwood[3]	Southampton	1958–9
Haslemere[3]	Southampton	1959
Winchester[4]	Southampton	from 1959
Normannia[3]	Southampton	1960, 1963
Brest[1]	Dieppe	1960–5
Brittany[2]	Southampton	1961
Isle of Guernsey[3]	Southampton	1961
Rennes[1]	Dieppe	1965
Colchester[1]	Harwich	1968–9

[1] Seasonal service.
[2] Isolated calls only.
[3] Service irregular and infrequent.
[4] Service irregular and infrequent until 1965, when transferred permanently (see also table 8).

Table 8 THE PRESENT FLEET

Name	*Date blt*	*Builder (a) ship (b) engines*	*L ft*	*B ft*	*D ft*	*Tons gross*	*Speed knots*
Winchester	1947	(a) (b) Wm. Denny & Bros, Dumbarton	241·0	36·1	13·4	1149	15
Elk / *Moose*	1959	(a) Brooke Marine, Lowestoft (b) Sulzer Bros, Winterthur	218·2	38·0	10·5	795	14
*Caesarea**	1960	(a) (b) J. Samuel White & Co, Cowes	308·4	51·2	16·5	3992	20
*Sarnia**	1961	(a) (b) J. Samuel White & Co, Cowes	308·4	51·2	16·5	3989	20

* Tonnage as built, 4174 gross.

The *Winchester*, *Elk* and *Moose*, augmented in season by charter, constitute the present cargo fleet. The *Winchester* was built for the Southern Railway; she visited Weymouth at intervals from 1959 and on 1 March 1965, on withdrawal of the *Roebuck*, became permanently Weymouth-based and manned. The *Elk* and *Moose*, the 'cargo half' of the 1957 replacement programme, are nominally Southampton-based but from the time of entering service have served both ports equally.

Appendix Two

THE GREAT WESTERN MARINE DEPARTMENT

The Great Western Marine Department was brought into being on 15 December 1870, while the Steam Vessels Bill was before Parliament, by the appointment of a Steamboat Committee. This committee met at irregular intervals until 1897; on more important questions, however, the marine superintendent appears to have reported direct to the board and from 1890 many steamship matters of a more routine nature were considered by the Traffic Committee. The Steamboat Committee was reconstituted with effect from 16 July 1908.

The company's first marine superintendent was Captain Jackson, whose services the company was pleased to retain 'for as long as might be necessary' when it took over the Milford steamers. He remained in an advisory capacity until the first permanent appointment was made, in July 1873. Successive holders of the post were as follows:

Feb 1872–Jul 1873	Thomas Thompson Jackson (manager)
Jul 1873–Dec 1882	William Henry Haswell, Capt RN (later Admiral)
Jan 1883–Oct 1898	Thornton Stratford Lecky
Nov 1898–Mar 1907	John Dunster (marine and docks superintendent)
Mar 1907–Dec 1909	C. Irvine Davidson (steamboat superintendent from Aug 1906)
Nov 1909–Sep 1920	John Humphreys
Oct 1920–Dec 1926	Richard Sharp

On the retirement of Captain Sharp the Marine Department was discontinued, responsibility for steamships being transferred to the Docks Department.

A separate Weymouth establishment was not created until 1889, the Cherbourg steamers being managed for the company by John Wimble, the Packet Company's manager. Wimble was appointed local marine superintendent in 1878 and while holding the double post transferred his office from Jersey to Weymouth.

Captain Hemmings, appointed as assistant marine superintendent for the Channel Islands steamers in 1889, served until 31 December 1915 and then retired, at the age of 71. From 1899 his responsibility embraced the staff and working of Weymouth Quay (formerly under the Passenger Department) as well as the steamers. He was succeeded by his erstwhile chief clerk, the 'very trustworthy' Percy Boyle, but the post of assistant marine superintendent was discontinued, Boyle being designated traffic and marine agent. At the time of his own retirement, on 31 December 1935, Boyle was Weymouth's sole surviving link with 1889 and had served the company for 52 years. His successors were, in turn, Mr Douglas Giles Hoppins until 1940 and, from 1943, Mr William George Salmon (designated quay superintendent).

The principal officers of the Weymouth & Channel Islands Steam Packet Company were as follows :

Chairman		Secretary and Manager	
1857–1859	Elias Neel	1857–1868	Joseph Maunders
1859–c1880	Abraham Bishop	1868–1878	Joseph Maunders (secretary) John Wimble (manager)
c1880–1891	— Le Gros		
		1878–1891	John Wimble (liquidator from 1889)

From 1868 to 1878 the company was in the odd situation of having a Jersey manager (Wimble) a Guernsey chairman (Bishop) and a Weymouth secretary (Maunders).

Appendix Three

SOME TRAFFIC STATISTICS

Comparative totals for Channel Islands passenger traffic via Weymouth and via Southampton, 1828–1938.

Year	*To and from G'sey and J'sey*		*Inter-island*	
	Via Wmth	*Via S'ton*	GWR	LSWR/SR
1828	6,900*	n/a	—	—
1839	5,212	n/a	—	—
1859	16,758	n/a	n/a	n/a
1892	29,319	54,056	18,315	13,802
1903	51,423	59,973	21,365	12,484
1913	63,589	81,444	22,095	17,525
1925	95,912	112,888	20,735	17,303
1938	111,639	177,592	21,556	n/a

* Approximate figure.
n/a—not available.

Comparative totals of Jersey and Guernsey passenger traffic by British Railways and by airlines, 1953–69.

Year	*British Railways*			
	Via Wmth	*Via S'ton*	*Total*	*By air*
1953	136,597	223,925	360,522	289,489
1955	145,865	229,805	375,670	382,160
1957	147,306	204,356	351,662	582,674
1959	152,888	176,446	329,334	575,000*
1960	133,879	126,436	260,315	680,000*
1967	304,186	—	304,186	1,244,000*
1968	384,959	—	384,959	1,172,000*
1969	451,855	—	451,855	1,165,000*

* Approximate figure.

Weymouth cross-channel excursion passengers, 1930–65.

Year	*Total*	*Year*	*Total*	*Year*	*Total*	*Year*	*Total*
1930	6,536	1949	13,541	1962	22,848	1965	3,658*
1938	6,527	1959	22,688	1964	9,702		

* SS *Lisieux.*

Goods and parcels traffic between Weymouth and the Channel Islands, 1890–1969 (tons).

Year	*Goods traffic*			*Parcels traffic*			*Total, all traffic*
	Inwards	*Outwards*	*Total*	*Inwards*	*Outwards*	*Total*	
1890	—	—	—	—	—	—	22,972
1900	18,717	13,206	31,923	960	568	1,528	33,451
1914	29,243	15,612	44,855	1,904	1,269	3,173	48,028
1925	35,509	21,219	56,728	2,055	1,873	3,928	60,656
1939	46,931	24,601	71,532	2,920	1,523	4,443	75,975
1947	32,703	33,761*	66,464*	1,131	849*	1,980*	68,444*
1960	50,859	29,329	80,188	5,106	1,838	6,944	87,132
1967	29,029	27,491	56,520	4,567	1,882	6,449	62,969
1968	25,787	28,261	54,048	5,688	2,030	7,718	61,766
1969	26,736	25,616	52,352	5,122	1,773	6,895	59,247

* Including shipments to Alderney.

Analysis of Weymouth–Channel Islands goods traffic, 1947–69 (tons).

Year	*Inwards*			*Outwards*			*Total in and out*
	Jersey	*Guernsey*	*Total*	*Jersey*	*Guernsey*	*Total*	
1947	—	—	32,703	19,818	13,753	33,571	66,274
1960	6,443	44,416	50,859	18,246	11,083	29,329	80,188
1967	1,320	27,709	29,029	14,736	12,755	27,491	56,520
1968	1,065	24,722	25,787	15,013	13,248	28,261	54,048
1969	1,132	25,604	26,736	14,249	11,367	25,616	52,352

Analysis of Weymouth–Channel Islands parcels traffic, 1947–69 (tons).

Year	*Inwards*			*Outwards*			*Total in*
	Jersey	*Guernsey*	*Total*	*Jersey*	*Guernsey*	*Total*	*and out*
1947	33	1,098	1,131	502	344	846	1,977
1960	1,142	3,964	5,106	1,187	651	1,838	6,944
1967	746	3,821	4,567	1,197	685	1,882	6,449
1968	823	4,865	5,688	1,311	719	2,030	7,718
1969	703	4,419	5,122	941	832	1,773	6,895

Appendix Four

WORKING THE TRAMWAY IN 1895

A letter* from locomotive inspector (?) John Birks to the outdoor assistant superintendent in the Locomotive & Carriage Department at Swindon :

December 7th 1895

Dear Sir,

Shunting Engine, Weymouth Quay

The following is a general statement of the everyday working of the engine booked out at 2.0 p.m. and taken charge of by a Pilotman, goes down at once and clear the Tramway and bring back any traffic which can be got at.

At 3.0 p.m. D. Elkins [the regular tramway driver at that time] take charge and takes down any Fruit Vans & Customs goods that may be on hand at the Cargo staging. Engine then proceeds to the Pier Station & is attached to the Boat train which it takes to Portland Jc., return light to the Quay & bring up the Fruit Vans for 5.20 passr. train, afterwards take down General Goods and return with Perishable Goods for 7.20 express London Goods down to the quay again with any L&SW Co's traffic or any that may be on hand, does shunting at the stage & bring away any surplus empties to the Station. Meets 12.45 p.m. Chippenham Goods & takes down & berths its traffic return again to station & takes traffic off 11.5 a.m. Bristol Goods & the steam coal for the company's boats. A sampling of the empty wagons for next day's use by the traders is made and what are not required are taken to the station. The engine then waits the arrival of the Down Boat train due 1.45 a.m., proceed to the Pier afterwards run round the train & propells it back into position for the afternoon. It then proceeds to berth the wagons selected for the days use and returns to shed about 3 a.m.

I have watched the working for last night and although not exactly to the programme on account of the Boat Train having a late start the men were fully occupied at their work & I fail to see that any improvement or save can be effected even with the road put in good condition, unless accompanied by a large increase in siding accommodation.

I may mention that one engine does the work for both companies & that a great deal of time is occupied in shunting the Merchants with the class of stock they require from both companies.

Yours truly

Thos. Simpson Esq. sgd. Jno. Birks

* From British Transport Historical Records.

ACKNOWLEDGEMENTS

Many books have been written about the Great Western Railway but none previously has dealt in detail with steamship services; the present work, I think, largely breaks new ground. In compiling it I have inevitably drawn on many sources and gratefully acknowledge my debt to the following: the Archivist and staff of British Transport Historical Records; Mr R. N. R. Peers, Curator, Dorset Natural History & Archaeological Society, for the use of society facilities; Mr J. A. C. West, Chief Librarian, Weymouth, for loan of the Boyle papers; Mr E. J. Jones, Town Clerk of Weymouth, for access to harbour and tramway agreements and the plans of the 1884 docks proposals; Mrs Jean Farrugia (Post Office Historical Records); Mr A. W. H. Pearsall (National Maritime Museum); Mr A. L. Pepper (British Rail, Weymouth Quay); Dr J. Renouf (Société Jersiaise); Mr J. Sheppard (Guille-Allès Library, Guernsey); the libraries of the Admiralty and Board of Trade; the Commissioners of Customs & Excise (shipping registers); the House of Lords Record Office; the Public Record Office; the Dorset County Record Office; and the editors of the *Salisbury Journal* and *Dorset Evening Echo*. Details of the Royal Engineers' train ferry terminal were kindly supplied by the Commandant, Longmoor, and statistics by the authorities in Jersey and Guernsey.

Former Great Western staff at Weymouth Quay have readily given me the benefit of their first-hand knowledge of the Channel Islands service in company days, among them in particular Messrs J. Bartlett, W. J. Bellamy, C. Gollop and H. Lowman, Captain R. R. Pitman, and Messrs W. G. Salmon and W. Symons. Valuable assistance of one kind or another has been received also from Mr P. Kelley, Dr P. Perry and Messrs P. J. T. Reed, C. E. C. Townsend, J. M. Y. Trotter and A. J. Wallis.

I especially wish to mention Mr Mark David, of Guernsey, who generously made available his extensive shipping notes from

Channel Islands newspapers, covering a period of many years, and Mr Eric Latcham, of Weymouth. The latter's vast collection of photographs was always at my disposal and no fewer than nine of the book's illustrations, including those credited to the late E. H. Seward, owe their inclusion to his generosity. To my regret I have to record that both these friends died before the book was finished. Mr Salmon and Captain Harry Walker, master of the British Rail steamer *Sarnia*, have read the manuscript, and lastly I pay tribute to my wife, without whose encouragement the rest could have come to nought.

There are many to whom the affairs of the Great Western Railway are of abiding interest; if the book fills a small gap in the company's published history my object will have been achieved.

Weymouth,
April 1970

INDEX

For references to individual ships see separate index on page 251. Page numbers in italics indicate illustrations.

INDEX OF SHIPS

Page numbers in italics indicate illustrations.